AFRICAN-AMERICAN POETRY
OF THE
NINETEENTH CENTURY

AFRICAN–AMERICAN

OF THE
NINETEENTH CENTURY

AN ANTHOLOGY

EDITED BY

Joan R. Sherman

UNIVERSITY OF ILLINOIS PRESS
Urbana and Chicago

Illini Books edition, 1992

© 1992 by the Board of Trustees of the University of Illinois

Manufactured in the United States of America

1 2 3 4 5 C P 5 4 3 2

Library of Congress Cataloging-in-Publication Data

African-American Poetry of the nineteenth century : an anthology /
   edited by Joan R. Sherman.
      p.   cm.
   Includes bibliographical references and indexes.
   ISBN 0-252-01917-2 (cl). — ISBN 0-252-06246-9 (pb).
   1. American poetry—Afro-American authors. 2. American
poetry—19th century. 3. Afro-Americans—Poetry. I. Sherman, Joan
R.
PS591.N4A35 1992
811′.308096073—dc20   91-41709
                                                              CIP

Contents

Introduction

In the Introduction to *Invisible Poets* (1974), I wrote: "Afro-Americans of the nineteenth century are the invisible poets of our national literature. . . . their achievements, impressive both in quantity and quality, remain unacknowledged." To remedy this neglect, I examined the lives and writings of twenty-six representative poets and briefly discussed some three dozen others. Fifteen years later, the second edition of *Invisible Poets* noted progress toward visibility of the poets through publication of literary histories, bibliographies, and anthologies that included the work of a few of them; occasional collective biographies and periodical articles that acknowledged their existence; and the reprinting of several rare volumes of their poetry. This welcome attention, however, remains highly selective, focusing on the same handful of "names" or a special group; moreover, the poetry itself is largely inaccessible. Therefore, this anthology brings together 171 poems by 35 poets, from the best known to the unknown, in one convenient volume.

In the last century, abolitionist and African-American periodicals published thousands of poems by black writers. Although these scattered poems may have merit, this anthology focuses on poets who produced one or more volumes of verse—all but three of the thirty-five poets here did so.[1] The collection can thus reveal the range of talents, techniques, and interests of individuals for whom poetry was a lifelong avocation, those who were unusually articulate and sensitive to racial experience, as is evidenced by the prose they also wrote—histories, biographies, autobiographies, dramas, short stories, novels, translations from French or German, sermons, and treatises. A dozen of the poets published, edited, and wrote for their own periodicals; almost all published essays, articles, and letters in African-American magazines and newspapers on such issues as race, religion, politics, economics, history, literature, temperance, astronomy, law, travel, and current events.

All thirty-five writers published poetry before 1900, and some continued writing into the twentieth century. Their outputs varied considerably in quantity and artistry.[2] The poets are presented chronologically in order of their first published poem, making it apparent how the body of African-American verse shifted in subject, style, and tone over the century to mirror accurately the currents in American life that determined the status of the race and modified the art of all black writers.[3]

The Poets

The life experiences, educations, vocations, and achievements of these thirty-five poets differ widely, as would be expected among individuals born during the course of almost a century, from 1796 to 1878, some in the South, others in the North or border states. Six poets were born slaves, several were freeborn of former slave parents, and others came from generations of free blacks. Many grew up in dire poverty, and a few in middle-class comfort. Their formal educations ranged from none at all for Horton and Cannon to McClellan's three higher degrees. Whitman had only one year of schooling, and Fortune three years. Six poets acquired less than a high school education; another seven completed the equivalent of high school and, in some cases, additional "adult" education or religious training; eight poets earned bachelor degrees at colleges or seminaries. Higher on the educational ladder, Ray and Coffin earned graduate degrees, and Vashon, Benjamin, and Beadle became lawyers.

With vocational choices of African Americans severely limited, almost half the poets were teachers or clergy, and several combined these vocations. Only Harper and Dunbar supported themselves by writing and lecturing; the rest earned a living as a plasterer, barber, manufacturer, manual laborer, printer, civil service clerk, newspaper or magazine editor, journalist, farmer, lawyer, politician, elevator operator, pharmacist, miner, social worker, bootmaker, postal worker, actress, herb doctor, or waiter. Most of the poets traveled extensively for schooling or employment throughout the United States and Canada, and a handful visited Europe, Africa, and South or Central America.

In addition to pursuing their occupations and writing, a majority of the poets actively participated in African-American literary and educational societies, state boards of religious denominations, lodges and welfare agencies, and national political and social organizations. Several were in the vanguard of antislavery and civil rights groups as officers, writers, and lecturers. In the course of these activities and in their daily work, many of the poets knew one another and also maintained close ties with African-American leaders and other writers. For example, Cotter and McClellan were colleagues in the Louisville, Kentucky, schools as were Reason and Ray in New York City, and Whitman and Payne at Wilberforce University. Bell and Whitfield were friends in San Francisco, and Reason and Vashon labored for civil rights alongside Frederick Douglass. Fortune worked with (and against) Douglass, Booker T. Washington, and W. E. B. DuBois; Harper campaigned with leading suffragettes, women's rights, and WCTU workers. Fortune, Cotter, Davis, James Campbell, and James Weldon Johnson were friends of Dunbar's. John E. Bruce, the New York journalist, and William Wells Brown, litterateur of his day, worked with many of the poets.

In sum, the lives of these men and women were as heterogeneous as their poetry and perhaps even more extraordinary. No group of writers in any place or time has struggled to surmount such obstacles— lowly birth, poverty, lack of educational, occupational, and publication opportunities, and lifelong discrimination—to produce a body of literature that attests to their remarkable courage and talent.

The Poetry

In the broadest view, African-American poetry from 1829 through 1900 is *American poetry* in subject, versification, and attitudes. Like the main body of white nineteenth-century verse, poetry by blacks reflects and responds to the changing political, social, and cultural scene, to the events, ideologies, heroes, and villains that constitute American history. Black poets share with their white contemporaries a variety of poetic and personal values: unambiguous thought and refined sentiments, elevated language, Christian piety and morality, and affectionate nostalgia for a simple, homely rural life. Their poetry also shares tendencies toward didacticism, diffuseness, intellectual and emotional banality, abstractness, sentimentality, and use of archaic diction and mythological-literary allusions. African-American poets employ every conventional verse form: the ode, sonnet, ballad, Spenserian stanza, ottava rima, heroic couplet, terza rima, rhymed triplet, quatrain, blank and free verse, and all standard combinations of meter and rhyme. Throughout the century, poetry by blacks is influenced not by other black poets but by such white American contemporaries as Longfellow, Whittier, and Riley, or by the British writers Shelley, Goldsmith, Scott,

Byron, and Tennyson. Finally, the African-American poets almost universally accept the century's dictum that poetry's province is to convey truth, to teach, uplift, reform, and, secondarily, to give pleasure.

Despite such close and consistent adherence to established literary practice, black voices do speak from the unique perspective of an alien race in white society. The fact that various African Americans at different times celebrate, or mask, or reject their blackness and race heritage significantly modifies their art. Emotions of despair, bitterness, and anger in antebellum verse, or hopeful accommodation later on, or irony in dialect verse distinguish black from white poems on the same subjects. And although two verses on the love of God, one black, one white, seem esthetically indistinguishable, the black writer's poem issues from unique racial experiences and always has additional sociohistorical value. Clearly, the corpus of nineteenth-century black verse is linked intimately with the era's other black literary products, and all shift literary postures in the same direction at the same time.

The finest militant race protest of the century, in terms of emotional and intellectual intensity, craftsmanship, and racial propaganda value, appears before the Civil War, from 1830 to 1860. From the pens of Horton, Rogers, Reason, Simpson, Whitfield, Harper, Vashon, Holly, and Alfred Campbell come impassioned denunciations of slavery and injustice and demands for freedom and civil rights.[4] The best of this aggressive poetry resounds with anguish and fury of a dream deferred; with lightning blasts of righteous indignation or bitter mockery; with threats of bloody vengeance and a nation's doom; and with a proud, all-encompassing concern for the race above the individual. The militant poetry belongs to an era dominated by African-American protest organizations, abolitionist literature, and eloquent orators. From pulpits and podiums, in petitions and calls, at meetings of the Free Negro Convention movement and a multitude of black and interracial antislavery societies, African Americans clamored for emancipation and equality: Douglass, Henry H. Garnet, David Ruggles, Alexander Crummell, Charles L. Remond, William Still, William C. Nell, Samuel R. Ward, James Forten, Daniel A. Payne, Charles B. Ray, Paul Cuffe, James McCune Smith, Robert Purvis, and dozens more. As early as 1827, *Freedom's Journal* sounded the liberation cry, followed by John B. Russwurm's *Rights of All* (1829), Ray's *Colored American* (1837), Ruggles's *Mirror of Liberty* (1838), William J. Whipper's *National Reformer* (1838), Martin R. Delany's *Mystery* (1843), Douglass's *North Star*, his

Paper and *Monthly* (1847–63). White newspapers, better known and more widely circulated, joined in protest: Benjamin Lundy and William Lloyd Garrison's *Genius of Universal Emancipation* (1829); Garrison's *Liberator* (1831) and *Emancipator* (1833), the journal of the American Anti-Slavery Society; and David L. Child's *National Anti-Slavery Standard* (1841).

Antebellum black writers concentrated on abolitionist and civil rights polemic, but they also produced a few literary works: Delany's *The Condition, Elevation, Emigration and Destiny of the Colored People of the United States* (1852) and Nell's *Colored Patriots of the American Revolution* (1855) are inspiring biographical histories. William Wells Brown's *Clotel; or The President's Daughter* (1853) and *The Escape* (1858), the first novel and play by a black man, expose the evils of slavery. Another novel, Frank Webb's *The Garies and Their Friends* (1857), was followed in 1859 by Harriet Wilson's *Our Nig,* the first novel by a black woman; Harper's tale, "The Two Offers," the first short story by a black woman; and Delany's second novel, *Blake; or The Huts of America* (1859). To provide additional outlets for fiction and poetry as well as protest writings, African Americans founded dozens of periodicals before the war, notably the *AME Church Magazine* (1841–47), Payne's *Repository of Religion and Literature and of Science and Art* (1858–63), and Robert Hamilton's *Anglo-African Magazine* (1859–60).

By far the most popular and influential writing from the 1830s through the 1850s were thousands of slave narratives, autobiographical accounts of life in slavery written by fugitives or from their dictation. Most appeared in widely read abolitionist newspapers and magazines, but several dozen were full-length books such as the stirring narratives of Frederick Douglass (1845); William Wells Brown (1847); Henry Bibb (1849), Josiah Henson (1849; 1858), Solomon Northup (1853), Ellen and William Craft (1860), and Harriet Jacobs (1861). Such vivid chronicles of human bondage and dramatic escapes became best-sellers; they fueled abolitionist fervor in the North and fearful antagonisms in the South as the fugitives' firsthand descriptions of slavery's horrors contradicted Southerners' propaganda for the benignity of their peculiar institution. Many former slaves became celebrities of the lecture circuit in the North and in Europe when their memoirs appeared, exacerbating sectional tensions. The fugitives' narratives not only provided an invaluable perspective on slavery but also gave impetus to a lasting African-American literary tradition of biography and autobiography.

Slave narratives differ radically from formal black poetry by their indebtedness to oral folkloristic and melodramatic traditions of race culture. Significantly, the only antebellum verse that partakes of these qualities are Simpson's antislavery song-poems, written for fugitives on the Underground Railroad. These songs (and many similar ones of the period) satirize hypocritical white preachers and naive masters and reveal the superstitions, amusements, pious emotionalism, and shrewd trickery of slaves. Like the slave narratives, Simpson's songs stress the race's alienation and slaves' continual ardent efforts to attain freedom, not in some kingdom after death but now, in the North or Canada. The folk qualities of slave narratives appear to a lesser degree in a few homespun verses by the slave poet Horton and the former slave Walden; and their folkways selectively surface again in dialect verse of the century's last two decades.

In contrast to the sly humor of Simpson's songs, antislavery verse by the other eight antebellum poets is uniformly serious, pragmatic, moralistic, historically oriented, and intellectual even when most fervid. Horton's antislavery poems differ from those of free poets, for Horton naturally laments *his* bondage and omits blood-curdling details of enslavement that were alien to his personal experience. Horton's voice is honest and moving, more intimately genuine than voices that anathematize the generic institution of slavery. Reason writes forceful appeals for black enfranchisement and universal liberty; Whitfield, the most indignant and powerful protest poet, decries national injustice and the crippling of a creative soul by race prejudice; Alfred Campbell, an avid Garrisonian, attacks the church, Constitution, Fugitive Slave Law, and Southern hypocrites; Harper, with less rancor than sorrowful melodrama, summons a fiery Jehovah and callous mankind to witness the suffering and heroism of slave mothers, abused black women, and fugitives; Holly invokes the muse of antislavery poets to call down God's vengeance upon a sinful nation; Vashon brilliantly dramatizes the Haitian insurrection; and Rogers courageously appeals to law and conscience to condemn proslavery legislation of the 1850s. These antebellum poets, and several after them, also write martial or sentimental tributes to champions of the race such as Douglass, Ulysses S. Grant, Abraham Lincoln, John Brown, Harriet Beecher Stowe, Charles Sumner, Thomas Clarkson, Robert Gould Shaw, and Toussaint L'Ouverture.

The villains of the century for all black poets are white society in general and, after the Civil War, President Andrew Johnson in particular. Bell, the most steadfast champion of race progress from 1862 to 1900, contributes a witty anti-Johnson satire of scathing effectiveness, while his lengthy odes trace black history and achievement in peace and war. Although proudly race conscious, Bell is a transitional figure, for he drowns the militant ardor and anger of antebellum poets in floods of abstract, pretentious, and defensive oratory.

Reconstruction (1866–77), when hopes for racial equality were raised and then shattered, was unfruitful for African-American poetry and culture. Poets like Whitfield, Vashon, and Simpson continue to be politically aware, writing poems in honor of Emancipation, the three constitutional amendments, and Civil Rights Acts, as poets after them also will. Harper surveys the life and death of Moses (1869), finding a parallel for her race's captivity and liberation in the biblical account of Israel's redemption from Egyptian bondage. This Bible story, sung in the popular spiritual "Go Down, Moses," is a favorite reference for poets throughout the century. Among others, Reason, Simpson, Whitfield, Campbell, and Bell allude to it; Menken's "Hear, O Israel!" and Dunbar's "An Antebellum Sermon" elaborate on it. Other publications during Reconstruction include Menken's poems (1868), which concentrate on personal conflicts and losses. Harper's witty sketches of freedmen, narrated by Aunt Chloe (1872), herald a new kind of race poetry in the vernacular.

Two major approaches to race that reflect the postwar condition of African Americans and would dominate their poetry until 1900 appear for the first time during Reconstruction. With abolition of slavery, the leading grievance for impassioned protest poetry vanished. The struggle for freedom had bonded black writers of North and South, free blacks and slaves, to each other and to like-minded white Americans. Freedom imposed uncertainties about racial identity and the role of blacks in America's future. Reconstruction brought an urgent need for racial solidarity, as newly won civil rights were undermined by trickery, intimidation, and the South's black codes; the race's social, economic, and political security seemed fearfully precarious.

African-American poets typically respond to postwar conditions in two ways: first, by avoiding racial issues as a subject, either altogether as in Whitman's first poem *Leelah Misled* (1873), a "whites only" love story, or by only minor acknowledgment of race (in a dedication or tribute) as in the volumes of Walden (1873, 1877). Walden's verse is pious and conciliatory in tone, or playfully witty; he never refers to his eighteen years in bondage. The second postwar response, also initiated by Whitman and characteristic of his work until 1900, is aggrandizement of the race. In *Not a Man, and Yet a Man* (1877) he portrays "America's *coming* colored man" as one endowed with suprahuman physical, mental, and moral powers. He combines this elevation of the race's image with subtle race protest and an optimistic vision of the future. *Not a Man* contrasts the superior mixed-race hero and heroine and virtuous Indians with brutish whites like Sir Maxey and his murderous gang. The poem ends with a plea for peace and brotherhood: "Free schools, free press, free speech and equal laws,/ A common country and a common cause."

Thus Reconstruction sounded the death knell of militant protest poetry and the birth of "integrationist" and "upward-bound" types. In the last two decades of the century, African-American poets would lower their voices, mask discontents, and write sober, genteel verse largely indistinguishable from their white contemporaries' art. They would portray noble black men and women for the race to emulate and for whites to recognize as capable, responsible citizens worthy of integration into American society.

Conditions from 1877 onward, especially after 1890, necessitated these poetic modes as African-Americans' status worsened in North and South. Through legislatures, courts, and public opinion they were systematically disfranchised, excluded from juries, stripped of civil and social gains, relegated to menial jobs and sharecropper farming, and effectively subordinated in American society. Jim Crow laws (and later the "separate but equal" doctrine of the Supreme Court [1896]) enforced segregation in public facilities, railroads, residential zones of cities, and impoverished black schools. Racial hostility flourished, and mob terrorism raged, with lynchings reaching their apex in 1892. Racial inferiority was "proved" on sociological, psychological, and physiological authority, as for two centuries past it had been proved on biblical authority. Minstrel show caricatures mocked black personhood, and popular white literature in the plantation tradition, which reached a nadir in the writings of Thomas Nelson Page (1887–92), portrayed childlike "darkies" and justified slavery.

African Americans responded to this crippling discrimination in several ways. Outside of the literary sphere, the race organized: unions of farmers and industrial workers; educational, cultural, historical, social welfare, legal aid, and fraternal benefit societies; civil rights and anti-lynching leagues; associations of club women, businessmen, editors, teachers, and doctors; schools for industrial and agricultural training; and church groups active in all areas of social and economic improvement. These organizations had the same goals as African-American writers of the period: to develop race pride and solidarity; to encourage cultivation of Christian morality and cultural gentility; to rise by self-help, education, hard work, and accumulation of wealth; and to prove to white society that blacks were ready for assimilation into the mainstream.

To these ends, African-American writers recounted the sacrifices and struggles to overcome prejudice, the strengths and achievements of talented black men and women in dozens of books—biographies, autobiographies, histories such as Henry O. Flipper's *The Colored Cadet at West Point* (1878), George W. Williams's *History of the Negro Race in America* (1883), William J. Simmons's *Men of Mark: Eminent, Progressive and Rising* (1887), Daniel A. Payne's *Recollections of Seventy Years* (1888), Joseph T. Wilson's *The Black Phalanx* (1890), I. Garland Penn's *The Afro-American Press and Its Editors* (1891), Monroe Majors's *Noted Negro Women: Their Triumphs and Activities* (1893), Mrs. N. F. Mossell's *The Work of Afro-American Women* (1894), John M. Langston's *From the Virginia Plantation to the National Capitol* (1894), G. F. Richings's *Evidences of Progress among Colored People* (1896), and the zenith of upward-bound literature, Booker T. Washington's *Up from Slavery* (1900). These works identify the race with America's middle-class ethical and economic values; they prove Washington's dictum that "the past and present teach but one lesson,—to the Negro's friends and to the Negro himself,—that there is but one way out, . . . that his pillar of fire by night and pillar of cloud by day shall be property, economy, education and Christian character."[5] Furthermore, such books made the African-American author publishable as militant propaganda would not. And finally, as Whitman's *Not a Man* did in 1877, they conveyed a new, more refined race protest by demonstrating the hypocrisy of discrimination against blacks who had lived by white America's sacred principles—democratic equality, Christian idealism, and self-reliance—and had contributed significantly to the nation's progress.

After a hiatus of fifteen years, dozens of black periodicals flourished nationwide from 1880 to 1900, all designed as showcases for black literary artists and as guides to race elevation. The three most successful (and enduring) magazines were church-sponsored: the *AME Church Review* (1884), *AME Zion Quarterly Review* (1890), and *National Baptist Magazine* (1894). These and many others dedicated themselves to the goal expressed in the subtitle of *Howard's American Magazine* (1895): "Devoted to the Educational, Religious, Industrial, Social, and Political Progress of the Colored Race."

With the same goals as the writers of prose, black poets after Reconstruction take new stances. Those who glance at race at all swipe weakly at the establishment; or cautiously plead for black civil rights; or honor dead race heroes; or publicize race achievements. Only two poems, Fortune's "Bartow Black" (1886) and Dunbar's "The Haunted Oak" (1900) approach the urgency of antebellum protest. From 1880 to 1900, black poetry is conservative in subject and manner, seeking approval from white readers for the race, its artists, and its assimilationist goals. The poets agree with Whitman, who claims the purpose of his art is to "correct the world's judgement and force its respect."[6]

Most African-American poets of the century's last two decades write inspirational, descriptive, or sentimental verses about love, poetic art, religion, nature, children, death, and the old, romanticized South. The work of Forten, Ray, Fortune, McClellan, Fordham, Dunbar, and Bibb shows a decided bias for neoclassical decorum, heightened poetic diction, and technical virtuosity, all far removed from the direct, ardent remonstrances of antebellum poets. Post-Reconstruction poets also shift allegiance from a wrathful Jehovah and retaliation through fire and sword to a gentle Jesus with his promise of justice in the next world. The poetry is integrationist, at times explicitly, more often through conscious adherence to culturally acceptable themes, techniques, and ethical attitudes. Only rarely, as in the work of McClellan and Dunbar, does a poet's anguished awareness of his double identity— as an American and a black man—disturb his verse and distinguish it from prevailing white verse.

Fortune's poems, written during the last quarter of the century and collected in 1905, lament the vanity of human wishes and unfulfilled love. In Menard's volume (1879) more than half the verses deal with love, and the few race poems are optimistic. Ray's art, rich in technical skills, treats the beauties and mysteries of nature, philosophical issues, and idealistic love of God and literature. Whitman continues the themes he initiated in 1877; in *The Rape of Florida* (1884) he exalts Seminole Indians and Maroons, whose struggles for freedom had ended forty years previously, and dramatizes the defeat of valiant men of color by treacherous whites. Similarly, Whitman's "The Octoroon" (1901) celebrates an honorable interracial love affair doomed by prejudice. Some stanzas in Whitman's epics and poems through the 1890s explicitly condemn racism and urge African Americans to become "fearless manly" men and defend their natural rights to citizenship. In general, however, Whitman sings most beautifully of God in Nature, love between man and woman, and the free mind's eternal power. With less talent but much sincerity, Rowe offers one volume of uplifting and consolatory sermons in verse (1887), and his *Our Heroes* (1890), which celebrates luminaries of the race, is the epitome of upward-bound literature, as a contemporary reviewer said: "We learn to look beyond the worldly envelope of a man to the integrity of his conscience. Here should begin our race pride, which, as the author wisely says, is necessary to the growth, progress, and prosperity of any people. It should especially be placed in the hands of the young."[7] Priscilla Jane Thompson's later hymn to the heroic black woman (1900) continues this tradition.

Very few of Dunbar's poems in standard English (1893–1905) vigorously protest injustice to the race; rather, with ambivalent feelings about his heritage, Dunbar looks nostalgically at the old South and sings with pathos about his own bitter disappointments. The graceful and refined poems of McClellan (1895–1916) reveal the struggles of a poet to honor his blackness while accommodating his art to white society's expectations. Other, lesser poets of the late 1800s focus on conventional topics. Heard concentrates on love and God (1890; 1901). One of her poems, "They Are Coming?" celebrates the rise of middle-class blacks, the "Doctors, Lawyers, Preachers; . . . Sculptors, Poets, Teachers," and is a paradigm of the era's upward-bound assimilationist verse. Fordham specializes in sentimental, melancholy verses about death and nature (1897); Coffin retells songs and stories of the past and urges the race to accept the burden of its future (1897); and McGirt writes didactic or maudlin verses that also recall the past, lament the poet's lack of success, and pray for a better future (1899, 1906).

The search for racial identity, race improvement, and society's approval drew several poets into the orbit of Booker T. Washington. In the work of Cotter, Davis, and the later Harper, the Tuskegean's upward-bound ideology reaches didactic perfection. Cotter sanctifies self-help, money-getting, patient accommodation, and education; Davis urges work and prayer as keys to racial progress and asks no favors from white society but only an "equal chance. . . . To make our home the fairest spot on earth" ("The Negro Meets to Pray"). An idea prevalent in several poems is that blacks' failures and white racism are the race's own fault and must be endured until blacks improve themselves and rise. This view is shared by Cotter and Davis and also appears in poems by McClellan, Beadle, and Thompson. As in every decade since 1850, Harper's work remains prototypical. As early as 1871, she forgave the oppressor and combined her appeals for civil rights with a confident vision of racial harmony. During the last two decades of the century, Harper leads black poets in uplifting verse directed not only at raising the race's moral, educational, and economic status, but also at reforming national evils of alcoholism and the double standard of sex.

The final development in nineteenth-century black poetry is dialect verse that mythologizes the Southern past. Beginning in the late 1880s, dialect poems by African Americans recreate characters and folkways of the plantation tradition popularized by white writers: in the antebellum novels of William Gilmore Simms and John Esten Cooke and in later works of Thomas Nelson Page; in poems by Irwin Russell and the Uncle Remus tales of Joel Chandler Harris; and in minstrel shows, revived in the 1890s after their heyday from 1850 to 1870. James Weldon Johnson describes the favorite "Negro" of plantation and minstrel myths: "a simple, indolent, docile, improvident peasant; a singing, dancing, laughing, weeping child; picturesque beside his log cabin and in the snowy field of cotton; naively charming with his banjo and his songs in the moonlight and along the lazy Southern rivers; a faithful, ever-smiling and genuflecting old servitor to the white folks of quality; a pathetic and pitiable figure."[8]

Although the plantation folk of African-American dialect verse do exhibit these stereotypical qualities, they are not objects of ridicule or pity as they were for white writers. Black poets stress admirable qualities of the "Negroes of the old regime," as James Campbell called them: they are deeply religious, loyal to and loving one another, and remarkably shrewd and realistic, with intimate links to the land and an often ironic sense of humor.

Dialect poetry became respectable, fashionable, and profitable for black poets when W. D. Howells's Introduction welcomed Dunbar's

Lyrics of Lowly Life (1896). Before that, in the late 1880s, James Campbell created original satiric folk poetry, free of minstrel and plantation caricatures. After Campbell came poems by Davis, Dunbar's several volumes, and contributions by Cotter, McGirt, and Thompson. In the first two decades of the twentieth century, dialect pieces by James Corrothers, J. Mord Allen, John Holloway, Ray Dandridge, and many others found honored niches in white periodicals that for two hundred years had wholly ignored the writings of African Americans.

Black poets at the end of the nineteenth century wrote in dialect for many reasons: to escape from oppressive realities, to earn money and recognition, for safety, to make African Americans acceptable to white America; that is, to paint the race as servile lackeys or happy-go-lucky children renders it harmless, thereby countermanding the image of demonic, menacing savages that took vicious forms in the novels of Thomas Dixon (1902–7). To mock the race's superstitions, exaggerate the proverbial talent for song and dance, gluttony, and head-scratching impotence creates delightful objects of laughter without either the intelligence or will to threaten Anglo-Saxon supremacy. In these senses, dialect poetry is a defensive mask. But dialect poets also had other motives and objectives. Some felt a genuine affection for bygone simple rural joys, sincere nostalgia for the Southland, love for black folkways and folklore, admiration for the pieties and humanity of the cabin folk, and an attraction to the music, color, and humor of minstrelsy. For these writers, dialect verse affirmed their own blackness and hereditary solidarity with Southern brothers and sisters, especially when the poets vivaciously performed their verses for African-American audiences, as did Dunbar, Campbell, and Davis. Finally, for some poets, dialect verses were teaching aids: on one hand, they illustrated positive qualities of the race for white readers to appreciate; on the other hand, they illustrated negative modes of behavior, the crippling legacy of slavery imposed by whites that modern African Americans had to liquidate.

With such complex motives behind dialect verse, it cannot be dismissed as solely a demeaning, inadequate sociohistorical record of antebellum black life, for it was never intended to be factually sound. Dialect poetry by African Americans not only served many emotional, political, and material needs of the poets and their communities; but also much of it has lasting esthetic merit: its passages of lyrical beauty, its rollicking satire, foot-tapping or haunting melodies, and folksy details of church-going, trickery, and merrymaking are indeed charming. This verse often recalls the folk and slave narrative traditions; but several decades after Emancipation, the seamy and brutal, demoralizing and killing aspects of antebellum slave life were buried by popular demand, and African-American poets trod the golden footsteps of Dunbar to offer an eager public roses without thorns.[9]

Notes

1. The bibliography at the end of the introduction for each poet includes only the volumes of poetry from which selections are anthologized. For every poet, representative selections are offered from all volumes published by 1900; for some poets, additional selections are taken from post-1900 volumes. A full bibliography of poetry and prose and more detailed biography and criticism for most of the poets can be found in *Invisible Poets* (Urbana, 1989).

2. Almost all the poems in this anthology date from the nineteenth century. Where selections come from the poet's only published volume, no dates follow the poems, and the date of the volume appears in the poet's introduction. Where selections come from two or more volumes, each poem is dated. If more than one date follows a poem, the first is the date a poem was written or appeared in a periodical, and the second is the date the poem was collected in a volume.

3. Often many years separate a poem's first publication and its inclusion in a collection. For example, Simpson's songs appeared in periodicals from 1848 through the early 1850s but were not collected until 1874; Alfred Campbell's verses first published in 1851–52 were collected in his 1883 volume. Because the work of both poets belongs to the antebellum era, it appears early in this anthology. Although a first-published poem may not be included in this anthology, its date, when known, still determines the poet's place in the chronological sequence.

4. Although they published before the Civil War, Cannon, Plato, and Payne did not write protest verse.

5. *Future of the American Negro* (Boston, 1899), 132.

6. *Twasinta's Seminoles; or, Rape of Florida* (St. Louis, 1885).

7. "Have You Seen Our Heroes?" *AME Church Review* 7 (Oct. 1890): back page.

8. "The Dilemma of the Negro Author," *American Mercury* 15 (1928): 478.

9. Some of the material in the Introduction and in the poets' biocritical sketches previously appeared in *Invisible Poets*.

A Note to the Reader

A biocritical sketch and list of selected primary works precedes the work of each of the thirty-five poets.

Each poem is accompanied by notes that refer to line numbers in the poem. The notes define unusual words, identify persons, places events, and mythological characters, explain historical circumstances and biblical references, and supply additional information. Because the poems are transcribed precisely as they first appeared, and their original spellings are maintained, the notes supply correct spellings.

A line of dots in a poem indicates the omission of several lines or one or more stanzas.

Following the poets' works is a bibliography of secondary sources and reference works for further study of nineteenth-century African-American literature, with emphasis on poetry, as well as sources specific to the anthologized poets.

GEORGE MOSES HORTON

George Moses Horton (1797?–1883?), the "Colored Bard of North Carolina," was the first Southern black man to publish a volume of poetry in America. Born a slave on the farm of William Horton in Northampton County, North Carolina, he moved with his master to Chatham and worked as a "cow-boy" and farm laborer throughout his teens. During these years, George taught himself to read and began composing verses and hymns in his head. From about 1817, he took weekend trips to the University of North Carolina, where students bought his love lyrics, composed to order and dictated to the buyers, and loaned him books to further his education. As Horton's fame as a poet spread through Chapel Hill in the 1820s, the novelist Caroline Lee Hentz transcribed his verse for publication — he could not write until 1832. With the university president and other notables, Hentz initiated the first of several futile campaigns to purchase Horton's freedom. In the early 1830s, Horton was earning more than $3 a week from sales of his love lyrics, and he arranged to hire his time from his master to become a full-time poet, handyman, hotel waiter, and servant to the university students and staff. For over thirty years until Emancipation, while he worked in Chapel Hill, Horton published poems in antislavery periodicals as well as in a second collection, and he continued to appeal for his freedom. After the Civil War, Horton traveled in North Carolina, composing dozens of new poems for his third volume, and about 1866 he went North to settle in Philadelphia. Here, it seems, he found liberty lonely and difficult for the seventeen years until his death.

With 150 poems in his three collections, Horton demonstrates a natural talent for the rhythms of verse, a perfect ear for rhyme, and a sensitive, often cynical awareness of what life, and thus poetry, is all about. His verse before 1865 is his best, including melodious love lyrics; neatly crafted religious verses that reveal his simple piety, often combined with love of poetry and nature; tender evocations of the rural sights and sounds of the seasons; and a few sincere antislavery poems, where hope for freedom is often linked to an exuberant tribute to the joys of poetizing. His personal and earthy folk verses (1845) are outstanding, lively with colloquial detail and wry humor. Most of his later work on the Civil War has more historical than esthetic value, but his overall lifelong achievement as Poet Horton was extraordinary.

The Hope of Liberty, Containing a Number of Poetical Pieces (Raleigh, N.C.: J. Gales & Son, 1829); *The Poetical Works* (Hillsborough, N.C.: D. Heartt, 1845); *Naked Genius* (Raleigh, N.C.: Wm. B. Smith, 1865).

Praise of Creation

Creation fires my tongue!
  Nature thy anthems raise;
And spread the universal song
  Of thy Creator's praise!

Heaven's chief delight was Man   5
  Before Creation's birth—
Ordained with joy to lead the van,
  And reign the lord of earth.

When Sin was quite unknown,
  And all the woes it brought,   10
He hailed the morn without a groan
  Or one corroding thought.

When each revolving wheel
  Assumed its sphere sublime,
Submissive Earth then heard the peal,   15
  And struck the march of time.

The march in Heaven begun,
  And splendor filled the skies,
When Wisdom bade the morning Sun
  With joy from chaos rise.   20

The angels heard the tune
  Throughout creation ring:
They seized their golden harps as soon
  And touched on every string.

When time and space were young,   25
  And music rolled along—
The morning stars together sung,
  And Heaven was drown'd in song.

Ye towering eagles soar,
    And fan Creation's blaze,   30
And ye terrific lions roar,
    To your Creator's praise.

Responsive thunders roll,
    Loud acclamations sound,
And show your Maker's vast control   35
    O'er all the worlds around.

Stupendous mountains smoke,
    And lift your summits high,
To him who all your terrors woke,
    Dark'ning the sapphire sky.   40

Now let my muse descend,
    To view the march below—
Ye subterraneous worlds attend
    And bid your chorus flow.

Ye vast volcanoes yell,   45
    Whence fiery cliffs are hurled;
And all ye liquid oceans swell
    Beneath the solid world.

Ye cataracts combine,
    Nor let the paean cease—   50
The universal concert join,
    Thou dismal precipice.

But halt my feeble tongue,
    My weary muse delays:
But, oh my soul, still float along   55
    Upon the flood of praise!
                       (1829)

Notes

Horton draws on the Bible (Gen. 1:1–31 and Job 38:7 ["morning stars," 27]
to celebrate God's creation of the universe, and he summons all created things

and his poetic art to join in praise. 13. *revolving wheel:* planet. 19. *Wisdom:* God. 20. *chaos:* the original disorder of formless matter and darkness. 41, 54. *muse:* in Greek myth, nine muses or goddesses presided over the arts and sciences; here the muse is Calliope of epic poetry or Erato of lyric poetry. 50. *paean:* a song of praise.

The Slave's Complaint

Am I sadly cast aside,
On misfortune's rugged tide?
Will the world my pains deride
   Forever?

Must I dwell in Slavery's night,   5
And all pleasure take its flight,
Far beyond my feeble sight,
   Forever?

Worst of all, must hope grow dim,
And withhold her cheering beam?   10
Rather let me sleep and dream
   Forever!

Something still my heart surveys,
Groping through this dreary maze;
Is it Hope? — then burn and blaze   15
   Forever!

Leave me not a wretch confined,
Altogether lame and blind —
Unto gross despair consigned,
   Forever!   20

Heaven! in whom can I confide?
Canst thou not for all provide?
Condescend to be my guide
   Forever:

And when this transient life shall end,   25
Oh, may some kind, eternal Friend
Bid me from servitude ascend,
   Forever!

      (1829)

On Summer

Esteville fire begins to burn;
  The auburn fields of harvest rise;
The torrid flames again return,
  And thunders roll along the skies.

Perspiring Cancer lifts his head,   5
  And roars terrific from on high;
Whose voice the timid creatures dread;
  From which they strive with awe to fly.

The night-hawk ventures from his cell,
  And starts his note in evening air;   10
He feels the heat his bosom swell,
  Which drives away the gloom of fear.

Thou noisy insect, start thy drum;
  Rise lamp-like bugs to light the train;
And bid sweet Philomela come,   15
  And sound in front the nightly strain.

The bee begins her ceaseless hum,
  And doth with sweet exertions rise;
And with delight she stores her comb,
  And well her rising stock supplies.   20

Let sportive children well beware,
  While sprightly frisking o'er the green;
And carefully avoid the snare,
  Which lurks beneath the smiling scene.

The mistress bird assumes her nest,   25
  And broods in silence on the tree,
Her note to cease, her wings at rest,
  She patient waits her young to see.

The farmer hastens from the heat;
   The weary plough-horse droops his head;   30
The cattle all at noon retreat,
   And ruminate beneath the shade.

The burdened ox with dauntless rage,
   Flies heedless to the liquid flood,
From which he quaffs, devoid of gauge,   35
   Regardless of his driver's rod.

Pomacious orchards now expand
   Their laden branches o'er the lea;
And with their bounty fill the land,
   While plenty smiles on every tree.   40

On fertile borders, near the stream,
   Now gaze with pleasure and delight;
See loaded vines with melons teem—
   'Tis paradise to human sight.

With rapture view the smiling fields,   45
   Adorn the mountain and the plain,
Each, on the eve of Autumn, yields
   A large supply of golden grain.

                  (1829)

Notes

1. *Esteville:* a town in North Carolina. 2. *auburn:* reddish brown. 5. *Cancer:* a sign of the zodiac (the Crab) which the sun enters on June 21, the first day of summer. 15. *Philomela:* the nightingale, from the classical myth of Philomela, an Athenian princess who was transformed into a nightingale. 32. *ruminate:* to chew the cud; cud: a mouthful of food from the first stomach chewed slowly for a second time, as a cow does. 35. *gauge:* means of measuring an amount. 37. *pomaceous:* of apples. 38. *lea:* a meadow.

Liberty and Slavery

Alas! and am I born for this,
  To wear this slavish chain?
Deprived of all created bliss,
  Through hardship, toil and pain!

How long have I in bondage lain,   5
  And languished to be free!
Alas! and must I still complain—
  Deprived of liberty.

Oh, Heaven! and is there no relief
  This side the silent grave—   10
To soothe the pain—to quell the grief
  And anguish of a slave?

Come Liberty, thou cheerful sound,
  Roll through my ravished ears!
Come, let my grief in joys be drowned,   15
  And drive away my fears.

Say unto foul oppression, Cease:
  Ye tyrants rage no more,
And let the joyful trump of peace,
  Now bid the vassal soar.   20

Soar on the pinions of that dove
  Which long has cooed for thee,
And breathed her notes from Afric's grove,
  The sound of Liberty.

Oh, Liberty! thou golden prize,   25
  So often sought by blood—
We crave thy sacred sun to rise,
  The gift of nature's God!

Bid Slavery hide her haggard face,
  And barbarism fly: 30
I scorn to see the sad disgrace
  In which enslaved I lie.

Dear Liberty! upon thy breast,
  I languish to respire;
And like the Swan unto her nest,   35
  I'd to thy smiles retire.

Oh, blest asylum—heavenly balm!
  Unto thy boughs I flee—
And in thy shades the storm shall calm,
  With songs of Liberty!   40
                              (1829)

Notes

20. *vassal:* slave. 21. *pinions:* wings. 34. *respire:* to breathe freely. 37. *balm:* anything healing to the mind.

On Hearing of the Intention of a Gentleman to Purchase the Poet's Freedom

When on life's ocean first I spread my sail,
I then implored a mild auspicious gale;
And from the slippery strand I took my flight,
And sought the peaceful haven of delight.

Tyrannic storms arose upon my soul,   5
And dreadful did their mad'ning thunders roll;
The pensive muse was shaken from her sphere,
And hope, it vanished in the clouds of fear.

At length a golden sun broke through the gloom,
And from his smiles arose a sweet perfume —   10
A calm ensued, and birds began to sing,
And lo! the sacred muse resumed her wing.

With frantic joy she chaunted as she flew,
And kiss'd the clement hand that bore her through;
Her envious foes did from her sight retreat,   15
Or prostrate fall beneath her burning feet.

'Twas like a proselyte, allied to Heaven —
Or rising spirits' boast of sins forgiven,
Whose shout dissolves the adamant away,
Whose melting voice the stubborn rocks obey.   20

'Twas like the salutation of the dove,
Borne on the zephyr through some lonesome grove,
When Spring returns, and Winter's chill is past,
And vegetation smiles above the blast.

'Twas like the evening of a nuptial pair,   25
When love pervades the hour of sad despair —
'Twas like fair Helen's sweet return to Troy,
When every Grecian bosom swell'd with joy.

The silent harp which on the osiers hung,
Was then attuned, and manumission sung;   30
Away by hope the clouds of fear were driven,
And music breathed my gratitude to Heaven.

Hard was the race to reach the distant goal,
The needle oft was shaken from the pole;
In such distress who could forbear to weep?   35
Toss'd by the headlong billows of the deep!

The tantalizing beams which shone so plain,
Which turned my former pleasures into pain—
Which falsely promised all the joys of fame,
Gave way, and to a more substantial flame.   40

Some philanthropic souls as from afar,
With pity strove to break the slavish bar;
To whom my floods of gratitude shall roll,
And yield with pleasure to their soft control.

And sure of Providence this work begun—   45
He shod my feet this rugged race to run;
And in despite of all the swelling tide,
Along the dismal path will prove my guide.

Thus on the dusky verge of deep despair,
Eternal Providence was with me there;   50
When pleasure seemed to fade on life's gay dawn,
And the last beam of hope was almost gone.
                                        (1829)

Notes

In 1828, several of Horton's friends initiated a campaign to buy his freedom;
although aided by the Manumission Society and an appeal for funds in *Freedom's
Journal,* the campaign failed. 12. *muse:* see Horton's "Praise of Creation" (41).
17. *proselyte:* a person converted to a belief. 19. *adamant:* hard stone. 22. *zephyr:*
soft gentle breeze; the west wind. 27. *Helen's sweet return to Troy:* When Paris,
a Trojan prince, abducted Helen, the wife of Menelaus, king of Sparta, the Greeks
laid siege to Troy for ten years. After the Greeks defeated Troy, Helen returned
to her husband and Sparta. The poet mistakenly returns Helen to Troy. 29. *osiers:*
willow tree branches. 41. *philanthropic:* charitable.

The Creditor to His Proud Debtor

Ha! tott'ring Johnny strut and boast,
But think of what your feathers cost;
Your crowing days are short at most,
   You bloom but soon to fade.
Surely you could not stand so wide,   5
If strictly to the bottom tried;
The wind would blow your plume aside,
   If half your debts were paid.
     Then boast and bear the crack,
     With the Sheriff at your back,   10
     Huzza for dandy Jack,
     My jolly fop, my Jo—

The blue smoke from your segar flies,
Offensive to my nose and eyes,
The most of people would be wise,   15
   Your presence to evade.
Your pockets jingle loud with cash,
And thus you cut a foppish dash,
But alas! dear boy, you would be trash,
   If your accounts were paid.   20
     Then boast and bear the crack, &c.

My duck bill boots would look as bright,
Had you in justice served me right,
Like you, I then could step as light,
   Before a flaunting maid.   25
As nicely could I clear my throat,
And to my tights, my eyes devote,
But I'd leave you bear, without coat,
   For which you have not paid.
     Then boast and bear the crack, &c.   30

I'd toss myself with a scornful air,
And to a poor man pay no care,

I could rock cross-legged in my chair,
    Within the cloister shade.
I'd gird my neck with a light cravat,   35
And creaming wear my bell-crown hat;
But away my down would fly at that,
    If once my debts were paid.
        Then boast and bear the crack,
        With the Sheriff at your back,   40
        Huzza for dandy Jack,
        My jolly fop, my Jo—

                                (1845)

Notes

13. *segar:* cigar. 22. *duck bill boots:* boots made of heavy cotton cloth. 34. *cloister:* a secluded place. 35. *cravat:* scarf or necktie.

Early Affection

I lov'd thee from the earliest dawn,
  When first I saw thy beauty's ray,
And will, until life's eve comes on,
  And beauty's blossom fades away;
And when all things go well with thee,   5
With smiles and tears remember me.

I'll love thee when thy morn is past,
  And wheedling gallantry is o'er,
When youth is lost in ages blast,
  And beauty can ascend no more,   10
And when life's journey ends with thee,
O, then look back and think of me.

I'll love thee with a smile or frown,
  'Mid sorrow's gloom or pleasure's light,
And when the chain of life runs down,   15
  Pursue thy last eternal flight,
When thou hast spread thy wing to flee,
Still, still, a moment wait for me.

I'll love thee for those sparkling eyes,
  To which my fondness was betray'd,   20
Bearing the tincture of the skies,
  To glow when other beauties fade,
And when they sink too low to see,
Reflect an azure beam on me.

                 (1845)

Notes
21. *tincture:* tint or light color. 24. *azure:* sky blue.

Troubled with the Itch and Rubbing with Sulphur

'Tis bitter, yet 'tis sweet;
    Scratching effects but transient ease;
Pleasure and pain together meet
    And vanish as they please.

My nails, the only balm,   5
    To every bump are oft applied,
And thus the rage will sweetly calm
    Which aggravates my hide.

It soon returns again:
    A frown succeeds to every smile;   10
Grinning I scratch and curse the pain
    But grieve to be so vile.

In fine, I know not which
    Can play the most deceitful game:
The devil, sulphur, or the itch.   15
    The three are but the same.

The devil sows the itch,
    And sulphur has a loathsome smell,
And with my clothes as black as pitch
    I stink where'er I dwell.   20

Excoriated deep,
    By friction played on every part,
If oft deprives me of my sleep
    And plagues me to my heart.
                (1845)

Notes

Sulphur: an element used in making medicine. 21. *excoriated:* one's skin scratched off.

Acrostics

Mistress of green in flowers arrayed
Alluring all my heart away
Replete with glory not to fade
Yet flourish in eternal May—
Eternalized by distant fame—   5
Void of a shade in bloom divine—
Pleasures await thy sacred name
Or bid thee still proceed(s) to shine
Who has surpassed thy heavenly mein
Expression will forbear to tell   10
Like thee not one I yet have seen
Let all adore *thee* lovely belle

So let our names togather blend
In floods of union to the end
Or flow togather soul in soul   15
Nor distance break the soft control—
How pleasing is the thought to me
A thought of such a nymph as thee
Reverts my language into song
That flows delightful soft along—   20
Return to me a soft reply
On which I must with joy rely
Give me thy hand and then thy heart
Entirely mingled not to part
Relume the tapor near expired   25
Seeking a friend so long desired—
(ca. 1845)

Notes

Acrostics are verses in which the first letters of each line, in order, spell out a name (in this case, two names). Horton wrote many acrostics; he did not supply a title for this acrostic. 8. *proceed.* 13, 15. *together.* 25. *taper:* candle.

Gen. Grant—the Hero of the War

Brave Grant, thou hero of the war,
Thou art the emblem of the morning star,
Transpiring from the East to banish fear,
Revolving o'er a servile Hemisphere,
At large thou hast sustained the chief command   5
And at whose order all must rise and stand,
To hold position in the field is thine,
To sink in darkness or to rise and shine.

Thou art the leader of the Fed'ral band,
To send them at thy pleasure through the land,   10
Whose martial soldiers never did recoil
Nor fail in any place to take the spoil,
Thus organized was all the army firm,
And led unwavering to their lawful term,
Never repulsed or made to shrink with fear,   15
Advancing in their cause so truly dear.

The love of Union burned in every heart,
Which led them true and faithful from the start,
Whether upon water or on land,
They all obeyed their marshal's strict command,   20
By him the regiments were all surveyed,
His trumpet voice was by the whole obeyed,
His order right was every line to form,
And all be well prepared to front the storm.

Ye Southern gentlemen must grant him praise,   25
Nor on the flag of Union fail to gaze;
Ye ladies of the South forego the prize,
Our chief commander here to recognize,
From him the stream of general orders flow,
And every chief on him some praise bestow,   30
The well-known victor of the mighty cause
Demands from every voice a loud applause.

What more has great Napoleon ever done,
Though many battles in his course he won?
What more has Alexander e'er achieved,   35
Who left depopulated cities grieved?
To him we dedicate the whole in song,
The verses from our pen to him belong,
To him the Union banners are unfurled,
The star of peace the standard of the world.   40
                                    (1865)

Notes

Ulysses Simpson Grant (1822–85), commander-in-chief of the Union armies and, succeeding Johnson, eighteenth president (1869–77). 33. *Napoleon:* Napoleon Bonaparte (1769–1821), French military genius, world conqueror, and emperor as Napoleon I. 35. *Alexander:* Alexander the Great (356–323 B.C.), king of Macedonia and conquerer of most of the ancient world.

Imploring to Be Resigned at Death

Let me die and not tremble at death,
　But smile at the close of my day,
And then at the flight of my breath,
　Like a bird of the morning in May,
　　Go chanting away.　　　　　　5

Let me die without fear of the dead,
　No horrors my soul shall dismay,
And with faith's pillow under my head,
　With defiance to mortal decay,
　　Go chanting away.　　　　　　10

Let me die like a son of the brave,
　And martial distinction display;
Nor shrink from a thought of the grave,
　No, but with a smile from the clay,
　　Go chanting away.　　　　　　15

Let me die glad, regardless of pain,
　No pang to this world betray,
And the spirit cut loose from its chains,
　So loath in the flesh to delay,
　　Go chanting away.　　　　　　20

Let me die, and my worst foe forgive,
　When death veils the last vital ray;
Since I have but a moment to live,
　Let me, when the last debt I pay,
　　Go chanting away.　　　　　　25

(1865)

George Moses Horton, Myself

I feel myself in need
  Of the inspiring strains of ancient lore,
My heart to lift, my empty mind to feed,
  And all the world explore.

I know that I am old   5
  And never can recover what is past,
But for the future may some light unfold
  And soar from ages blast.

I feel resolved to try,
  My wish to prove, my calling to pursue,   10
Or mount up from the earth into the sky,
  To show what Heaven can do.

My genius from a boy,
  Has fluttered like a bird within my heart;
But could not thus confined her powers employ,   15
  Impatient to depart.

She like a restless bird,
  Would spread her wing, her power to be unfurl'd,
And let her songs be loudly heard,
  And dart from world to world.   20

                    (1865)

NOAH CALWELL CANNON

Noah Calwell W. Cannon (1796?–1850) was a self-educated itinerant African Methodist Episcopal exhorter. Cannon and both of his parents were born in Sussex County, Delaware, where he spent his youth. As a result of a vision, he determined to become a minister. About 1818, in Philadelphia, Cannon joined the A.M.E. church and soon received a license to preach. For the next three decades he preached at camp meetings throughout the eastern A.M.E. circuit. He died in Canada.

The stated goal of *The Rock of Wisdom* is "to try to save souls." To this end, Cannon expounds and reinterprets the Old and New Testaments, Methodist doctrines, and world history in vivid, rhythmic prose, and he appends sixteen hymns and "The Ark." His prose is often enigmatic, the hymns traditional in form and content, and "The Ark" is a lively summons to praise God and pray for one another as did the biblical heroes he names.

The Rock of Wisdom; An Explanation of the Sacred Scriptures, . . . To Which Are Added Several Interesting Hymns (N.p., 1833).

The Ark

Dear brothers and sisters, we love one another,
And have done, for years that have gone;
How often we've met him in sweet heavenly union,
Who opens the way to God's throne;
With joy and thanksgiving we'll praise him that lov'd us,   5
While we run the bright shining way;
Though we part here in body, we're bound for one glory,
And bound for each other to pray.
There Joshua and Joseph, Elias and Moses,
Who pray'd and God heard from this throne.   10
There was Abram, and Isaac, and Jacob, and David,
And Solomon, Stephen and John.
There was Simeon and Anna—I don't know how many,
Who pray'd as they journey'd along;
Some cast among lions—some bound with rough irons;   15
Yet praises and glory they sung.
Some tell us that praying, and also that praising,
Is labor that's all spent in vain:
But we have such witness, that God hears with sweetness;
From praying we will not refrain.   20
There was old father Noah and ten thousand more,
Who witness'd that God heard them pray;
There was Samuel and Hannah, Paul, Silas and Peter,
And Daniel and Jonah, we'll say,
That God by his Spirit, and angel did visit   25
Their souls while in this happy frame.
Shall we all go a fainting, while they went a praising,
And glorified God in a flame!
God grant us inherit the same praying spirit,
While we shall be toiling below,   30
That when we've done praying, we shall not cease praising,
But around God's throne we shall bow.
   [And now pious friends, when you read these lines which
have been penned by me, think of me in solemn prayer;

let me be on land or sea, I intend to stand for liberty, for   35
Christ has set me free.]
      For this love let rocks and mountains;
      Purling streams and crystal fountains;
      Roaring thunders, lightning blazes,
      Shout the great Messiah's praises. Amen.   40

Note

   The Ark of the Covenant was originally a box built by the Israelites to house the Ten Commandments. This Ark came to represent the Deity. Cannon names patriarchs, prophets, kings, sages, martyrs, and apostles of the Old and New Testaments who glorified God.

CHARLES LEWIS REASON

Charles Lewis Reason (1818–93), an educator, reformer, essayist, and poet, was born in New York City of West Indian parents, Elizabeth and Michiel Reason. He studied and taught at the African Free School in the city, graduated from McGrawville College (New York), and from 1849 to 1850 he taught belles lettres, Greek, Latin, French, and mathematics at New York Central College. Reason campaigned for black enfranchisement in New York City and state. He was secretary of the Political Improvement Association (1837), New York State Convention for Negro Suffrage (1840), National Negro Convention (1853), and New York's Citizens Civil Rights Committee.

In Philadelphia, Reason was principal of the Institute for Colored Youth (1852–55); then for thirty-eight years he served as a teacher and principal at several colored schools in New York City. From the 1830s until his death, Reason fought for abolitionism, black civil rights, suffrage, and education as an officer, writer, and lecturer for leading African-American organizations. His essays and poems appeared in periodicals and remain uncollected. Reason died of nephritis and heart disease in his New York City home.

Reason's poems illustrate his sincere dedication to reform, his vast learning, and adroit poetic techniques. With direct, stirring language he links ancient and modern worldwide battles for freedom in admirable examples of antebellum protest verse.

The Spirit Voice;
or Liberty Call to the Disfranchised
(State of New York)

Come! rouse ye brothers, rouse! a peal now breaks
From lowest island to our gallant lakes:
'Tis summoning you, who long in bonds have lain,
To stand up manful on the battle plain,
Each as a warrior, with his armor bright,   5
Prepared to battle in a bloodless fight.
Hark! How each breeze that blows o'er Hudson's tide
Is calling loudly on your birth-right pride
And each near cliff, whose peak fierce storms has stood,
Shouts back responsive to the calling flood.   10
List! from those heights that once with freedom rung,
And those broad fields, where Earth has oft-times sung,
A voice goes up, invoking men to prove
How dear is freedom, and how strong their love.
From every obscure vale and swelling hill   15
The spirit tones are mounting; louder still
From out the din where noble cities rise
On Mohawk's banks, the peal ascends the skies.
Responding sweet with morning's opening praise,
The sounds commingle, far, to where the rays   20
Of light departing, sink to partial sleep,
'Mid caverned gems in Erie's bosomed deep.
Nor yet less heard, from inland slopes it swells,
In chiming music, with the village bells,
And mixes loud e'en with the ocean's waves,   25
Like shrill-voiced echo in the mountain caves.
'Tis calling you, who now too long have been
Sore victims suffering under legal sin,
To vow, no more to sleep, till raised and freed
From partial bondage, to a life indeed.   30
Behold ye now! here consecrate from toil
And love, your homes abide on holy soil.
To these, as sacred temples, fond you cling:
For, thence alone, life's narrow comforts spring,

'Tis here the twilight of existence broke,   35
The first warm throbbings of your hearts awoke.
Here first o'er you, fond mothers watch'd and pray'd,
Here friendship rose and holy vows were made.
On yon familiar height or gentle stream,
You first did mark the pleasant moonlight gleam.   40
Here, happy, laugh'd o'er life in cradled bloom
And here, first pensive, wept at age's tomb,
Yes; many a sire, with burnt and furrowed brow
Here died, in hope that you in freedom now
Would feel the boasted pledge your country gave,   45
That her defender should not be her slave.
And wherefore, round your homes has not been thrown
That guardian shield, which strangers call their own?
Why, now, do ye, as your poor fathers did,
Bow down in slience to what tyrants bid?   50
And sweat and bleed from early morn till eve,
To earn a dower less than beggars leave?
Why are ye pleased to delve at mammon's nod?
To buy that manhood which is yours from God,
Free choice to say who worthy is to lead   55
Your country's cause, to give your heart-felt meed
Of praise to him that, barring custom's rule,
Would nobly dare attack the cringing tool
That with a selfish aim and ruthless hand,
Would tear in twain love's strong and holy band: 60
Why can ye not, as men who know and feel
What most is needed for your nation's weal,
Stand in her forums, and with burning words
Urge on the time, when to the bleeding herds,
Whose minds are buried now in polar night,   65
Hope shall descend; when freedom's mellow light
Shall break, and usher in the endless day,
That from Orleans to Pass'maquoddy Bay,
Despots no more may earthly homage claim,
Nor slaves exist, to soil Columbia's name.   70
Then, up! awake! nor let dull slumber waste
Your soul's devotion! life doth bid you haste;
The captive in his hut, with watchful ear,

Awaits the sweet triumphant songs to hear,
That shall proclaim the glorious jubilee   75
When crippled thousands shall in truth be free.
Come! rouse ye brothers, rouse! nor let the voice
That shouting, calls you onward to rejoice,
Be heard in vain! but with ennobled souls,
Let all whom now an unjust law controls,   80
Press on in strength of mind, in purpose bent,
To live by right; to swell the free tones sent
On Southern airs, from this, your native State,
A glorious promise for the captive's fate.
Then up! and vow no more to sleep, till freed   85
From partial bondage to a life indeed.
                    (New York, July 20, 1841)

Notes

7, 18, 22. *Hudson's . . . Mohawk's . . . Erie's:* rivers and lakes in New York. 68.
Orleans to Pass'maquoddy Bay: New Orleans, Louisiana, on the Mississippi River
to Passamaquoddy Bay, an inlet of the Bay of Fundy between Maine and New
Brunswick, Canada.

CHARLES LEWIS REASON

from Freedom

* * * * * * *

"Sans Toi l'univers est un temple
Qui n'a plus ni parfums, ni chants."
LAMARTINE

* * * * * *

O Freedom! Freedom! O! how oft
Thy loving children call on Thee!
In wailings loud, and breathings soft,
Beseeching God, Thy face to see.

With agonizing hearts we kneel,   5
While 'round us howls the oppressor's cry,—
And suppliant pray, that we may feel
The ennob'ling glances of Thine eye.

We think of Thee as once we saw
Thee, jewel'd by Thy Father's hand,   10
Afar beside dark Egypt's shore,
Exulting with Thy ransom'd band.

We hear, as then, the thrilling song,
That hail'd Thy passage through the sea,—
While distant echoes still prolong   15
The cymbal'd anthem, sung to Thee.

And wafted yet, upon the gales
Borne pure and fresh from sunny skies,
Come startling words! that 'long the vales
Where Pelion and Ossa rise,   20

Were shouted by Thine own clear voice!
And Grecian hearts leap'd at the call:
E'en as now Patriot souls rejoice,
To see invading tyrants fall.

We view Thy stately form, loom o'er 25
The topmost of the seven hills!
While 'round Thee glittering eagles soar—
The symbol'd rise of freeborn wills.

Down in the plains, we still behold
The circled forums built to Thee;— 30
Hear Tully's strains, and Brutus bold,
Call on his country to be free.

When from those groves of citron bloom,
And classic Helle's vine clad shore,—
Through countries hung in castled gloom, 35
Attending winds Thy chariot bore,—

We followed Thee o'er all the fields
Of Europe, crimson-dyed with blood;
Where broken spears, and buried shields,
Now mark the spots where Thou hast stood. 40

. . . .

Exulting in their mission high,
Columbia's sons had pledged Thy cause—
Thy first endeavor,—"to untie
The cords of caste and slavish laws."

Long years roll'd by, and still went on 45
The strife of man, 'gainst regal power:
Till, falsely, in Thy strength, was won
Thy since, polluted, blood-stained dower.

We mourn for this! yet joyfully
O Freedom! we loud praises give, 50
That on Thine altar in the sea,
For us Thy holy fires live.

O! grant! unto our parent home,
Thy constant presence and Thy shield!

That when again rude hirelings come,   55
Though starr'd from every battle field,

The spirit of the patriot true,
Toussaint, the "man of men," may ring
The shrill war cry the welkin through,
And plain to mount the echo sing.   60

. . . .

When from the slave's crush'd, aching heart,
The cry went up to Sabaoth's God,—
And man, with his immortal part,
Alike, were thrust beneath the sod,

We saw Thee wield convictions strength,   65
And heard Thy blows fall thick and fast;
While loud and clear through all the length
Of Britain, blew Thy trumpet blast.

Thou wast the answer! CLARKSON! *thou*
The mighty soul that woke to life!   70
That took the consecrated vow,
To conquer—perish in the strife.

Well hast thou fought, great pioneer!
The snows of age upon thy head,
Were Freedom's wreaths; by far, more dear,   75
Than finest sculpture o'er the dead.

We leave thee to thy long repose!
Thou hast the blessings of the slave:
We pray that at the world's dread close,
Thou rise *a freeman* from the grave.   80

What more can we O! Freedom! speak
In praise of Thee? our hearts grow faint!
Where else shall we Thy triumphs seek?
What fairer pictures can we paint?

We stand upon the shaking ground   85
Of tyranny! we call it home:
The earth is strewn with Christians bound,—
We've cried to Thee—Thou dost not come.

We know Thou has Thy chosen few,—
The men of heart, who live by right,—   90
Who steadily their way pursue,
Though round them pall the shades of night.

We hold them dear: defamed, beset,
They fight the civil war of man:
The fiercest struggle, that has yet   95
Been waged against oppressions ban.

We give them thanks: the bondman's prayer
As holy incense soars on high,
That nought to Thee their love impair,
'Till shall be gained the victory.   100

But, O! Great Spirit! see'st Thou
Thy spotless ermine men defile?
God's civil rulers cringing bow
To hate, and fraud, and customs vile!

The CHURCH, to her great charge untrue,   105
Keeps Christian guard, o'er slavery's den!
Her coward laymen, wrong pursue,
Her recreant priesthood, say—amen.

O! purify each holy court!
The ministry of law and light!   110
That man, no longer, may be bought
To trample down his brother's right.

We lift imploring hands to Thee!
We cry for those in prison bound!
O! in Thy strength, come! Liberty!   115
And 'stablish right the wide world round.

We pray to see Thee, face to face:
To feel our souls grow strong and wide:
So ever shall our injured race,
By Thy firm principles abide.   120
(New York, December 1846)

Notes

The poem eulogizes Thomas Clarkson (1760–1846), pioneer English abolitionist. Reason recited "Freedom" at a commemorative service in New York at Clarkson's death (1846). The epigraph is translated as: "Without you the universe is a temple that has neither perfume nor music." Alphonse de Lamartine (1790–1869) was a French poet and politician. 11–14. *dark Egypt's shore ... through the sea:* the Israelites were freed from Egyptian bondage as the waters of the Red Sea parted (Exod. 14: 21–22). 20–22. *Pelion and Ossa rise. ... Grecian hearts:* in Greek myth, the Giants, at war with the gods, attempted to climb into heaven by piling the mountain Ossa on the mountain Pelion, but the gods subdued the invaders. 26–30: *seven hills ... eagles soar ... circled forums:* ancient Rome, whose emblem was the eagle, was built on seven hills; governmental bodies and the populace assembled in forums, the public squares of the city. 31. *Tully's strains:* Marcus Tullius (106–43 B.C.), known as *Cicero,* an eloquent Roman orator, statesman, philosopher, and writer. 31. *Brutus:* Marcus Junius Brutus (85?–42 B.C.), a Roman statesman and general, one of the assassins of Julius Caesar. 33. *citron:* a fruit similar to a lemon but larger. 34. *Helle's vine:* the grapevine of ancient Greece. 58. *Toussaint:* Pierre François Dominique Toussaint L'Ouverture (1743–1803), leader of the successful slave revolt, 1790–91, in Saint-Domingue (now Haiti). Toussaint, a slave for almost fifty years, was a brilliant military strategist, diplomat, and administrator. The Haitian rebellion and Toussaint's deeds inspired many literary tributes. See Vashon's "Vincent Ogé" and Rogers' "Toussaint L'Overture" and their notes. 62. *Sabaoth's God:* Sabaoth, derived from the Hebrew, means armies or hosts; in the Bible it appears in the phrase "the Lord of Sabaoth." Although Reason here reverses the word order, he is referring to the Old Testament God of the Israelites, the Lord of Hosts. See usage in Menken's "Hear, O Israel!" 102. *ermine:* a rare white fur used to trim the robes of royalty and judges.

ANN PLATO

Ann Plato (1820?–?) was a teenage girl when she published a collection of sixteen moral essays, four biographical sketches, and twenty poems. The Reverend James W. C. Pennington, her pastor at the Colored Congregational Church of Hartford, Connecticut, a leading abolitionist and clergyman, introduced the volume, which he accurately describes as "the pious sentiments of a youth devoted to the glory of God, and the best good of her readers." Nothing is known about Plato's life. She combines a Puritan religiosity and romantic imagination in her poems, most of them in neat iambic tetrameter. Plato's verses generally moralize about religion and death and teach the virtues of obedience, "order, industry, and perseverance," benevolence, and love of God.

Essays: Including Biographies and Miscellaneous Pieces, in Prose and Poetry (Hartford, Conn.: Author, 1841).

Advice to Young Ladies

Day after day I sit and write,
  And thus the moments spend—
The thought that occupies my mind,—
  Compose to please my friend.

And then I think I will compose,   5
  And thus myself engage—
To try to please young ladies minds,
  Which are about my age.

The greatest word that I can say,—
  I think to please, will be,   10
To try and get your learning young,
  And write it back to me.

But this is not the only thing
  That I can recommend;
Religion is most needful for   15
  To make in us a friend.

At thirteen years I found a hope,
  And did embrace the Lord;
And since, I've found a blessing great,
  Within his holy word.   20

Perchance that we may ne'er fulfill,
  The place of aged sires,
But may it with God's holy will,
  Be ever our desires.

The Natives of America

Tell me a story, father please,
And then I sat upon his knees.
Then answer'd he,—"what speech make known,
Or tell the words of native tone,
Of how my Indian fathers dwelt,   5
And, of sore oppression felt;
And how they mourned a land serene,
It was an ever mournful theme."

Yes, I replied,—I like to hear,
And bring my father's spirit near;   10
Of every pain they did forego,
Oh, please to tell me all you know.
In history often I do read,
Of pain which none but they did heed.

He thus began. "We were a happy race,   15
When we no tongue but ours did trace,
We were in ever peace,
We sold, we did release—
Our brethren, far remote, and far unknown,
And spake to them in silent, tender tone.   20
We all were then as in one band,
We join'd and took each others hand;
Our dress was suited to the clime,
Our food was such as roam'd that time,
Our houses were of sticks compos'd;   25
No matter,—for they us enclos'd.

But then discover'd was this land indeed
By European men; who then had need
Of this far country. Columbus came afar,
And thus before we could say Ah!   30
What meaneth this?—we fell in cruel hands.

Though some were kind, yet others then held bands
Of cruel oppression. Then too, foretold our chief,—
Beggars you will become—is my belief.
We sold, then some bought lands,   35
We altogether moved in foreign hands.

Wars ensued. They knew the handling of firearms.
Mothers spoke,—no fear this breast alarms,
They will not cruelly us oppress,
Or thus our lands possess.   40
Alas! it was a cruel day; we were crush'd:
Into the dark, dark woods we rush'd
To seek a refuge.

My daughter, we are now diminish'd, unknown,
Unfelt! Alas! No tender tone   45
To cheer us when the hunt is done;
Fathers sleep,—we're silent every one.

Oh! silent the horror, and fierce the fight,
When my brothers were shrouded in night;
Strangers did us invade—strangers destroy'd   50
The fields, which were by us enjoy'd.

Our country is cultur'd, and looks all sublime,
Our fathers are sleeping who lived in the time
That I tell. Oh! could I tell them my grief
In its flow, that in roaming, we find no relief.   55

I love my country; and shall, until death
Shall cease my breath.

Now daughter dear I've done,
Seal this upon thy memory; until the morrow's sun
Shall sink, to rise no more;   60
And if my years should score,
Remember this, though I tell no more."

JOSHUA McCARTER SIMPSON

Joshua McCarter Simpson (1820?–76) was freeborn in Morgan County, Ohio, and suffered a childhood of poverty and harsh treatment. Bound out at a very young age, first to a stonemason, then to a farmer until he was twenty-one, Simpson had only three months of schooling. He taught himself to write, sang his first poem in public in 1842, and published a small pamphlet of antislavery songs before 1852. Hoping to become a teacher, Simpson studied at Oberlin College (1844–48) but could not attain his goal. He married in Zanesville, Ohio (1847), and in the next two decades wrote the two satirical essays and fifty-three song poems collected in 1874. In that year, Simpson was an elder in charge of the Zion Baptist Church and an herb doctor in Zanesville, where he died.

Simpson artfully clothes angry race protest in sardonic humor for his song poems, which are both hearty folk poetry and forceful literary propaganda for emancipation and freedmen's rights. The songs share simple diction, repetition of phrases and refrains, topicality, and humorous, pathetic, or militant tones. Simpson's choice of tunes—familiar hymns, folk songs, and patriotic airs—is often shrewdly ironic, as when he warns white people that judgment is coming to the melody of "Massa's in the Cold Cold Ground," or he condemns July Fourth celebrations to the tune of "America." The sly wit, drama, nimble dialog, colorful detail, and truth to experience of these songs made them very popular among fugitives on the Underground Railroad in the 1850s.

The Emancipation Car (Zanesville, Ohio: Sullivan and Brown, 1874).

The First of August in Jamaica

Air—*"Hail Columbia"*

Hail thou sweet and welcome day,
Let the angels join the lay,
   And help us swell the anthems high.
   Tune all your golden harps once more,
And strike to notes ne'er struck before,   5
Yea let the morning's zephry-breeze,
   Bear the echo o'er the seas;
   Let all the islands bond and free,
   Proclaim Jamaica's liberty,
   And while we praise the God most high   10
Who rules the heavens, the earth and sky,
Let Queen Victoria honored be
As mother of our liberty.

To-day we gladly congregate,
A happy band to celebrate   15
   The day we rose from slavery's tomb.
   Our clanking chains no more are heard;
Our limbs no more by fetters scarred;
Our backs no more are drenched with blood;
   Our tears have ceased our cheeks to flood;   20
   Our wives and children, all so dear,
   Are bowed around the altar here.
   May Hayti gladly catch the gale,
And Portorico tell the tale;
Let the Atlantic's dancing spray   25
Salute this new-born happy day.

The knee with sacred awe we bend,
With melting hearts once more to spend
   This day in free, unfettered praise;
   Our thanks belong to God alone,   30
For He this mighty work has done.
He saw the tyrant wield the lash;

He counted every bleeding gash;
He heard our children beg for bread
Which o'er our master's table spread,   35
Our scalding tears in silence shed,
Were coals of fire upon his head.
Wake the psaltry, lute and lyre,
And let us set the world on fire.
   And may Jehovah blow the flame,   40
   Till all mankind shall see the light
Of knowledge, liberty and right!
Our hands are clear of human blood;
   We bought our liberty from God.
   Love, joy and peace are now combined   45
   With freedom's golden chain entwined,
   Firm united may we stand,
A happy, free and social band;
Each brother feels his brother's care.
And each his brother's burthen bear.   50
       (*North Star,* 1848; 1874)

Notes

In 1833, Great Britain abolished slavery in the British West Indies by paying
£20 million to slaveholders. The Parliamentary act of emancipation went into
effect on August 1, 1834; thereafter, American blacks and abolitionists celebrated
the first of August. 12. *Queen Victoria:* the reigning monarch of Great Britain
(1837–1901) and the personification of freedom in many popular song poems. 23,
24. *Hayti . . . Portorico:* The slaves of Haiti were liberated from French control
in 1791, and in Puerto Rico, a colony of Spain, slavery was abolished in 1873.
38. *psaltry, lute and lyre:* ancient musical instruments. 40. *Jehovah:* God (Old
Testament); modern version of the Hebrew "Yahweh."

Away to Canada

Adapted to the case of Mr. S.,
Fugitive from Tennessee.

I'm on my way to Canada,
   That cold and dreary land;
The dire effects of slavery,
   I can no longer stand.
My soul is vexed within me so,   5
   To think that I'm a slave;
I've now resolved to strike the blow
   For freedom or the grave.

     O righteous Father,
       Wilt thou not pity me?   10
     And aid me on to Canada,
       Where colored men are free.

I heard Victoria plainly say,
   If we would all forsake
Our native land of slavery,   15
   And come across the Lake.
That she was standing on the shore,
   With arms extended wide,
To give us all a peaceful home,
   Beyond the rolling tide.   20

     Farewell, old master!
       That's enough for me—
     I'm going straight to Canada,
       Where colored men are free.

I heard the old-soul driver say,   25
   As he was passing by,
That darkey's bound to run away,
   I see it in his eye.

My heart responded to the charge,
   And thought it was no crime;   30
And something seemed my mind to urge,
   That now's the very time.

    O! old driver,
       Don't you cry for me,
    I'm going up to Canada,   35
       Where colored men are free.

Grieve not, my wife—grieve not for me,
   O! do not break my heart,
For nought but cruel slavery
   Would cause me to depart.   40
If I should stay to quell your grief,
   Your grief I would augment;
For no one knows the day that we
   Asunder might be rent.

    O! Susannah,   45
       Don't you cry for me—
    I'm going up to Canada,
       Where colored men are free.

I heard old master pray last night—
   I heard him pray for me;   50
That God would come, and in his might
   From Satan set me free;
So I from Satan would escape,
   And flee the wrath to come—
If there's a fiend in human shape,   55
   Old master must be one.

    O! old master,
       While you pray for me,
    I'm doing all I can to reach
       The land of Liberty.   60

Ohio's not the place for me;
    For I was much surprised,
So many of her sons to see
    In garments of disguise.
Her name has gone out through the world,   65
    Free Labor, Soil, and Men;
But slaves had better far be hurled
    Into the Lion's Den.

    Farewell, Ohio!
        I am not safe in thee;   70
    I'll travel on to Canada,
        Where colored men are free.

I've now embarked for yonder shore,
    Where man's a *man by law,*
The vessel soon will bear me o'er,   75
    To shake the Lion's paw.
I no more dread the Auctioneer,
    Nor fear the master's frowns,
I no more tremble when I hear
    The beying negro-hounds.   80

    O! old Master,
        Don't think hard of me—
    I'm just in sight of Canada,
        Where colored men are free.

I've landed safe upon the shore,   85
    Both soul and body free;
My blood and brain, and tears no more
    Will drench old Tennesse.
But I behold the scalding tear,
    Now stealing from my eye,   90
To think my wife—my only dear,
    A slave must live and die.

    O, Susannah!
        Don't grieve after me—

For ever at a throne of grace,   95
I will remember thee.
(*Liberator,* 1852; 1874)

Notes

This poem is sung to the tune of "Oh, Susanna." In 1848, an antislavery Free Soil party was formed in the North; it took as its slogan "Free soil, free speech, free labor, and free men." As Simpson says, Ohio was known as the State of Free Labor, Free Soil, and Free Men (66). It was the first goal of fugitive slaves, but Ohio's proximity to slave territory made it a favorite hunting-ground of slave-catchers; therefore, escaped slaves and free blacks fled from Ohio across Lake Erie into Canada "where colored men are free" by British law. Some thirty thousand fugitives from American slavery lived in Canada in 1860. (See Simpson's " 'No, Master, Never!' "; see also Topic Index, Slavery and Abolitionism: Laws.) 68. *Lion's Den:* Daniel the prophet was hurled into a lion's den to be devoured; God's angel saved him (Dan. 6:16–23). Daniel's life-threatening situation images that of the slaves in Ohio. 76. *Lion's paw:* The lion is the national emblem of Great Britain. 80. *baying.* 88. *Tennessee.*

The Twilight Hour

Air—"*Alabama Again*"

As I sat one evening in sweet meditation,
  My mind not encompassed by land or by sea;
I soon was amused by a sweet conversation,
  Of Nature, while boasting herself to be free.

"I am free," said the stream, while the chrys-   5
    taline fountain
  Came dancing its bubbles along by my feet;
"I was free from my birth, and I came from
    the mountain,
  And now I am going the old ocean to greet."

"I am 'free,'" said the fish, "I can catch at the
    bubble,
  And if there a worm should happen to be,   10
I make him my supper, and it costs me no
    trouble,
  For God has created me happy and free."

"We are free," said the Nightingales, joining
    their chorus;
  (While over me gently they poised on the
    wing;)
Our parents and kinsmen were all free before   15
    us,
  And we will the anthems of liberty sing.

"I am free," said the breeze, loaded down with
    sweet odour,
  As it through the willows came rustling by.
"I can pass when I please, and return at my
    leisure;
  The power of monarchs or kings I defy."   20

"I am free," said the bee, as from flower to flower,
　It buzzed in pursuit of its evening store.
"I am happy though life is to me but an hour;
　God gives me my freedom, and I ask for no
　　more."

"I am free," said the lightning, while rending the　25
　Heavens;
　"A sceptre I sway, over land and the sea;
To kill and to cure, to me it is given;
　I act my own pleasure, I'm mighty and free."

Then, shouted all nature, with loud exultation;
　The voice was re-echoed o'er mountain and　30
　plain;
"I am free as my Maker—I'm queen of all na-
　tions,
　But poor suffering mortals I love to sustain."

Part II

The white man united his voice in the chorus,
　With jarring and discord, he sang to the
　　glee.
Of heroes that fought and who bled long before　35
　us,
　To purchase their offspring such sweet liberty.

I would have united in praise and devotion,
　But ere a long tear could escape from my
　　eye,
I thought of my brethren, a down-trodden na-
　tion,
　Poor bondsmen, like brutes, they must suffer　40
　　and die.

My soul I exclaimed, and is God thus ordain-
　ing,
　From angels and nature perpetual praise;

While Africa's sons are in bondage complain-
ing,
And dare not their voice to His Majesty
raise?

Will not the Almighty descend in great power,   45
And bid the poor slave from captivity go?
Will he not his vengeance on slave-holders
shower,
Until as a God they His power shall know?

Yea! now! even now is the "day star" arising;
The morning of freedom now dawns in the   50
East.
The sun which illumins the eastern horizon,
The captive from bondage, will shortly re-
lease.

Old Liberia Is Not the Place for Me

Air—"*Come to the Old Gum Tree*"

Come all ye Colonizationists,
　My muse is off to-day—
Come, listen while she's singing
　Her soft and gentle lay.
Before she's done you'll understand　　　　　　5
　Whoever you may be,
That Old Liberia
　Is not the place for me.

Although I'm trodden under foot,
　Here in America—　　　　　　　　　　　　10
And the right to life and liberty,
　From me you take away.
Until my brethren in the South
　From chains are all set free—
The Old Liberia　　　　　　　　　　　　　　15
　Is not the place for me.

Although (as Moses Walker says,)
　There, children never cry:
And he who can well act the hog,
　For food will never die;　　　　　　　　　20
For there the yams and cocoa-nuts,
　And oranges are free—
Yet old Liberia
　Is not the place for me.

You say it is a goodly land,　　　　　　　　25
　Where milk and honey flows,
And every "Jack" will be a man,
　Who there may choose to go.
You say that God appointed there
　The black man's destiny—　　　　　　　　30

Yet old Liberia
   Is not the place for me.

The sweet potatoes there may grow,
   And rice in great supplies;
And purest waters ever flow,   35
   Which dazzle quite your eyes.
Though there they have the sugar-cane,
   Also the coffee tree,
Yet old Liberia
   Is not the place for me.   40

Three millions slaves are in the South,
   And suffering there to-day:
You've gagged them, yes, you've stopped
      their mouth,
   They dare not even pray!
We, who in art and enterprise,   45
   Are trudging on our way,
You'd have us all to colonize,
   In old Liberia.

Give joy or grief—give ease or pain,
   Take life or friends away;   50
I deem this as my native land,
   And here I'm bound to stay,
"I have a mind to be a man
   Among white men and free;
And OLD LIBERIA!   55
   Is not the place for me!"

My muse has chanted now too long,
   And spent her breath in vain,
In singing of that "Negro Den,"
   Across the raging main.   60
Our blood is now so far dispersed
   Among the Anglo-race,
To rid the country of this curse,
   Would need a larger space,

And old Liberia   65
Is rather far away;
I'd rather find a peaceful home
In old America!

Note

1. *Colonizationists:* The American Colonization Society, formed in 1816, worked to establish a colony on Africa's West Coast for free blacks and for slaves who would be emancipated if they emigrated. By 1865, about ten thousand African Americans had colonized Liberia. Previously, from the late eighteenth century to 1865, many other efforts were made to remove blacks from the United States to colonies in Africa, Haiti, Canada, and Central America, including Lincoln's project to colonize Panama. However, most blacks and white abolitionists opposed separatism and colonization schemes. The poets Whitfield and Menard supported colonization, but others like Simpson rejected it. (See Subject Index, African-American Race: Colonization.)

"No, Master, Never!"

Or the true feelings of those slaves who say they
would not be free. The following shows their
feelings when they are free.

Air—*"Pop Goes the Weasel"*

Old master always said,
    Jack will never leave me:
He has a noble head,
    He will not deceive me.
I will treat him every day   5
    Kindly and clever,
Then he will not run away—
    No, master, never!

One night I heard him say,
    He was going to Cleveland,   10
A thought struck me right away,
    That this was a free land.
I thought if I too could go,
    The dearest ties I'd sever.
And never would come back no more—   15
    Never! no, never!

The next morn at early dawn,
    I heard old master knocking:
He says, "Jack, we must be gone—
    Put on your shoes and stockings."   20
Quickly I bounded out,
    And got my clothes together,
And told my wife I'd not come back
    No, Lizzie, never!

Soon we were on the way,   25
    Toward the Forest City;
There to leave my wife a slave,
    I thought it was a pity.

I heard mistress slightly say,
  We'll all keep together,   30
Or Jack will go to Canada,
  No, says master, never!

Jack, says he, be wide awake,
  And let nobody tease you;
And don't go too near the lake—   35
  The cold winds will freeze you!
Do you think I would run away,
  And leave a man so clever,
And seek a home in Canada?
  "No, master, never!"   40

We stopped at the Weddell House,
  The thought then came o'er me,
That now's the time to go across,
  As many have gone before me.
I went down to the steamboat wharf   45
  Got on the Jacob Astor,
And cried aloud as she shoved off,
  Farewell, old master.

The next day, in Malden town,
  Who should I see but master,   50
He says, Jack, you must go home,
  You'll starve and freeze to death sir.
Says I, you are a nice old man;
  Very kind and clever;
But think I'll wear my chains again?   55
  "No, master, never!"

To the White People of America

Air — *"Massa's in the Cold, Cold Ground"*

O'er this wide extended country,
    Hear the solemn echoes roll,
For a long and weary century,
    Those cries have gone from pole to pole;
See the white man sway his sceptre,   5
    In *one* hand he holds the rod —
In the *other* hand the Scripture,
    And says that he's a man of God.

    Hear ye that mourning?
        'Tis your brothers' cry!   10
    O! ye wicked men take warning,
        The day will come when you must die.

Lo! Ten thousand steeples shining
    Through this mighty Christian land,
While four millions slaves all pining   15
    And dying 'neath the Tyrant's hand.
See the *"blood-stained"* Christian banner
    Followed by a host of saints (?)
While they loudly sing Hosannah,
    We hear the dying slave's complaints: 20

    Hear ye that mourning?
        Anglo-sons of God,
    O! ye Hypocrites take warning,
        And shun your sable brothers blood.

In our Legislative members,   25
    Few there are with humane souls,
Though they speak in tones of thunder
    'Gainst sins which they cannot control,
Women's rights and annexation,
    Is the topic by the way,   30

While poor Africa's sable nation
For mercy, cry both by night and day.

    Hear ye that mourning?
    'Tis a solemn sound,
    O! ye wicked men take warning,   35
    For God will send his judgment down.

Tell us not of distant Island —
    Never will we colonize:
Send us not to British Highlands,
    For this is neither just nor wise,   40
Give us equal rights and chances,
    All the rights of citizens —
And as light and truth advances,
    We'll show you that we all are men.

    Hear ye that mourning?   45
    'Tis your brothers sigh,
    O! ye wicked men take warning,
    The judgment day will come by and by.

JAMES MONROE WHITFIELD

James Monroe Whitfield (1822–71), a major propagandist for black separatism and racial justice, worked as a barber all his life, and the bitter tone of much of his verse reflects his abortive attempts to become a man of letters while obliged to earn a living in a barber shop. He was born in New Hampshire, and little is known about his youth or later private life. Whitfield was a barber in Buffalo, New York (1854–59) and in California (1862–71), with brief sojourns in his later years in Oregon, Idaho, and Nevada. His public support for colonization began in 1854 when he wrote the call for the National Emigration Convention and a series of letters to the *North Star* supporting separatism. Continuing this work, in 1859–61 he probably traveled in Central America, seeking land for a black colony. From 1849 until his death, Whitfield's impassioned protest poetry, prose, and letters appeared often in African-American periodicals; the majority of his work remains uncollected. He also read several of his commemorative odes in public. Whitfield was Grand Master of California's Prince Hall Masons, and when he died of heart disease, he was buried in the Masonic Cemetery of San Francisco.

Whitfield's verse is outstanding for its metrical control, breadth of classical imagery, commanding historical sense, and for the biting cynicism of his antislavery tirades and the anguished pessimism of his self-portraits. He denounces oppression worldwide, scourges America's morally corrupt church and state, and dramatizes the estrangement and defeat by race prejudice of an African American who aspires to high ideals and poetic art. No poet of his time combines anger and artistry as well as Whitfield does in his intense and convincing poems.

America and Other Poems (Buffalo, N.Y.: James S. Leavitt, 1853); "A Poem," in Ezra Rothschild Johnson, *Emancipation Oration . . . and Poem. . . .* (San Francisco: *Elevator* Office, 1867), pp. 23–32.

How Long

How long, oh gracious God! how long
    Shall power lord it over right?
The feeble, trampled by the strong,
    Remain in slavery's gloomy night.
In every region of the earth,   5
    Oppression rules with iron power,
And every man of sterling worth,
    Whose soul disdains to cringe, or cower
Beneath a haughty tyrant's nod,
And, supplicating, kiss the rod,   10
That, wielded by oppression's might,
Smites to the earth his dearest right,
The right to speak, and think, and feel,
    And spread his uttered thoughts abroad,
To labor for the common weal,   15
    Responsible to none but God—
Is threatened with the dungeon's gloom,
The felon's cell, the traitor's doom;
And treacherous politicians league
    With hireling priests, to crush and ban   20
All who expose their vile intrigue,
    And vindicate the rights of man.
How long shall Afric raise to thee
    Her fettered hand, oh Lord, in vain?
And plead in fearful agony,   25
    For vengeance for her children slain.
I see the Gambia's swelling flood,
    And Niger's darkly rolling wave,
Bear on their bosoms stained with blood,
    The bound and lacerated slave;   30
While numerous tribes spread near and far,
Fierce, devastating, barbarous war—
Earth's fairest scenes in ruin laid
To furnish victims for that trade,

Which breeds on earth such deeds of shame   35
As fiends might blush to hear or name.
I see where Danube's waters roll,
    And where the Magyar vainly strove,
With valiant arm, and faithful soul,
    In battle for the land he loved —   40
A perjured tyrant's legions tread
The ground where Freedom's heroes bled,
And still the voice of those who feel
Their country's wrongs, with Austrian steel.
I see the "Rugged Russian Bear"   45
Lead forth his slavish hordes, to War
Upon the right of every State
Its own affairs to regulate:
To help each Despot bind the chain
Upon the people's rights again,   50
And crush beneath his ponderous paw
All Constitutions, rights and law.
I see in France, oh, burning shame!
The shadow of a mighty name,
Wielding the power her patriot bands   55
Had boldly wrenched from kingly hands,
With more despotic pride of sway
Than ever monarch dared display.
The Fisher, too, whose world-wide nets
Are spread to snare the souls of men.   60
By foreign tyrant's bayonets
    Established on his throne again,
Blesses the swords still reeking red
    With the best blood his country bore,
And prays for blessings on the head   65
    Of him who wades through Roman gore.
The same unholy sacrifice,
Where'er I turn, bursts on mine eyes,
Of princely pomp, and priestly pride.
    The people trampled in the dust,   70
Their dearest, holiest rights denied,
    Their hopes destroyed, their spirit crushed;

But when I turn the land to view,
   Which claims, par excellence, to be
The refuge of the brave and true,   75
   The strongest bulwark of the free,
The grand asylum for the poor
   And trodden-down of every land,
Where they may rest in peace secure,
   Nor fear th' oppressor's iron hand —   80
Worse scenes of rapine, lust and shame,
Than e'er disgraced the Russian name,
Worse than the Austrian ever saw,
Are sanctioned here as righteous law.
Here might the Austrian Butcher make   85
   Progress in shameful cruelty,
Where women-whippers proudly take
   The meed and praise of chivalry.
Here might the cunning Jesuit learn —
   Though skilled in subtle sophistry,   90
And trained to persevere in stern,
   Unsympathizing cruelty,
And call that good, which, right or wrong,
Will tend to make his order strong —
He here might learn from those who stand   95
   High in the gospel ministry,
The very magnates of the land
   In evangelic piety,
That conscience must not only bend
   To every thing the Church decrees,   100
But it must also condescend,
   When drunken politicians please
To place their own inhuman acts
   Above the "higher law" of God,
And on the hunted victim's tracks   105
   Cheer the malignant fiends of blood;
To help the man-thief bind the chain
   Upon his Christian brother's limb,
And bear to Slavery's hell again
   The bound and suffering child of Him   110

Who died upon the cross, to save
Alike, the master and the slave.
While all th' oppressed from every land
Are welcomed here with open hand,
And fulsome praises rend the heaven   115
For those who have the fetters riven
Of European tyranny,
And bravely struck for liberty;
And while from thirty thousand fanes
   Mock prayers go up, and hymns are sung,   120
Three millions drag their clanking chains,
   "Unwept, unhonored and unsung;"
Doomed to a state of slavery
   Compared with which the darkest night
Of European tyranny,   125
   Seems brilliant as the noonday light;
While politicians, void of shame,
   Cry, this is law and liberty,
The clergy lend the awful name
   And sanction of the Deity,   130
To help sustain the monstrous wrong,
And crush the weak beneath the strong.
Lord! thou hast said, the tyrant's ear
   Shall not be always closed to thee,
But that thou wilt in wrath appear,   135
   And set the trembling captive free;
And even now dark omens rise
   To those who either see or hear,
And gather o'er the darkening skies
   The threatening signs of fate and fear.   140
Not like the plagues which Egypt saw,
   When rising in an evil hour,
A rebel 'gainst the "higher law,"
   And glorying in her mighty power—
Saw blasting fire, and blighting hail,   145
Sweep o'er her rich and fertile vale,
And heard on every rising gale,
Ascend the bitter, mourning wail;
And blighted herd, and blasted plain,

Through all the land the first-born slain,   150
Her priests and magi made to cower
In witness of a higher power,
And darkness, like a sable pall,
 Shrouding the land in deepest gloom,
Sent sadly through the minds of all   155
 Forebodings of approaching doom.
What though no real shower of fire
 Spreads o'er this land its withering blight,
Denouncing wide Jehovah's ire
 Like that which palsied Egypt's might;   160
And though no literal darkness spreads
 Upon the land its sable gloom,
And seems to fling around our heads
 The awful terrors of the tomb:
Yet to the eye of him who reads   165
 The fate of nations past and gone,
And marks with care the wrongful deeds
 By which their power was overthrown,
Worse plagues than Egypt ever felt
 Are seen wide-spreading through the land,   170
Announcing that the heinous guilt
 On which the nation proudly stands,
Has risen to Jehovah's throne
 And kindled his avenging ire,
And broad-cast through the land has sown   175
 The seeds of a devouring fire.
Tainting with foul, pestiferous breath
 The fountain-springs of moral life,
And planting deep the seeds of death,
 And future germs of deadly strife;   180
And moral darkness spreads its gloom
 Over the land in every part
And buries in a living tomb
 Each generous prompting of the heart.
Vice in its darkest, deadliest stains,   185
 Here walks with brazen front abroad,
And foul corruption proudly reigns
 Triumphant in the Church of God;

And sinks so low the Christian name,
In foul, degrading vice, and shame,   190
That Moslem, Heathen, Atheist, Jew,
    And men of every faith and creed,
To their professions far more true,
    More liberal both in word and deed,
May well reject, with loathing scorn,   195
    The doctrines taught by those who sell
Their brethren in the Saviour born,
    Down into slavery's hateful hell;
And with the price of Christian blood
Build temples to the Christian's God;   200
And offer up as sacrifice,
    And incense to the God of heaven,
The mourning wail, and bitter cries,
    Of mothers from their children riven;
Of virgin purity profaned   205
    To sate some brutal ruffian's lust,
Millions of Godlike minds ordained
    To grovel ever in the dust;
Shut out by Christian power and might,
From every ray of Christian light.   210
How long, oh Lord! shall such vile deeds
    Be acted in thy holy name,
And senseless bigots, o'er their creeds,
    Fill the whole earth with war and flame?
How long shall ruthless tyrants claim   215
    Thy sanction to their bloody laws,
And throw the mantle of thy name,
    Around their foul, unhallowed cause?
How long shall all the people bow
    As vassals of the favored few,   220
And shame the pride of manhood's brow,
    Give what to God alone is due —
Homage, to wealth, and rank, and power
Vain shadows of a passing hour?
Oh for a pen of living fire,   225
    A tongue of flame, an arm of steel,

To rouse the people's slumbering ire,
    And teach the tyrant's heart to feel.
Oh Lord! in vengeance now appear,
    And guide the battles for the right,   230
The spirits of the fainting cheer,
    And nerve the patriot's arm with might;
Till slavery banished from the world,
And tyrants from their powers hurled,
And all mankind from bondage free,   235
Exult in glorious liberty.

Notes

27, 28. *Gambia's . . . Niger's:* rivers in West Africa. Most slaves imported to North America came from the regions of these rivers. 37, 38, 44, 45–52: *Danube's waters; the Magyar; Austrian steel; "Rugged Russian Bear" . . . rights and law:* The Danube River flows through Hungary and Austria. The Hungarian (Magyar) Revolution of 1848–49 was ruthlessly suppressed by the Austrians with the aid of Russia's Tsar Nicholas. From 1826, Russia had waged war on Persia, Turkey, and Poland; in the Crimean War, which began in 1853, Russia fought Great Britain, France, Turkey, and Sardinia. 54. *shadow of a mighty name:* In 1848–52, Prince Louis Napoleon Bonaparte, nephew of the "mighty" Napoleon I, as president of the Second French Republic established a repressive dictatorship; late in 1852, he became Napoleon III, emperor of the Second Empire. 59–66, 82, 83, 85. *Fisher . . . Roman gore:* The Fisher is the pope as imaged by Jesus' summons to the fishermen Simon (Peter) and Andrew: "Follow me, and I will make you fishers of men" (Matt. 4:18–19). During the Italian War of Independence against Austria (1848–49), Pope Pius IX declared his neutrality in the conflict; the Italians branded him a traitor and forced him to flee from Rome, however the French and Austrians restored his throne. 89. *cunning Jesuit:* Jesuits are members of a Roman Catholic religious order, the Society of Jesus, founded by Ignatius of Loyola in 1534. For their opponents, the Jesuits' debating skills and political intrigues throughout Europe made their name synonymous with crafty, unethical, or equivocal practices. Terms with these meanings, for example, "jesuitism," "jesuitry," and "jesuitical," remain in use today. 141–60. *plagues which Egypt saw . . . palsied Egypt's might:* When the pharaoh of Egypt refused to let Moses lead the Hebrews out of bondage into the wilderness, God sent ten afflictions on the Egyptians: water turned to blood; plagues of frogs, lice, and flies; death of cattle; boils; hail and fire; locusts; darkness; and the death of every Egyptian first-born male child (Exod. 4:29–15:21). The Egyptian captivity, sufferings, and escape of the children of Israel became for many black poets the prototype of American slavery. (See Subject Index, Religion: Moses.) 177. *pestiferous:* carrying disease.

To ———

Approaching night her mantle flings
   O'er plain and valley, rock and glen,
When borne away on fancy's wings,
   Imagination guides my pen.
I soar away to glittering spheres,   5
   And leave behind the sons of earth;
Lo! my enraptured fancy hears
   Seraphic strains of heavenly mirth.
A vision as of angel bright
   Sudden appears before my face,   10
A beauteous, fascinating sprite,
   Endowed with every charm and grace.
Majestic Juno's lofty mien,
   With beauteous Venus' form and face,
And chaste Diana's modesty,   15
   Adorned with wise Minerva's grace,
United in thy form divine,
With most resplendent luster shine.
And when those matchless charms I viewed,
   Thy faultless form, and graceful mien,   20
Surprised, amazed, entranced I stood,
   And gazed with rapture on the scene.
And when thy lips were ope'd to speak,
   In tones so sweet, so soft and clear,
Gabriel his golden harp might break,   25
   And seraphs lean from heaven to hear.
'Tis the pure mind which dwells within,
   Displays itself in act and word,
And raises thee from every sin
   Far, *far* above the common herd.   30
And when the term of life is past,
   And thy pure soul returns to heaven,
The memory of thy worth shall last,
   While thought or mind to man are given.

Notes

The poet's beloved shares attributes of mythological Roman deities: 13. *Juno:* queen of heaven; 14. *Venus:* goddess of love and beauty; 15. *Diana:* virgin goddess of the moon and the hunt; 16. *Minerva:* goddess of wisdom; 25. *Gabriel:* The biblical archangel, a divine messenger.

The Misanthropist

In vain thou bid'st me strike the lyre,
   And sing a song of mirth and glee,
Or, kindling with poetic fire,
   Attempt some higher minstrelsy;
In vain, in vain! for every thought   5
   That issues from this throbbing brain,
Is from its first conception fraught
   With gloom and darkness, woe and pain.
From earliest youth my path has been
   Cast in life's darkest, deepest shade,   10
Where no bright ray did intervene,
   Nor e'er a passing sunbeam strayed;
But all was dark and cheerless night,
   Without one ray of hopeful light.
From childhood, then, through many a shock,   15
   I've battled with the ills of life,
Till, like a rude and rugged rock,
   My heart grew callous in the strife.
When other children passed the hours
   In mirth, and play, and childish glee,   20
Or gathering the summer flowers
   By gentle brook, or flowery lea,
I sought the wild and rugged glen
   Where Nature, in her sternest mood,
Far from the busy haunts of men,   25
   Frowned in the darksome solitude.
There have I mused till gloomy night,
   Like the death-angel's brooding wing,
Would shut out every thing from sight,
   And o'er the scene her mantle fling;   30
And seeking then my lonely bed
   To pass the night in sweet repose,
Around my fevered, burning head,
   Dark visions of the night arose;

And the stern scenes which day had viewed   35
   In sterner aspect rose before me,
And specters of still sterner mood
   Waved their menacing fingers o'er me.
When the dark storm-fiend soared abroad,
   And swept to earth the waving grain,   40
On whirlwind through the forest rode,
   And stirred to foam the heaving main,
I loved to mark the lightning's flash,
   And listen to the ocean's roar,
Or hear the pealing thunder's crash,   45
   And see the mountain torrents pour
Down precipices dark and steep,
   Still bearing, in their headlong course
To meet th' embrace of ocean deep,
   Mementoes of the tempest's force;   50
For fire and tempest, flood and storm,
   Wakened deep echoes in my soul,
And made the quickening life-blood warm
   With impulse that knew no control;
And the fierce lightning's lurid flash   55
   Rending the somber clouds asunder,
Followed by the terrific crash
   Which marks the hoarsely rattling thunder,
Seemed like the gleams of lurid light
   Which flashed across my seething brain,   60
Succeeded by a darker night,
   With wilder horrors in its train.
And I have stood on ocean's shore,
   And viewed its dreary waters roll,
Till the dull music of its roar   65
   Called forth responses in my soul;
And I have felt that there was traced
   An image of my inmost soul,
In that dark, dreary, boundless waste,
   Whose sluggish waters aimless roll—   70
Save when aroused by storms' wild force
   It lifts on high its angry wave,

And thousands driven from their course
    Find in its depths a nameless grave.
Whene'er I turned in gentler mood   75
    To scan the old historic page,
It was not where the wise and good,
    The Bard, the Statesman, or the Sage,
Had drawn in lines of living light,
Lessons of virtue, truth and right;   80
But that which told of secret league,
    Where deep conspiracies were rife,
And where, through foul and dark intrigue,
    Were sowed the seeds of deadly strife.
Where hostile armies met to seal   85
    Their country's doom, for woe or weal;
Where the grim-visaged death-fiend drank
    His full supply of human gore,
And poured through every hostile rank
    The tide of battle's awful roar;   90
For then my spirit seemed to soar
    Away to where such scenes were rife,
And high above the battle's roar
    Sit as spectator of the strife—
And in those scenes of war and woe,   95
A fierce and fitful pleasure know.
There was a time when I possessed
    High notions of Religion's claim,
Nor deemed its practice, at the best,
    Was but a false and empty name;   100
But when I saw the graceless deeds
    Which marked its strongest votaries' path,
How senseless bigots, o'er their creeds,
    Blazing with wild fanatic wrath,
Let loose the deadly tide of war,   105
Spread devastation near and far,
Through scenes of rapine, blood and shame,
Of cities sacked, and towns on flame,
Caused unbelievers' hearts to feel
The arguments of fire and steel   110

By which they sought t' enforce the word,
   And make rebellious hearts approve
Those arguments of fire and sword
   As mandates of the God of love—
How could I think that such a faith,   115
   Whose path was marked by fire and blood,
That sowed the seeds of war and death,
   Had issued from a holy God?
There was a time when I did love,
   Such love as those alone can know,   120
Whose blood like burning lava moves,
   Whose passions like the lightning glow;
And when that ardent, truthful love,
   Was blighted in its opening bloom,
And all around, below, above,   125
   Seemed like the darkness of the tomb,
'Twas then my stern and callous heart,
Riven in its most vital part,
Seemed like some gnarled and knotted oak,
That, shivered by the lightning's stroke,   130
Stands in the lonely wanderer's path,
A ghastly monument of wrath.
Then how can I attune the lyre
   To strains of love, or joyous glee?
Break forth in patriotic fire,   135
   Or soar on higher minstrelsy,
To sing the praise of virtue bright,
Condemn the wrong, and laud the right;
When neither vice nor guilt can fling
   A darker shadow o'er my breast,   140
Nor even Virtue's self can bring,
   Unto my moody spirit, rest.
It may not be, it cannot be!
   Let others strike the sounding string,
And in rich strains of harmony,   145
   Songs of poetic beauty sing;
But mine must still the portion be,
   However dark and drear the doom,

To live estranged from sympathy,
　　Buried in doubt, despair and gloom;　　　　　150
To bare my breast to every blow,
To know no friend, and fear no foe,
Each generous impulse trod to dust,
Each noble aspiration crushed,
Each feeling struck with withering blight,　　　155
With no regard for wrong or right,
No fear of hell, no hope of heaven,
Die all unwept and unforgiven,
Content to know and dare the worst
Which mankind's hate, and heaven's curse,　　160
Can heap upon my living head,
Or cast around my memory dead;
And let them on my tombstone trace,
Here lies the Pariah of his race.

from A Poem

Written for the Celebration of the Fourth Anniversary of
President Lincoln's Emancipation Proclamation.

More than two centuries have passed
  Since, holding on their stormy way,
Before the furious wintry blast,
  Upon a dark December day,
Two sails, with different intent,   5
  Approached the Western Continent.
One vessel bore as rich a freight
  As ever yet has crossed the wave;
The living germs to form a State
  That knows no master, owns no slave.   10
She bore the pilgrims to that strand
  Which since is rendered classic soil,
Where all the honors of the land
  May reach the hardy sons of toil.
The other bore the baleful seeds   15
  Of future fratricidal strife,
The germ of dark and bloody deeds,
  Which prey upon a nation's life.
The trafficker in human souls
  Had gathered up and chained his prey,   20
And stood prepared to call the rolls,
  When, anchored in Virginia's Bay—
His captives landed on her soil,
  Doomed without recompense to toil,
Should spread abroad such deadly blight,   25
That the deep gloom of mental night
Spreading its darkness o'er the land,
And paralizing every hand
Raised in defence of Liberty,
Should throw the chains of slavery   30
O'er thought and limb, and mind and soul,
And bend them all to its control.

New England's cold and sterile land
Gave shelter to the pilgrim band;
Virginia's rich and fertile soil   35
Received the dusky sons of toil.
The one bore men whose lives were passed
In fierce contests for liberty—
Men who had struggled to the last
'Gainst every form of tyranny.   40
Vanquished in many a bloody fight,
Yet still in spirit unsubdued;
Though crushed by overwhelming might,
With love of freedom still imbued,
They bore unto their Western home,   45
The same ideas which drove them forth,
As houseless fugitives to roam
In endless exile o'er the earth.
And, on New England's sterile shore,
Those few and feeble germs took root,   50
To after generations bore
Abundance of the glorious fruit—
Freedom of thought, and of the pen,
Free schools, free speech, free soil, free men.
Thus in that world beyond the seas,   55
Found by the daring Genoese,
More than two centuries ago
A sower wandered forth to sow.
He planted deep the grains of wheat,
That generations yet unborn,   60
When e'er they came to reap and eat,
Might bless the hand that gave the corn;
And find it yield that priceless bread
With which the starving soul is fed;
The food which fills the hungry mind,   65
Gives mental growth to human kind,
And nerves the sinews of the free
To strike for Truth and Liberty.
Yet, planted at the self-same time
Was other seed by different hands,   70
To propagate the deadliest crime

That ever swept o'er guilty lands—
The crime of human slavery,
With all its want and misery—
The harrowing scenes of woe and pain,   75
Which follow in its ghastly train.
The same old feud that cursed the earth
Through all the ages of the past,
In this new world obtained new birth,
And built again its walls of caste,   80
More high and deep, more broad and strong,
On ancient prejudice and wrong.

. . . .

From year to year the contest grew,
Till slavery, glorying in her strength,
Again war's bloody falchion drew,   85
And sluggish freedom, roused at length,
Waked from her stupor, seized the shield,
And called her followers to the field.
And at that call they thronging came,
With arms of strength, and hearts on flame;   90
Answering the nation's call to arms,
The northern hive poured forth its swarms;
The lumbermen of Maine threw down
The axe, and seized the bayonet;
The Bay State's sons from every town,   95
Left loom and anvil, forge and net;
The Granite State sent forth its sons,
With hearts as steadfast as her rocks;
The stern Vermonters took their guns,
And left to others' care their flocks;   100
Rhode Island and Connecticut
Helped to fill up New England's roll,
And showed the pilgrim spirit yet
Could animate the Yankee soul.
The Empire State sent forth a host,   105
Such as might seal an empire's fate;

Even New Jersey held her post,
   And proved herself a Union State.
The Key-Stone of the Union arch
   Sent forth an army true and tried;   110
Ohio joined the Union march,
   And added to the Nation's side
   A force three hundred thousand strong,
   While Michigan took up the song;
   Wisconsin also, like the lakes,   115
   When the autumnal gale awakes,
   And rolls its surges on the shore,
   Poured forth its sons to battle's roar.
The gallant State of Illinois
   Sent forth in swarms its warlike boys.   120
On Indiana's teeming plain,
   Thick as the sheaves of ripened grain,
   Were soldiers hurrying to the wars
   To battle for the Stripes and Stars.
From Iowa fresh numbers came,   125
   While Minnesota joined the tide,
And Kansas helped to spread the flame,
   And carry o'er the border side
   The torch the ruffians once applied
   When fiercely, but in vain, they tried   130
   The people of their rights to spoil,
   And fasten slavery on her soil.
From East unto remotest West,
   From every portion of the North,
The true, the bravest, and the best,   135
   Forsook their homes and sallied forth;
   And men from every foreign land
   Were also reckoned in that band.
The Scandinavians swelled the train,
   The brave Norwegian, Swede, and Dane,   140
   And struck as though Thor rained his blows
   Upon the heads of haughty foes;
   Or Odin's self had sought the field
   To make all opposition yield.

Italia's sons, who once had cried   145
   Loud for united Italy,
And struck by Garibaldi's side
   For union and equality—
   Obtained another chance to fight
   For nationality and right.   150
The Germans came, a sturdy throng,
   And to the bleeding country brought
Friends of the right, foes of the wrong,
   Heroes in action as in thought,
Sigel, and Schurz, and many others,   155
   Whose names shall live among the brave,
Till all men are acknowledged brothers,
   Without a master or a slave.
Ireland's sons, as usual, came
   To battle strife with shouts of joy,   160
With Meagher and Corcoran won such fame
   As well might rival Fontenoy.
Briton and Frank, for centuries foes,
   Forgot their struggles, veiled their scars,
To deal on slavery's head their blows,   165
   Fighting beneath the Stripes and Stars.

. . . .

Though East, and West, and North combined,
   And foreigners from every land
With all that art and skill could find,
   They could not crush the rebel band.   170
They clung unto th' accursed thing,
   That which they knew accursed of God,
Nor strength, nor skill could victory bring
   With that accursed thing abroad.
When Abraham, the poor man's friend,   175
   Assumed the power to break the chain.

. . . .

As storms and thunder help to clear
And purify the atmosphere,

E'en so the thunders of the war,
Driving malaria afar,   180
Have purged the moral atmosphere,
And made the dawn of freedom clear.
From swamps and marshes left undrained
  Malarious vapors will arise,
From human passions, unrestrained,   185
  Rise fogs to cloud our moral skies:
So now, from portions of the land
  Where lately slavery reigned supreme,
Its conquered chiefs together band,
  Concocting many an artful scheme,   190
By which Oppression's tottering throne
  May be restored to pristine power,
And those who now its rule disown
  Be made submissive to its power.
The self-styled Moses brings the aid   195
  Of power and place to help them through,
To crush the race by him betrayed,
  And every man who, loyal, true,
  And faithful to his country's laws—
Declines to aid the tyrants cause.   200
Our real Moses, stretched his rod
  Four years ago across the sea,
And through its blood-dyed waves we trod
  The path that leads to Liberty.
His was the fiery column's light,   205
  That through the desert showed the way,
Out of oppression's gloomy night,
  Toward the light of Freedom's day;
And, like his prototype of old,
  Who used his power, as Heaven had told,   210
  To God and to the people true,
  Died with the promised land in view.
And we may well deplore his loss,
  For never was a ruler given,
More free from taint of sinful dross,   215
  To any Nation under Heaven.

And ever while the earth remains,
   His name among the first shall stand
Who freed four million slaves from chains,
   And saved thereby his native land.   220

  . . . .

Yet once again our moral air
   Is tainted by that poisonous breath,
Which Freedom's lungs can never bear,
   Which surely ends in moral death.
Then let the people in their might   225
   Arise, and send the fiat forth,
That every man shall have the right
   To rank according to his worth;
That north and south, and west and east,
All, from the greatest to the least,   230
Who rally to the nation's cause,
Shall have the shield of equal laws.
Wipe out the errors of the past,
Nursed by the barbarous pride of caste,
And o'er the nation's wide domain,   235
Where once was heard the clanking chain,
And timorous bondmen crouched in fear,
Before the brutal overseer,
Proclaim the truth that equal laws
Can best sustain the righteous cause;   240
And let this nation henceforth be
In truth the country of the free.

                (1867)

Notes

Emancipation Proclamation: effective January 1, 1863, it freed slaves in eleven rebellious Confederate states. Since the Proclamation did not affect slaves in other areas such as the Border States and Mississippi Valley, and since rebel territories were not under Union control, it was not until December 1865 that all slaves were effectively freed by the Thirteenth Amendment. The Emancipation Proclamation did have two major effects: it encouraged the North and Union forces to pursue war efforts and slaves to rebel and fight for the Union, and it discouraged foreign nations like Britain and France from granting diplomatic recognition to the Confederacy. 5–54. *Two sails* . . . : In 1619, a Dutch ship delivered the first black slaves to Virginia at Point Comfort, a few miles from Jamestown. In 1620, the "pilgrim band," English Puritans, sailed the *Mayflower* into Plymouth, Massachusetts, where under the leadership of William Bradford they established the first New England colony. These voyages sowed the seeds of slavery in the South and freedom in the North. 28. *paralyzing.* 56. *daring Genoese:* Christopher Columbus. 83 ff. *From year to year the contest grew* . . . : The Civil War (1861–65). Nicknames of states fighting for the Union are: 95. *Bay:* Massachusetts; 97. *Granite:* New Hampshire; 105. *Empire:* New York; 109. *Key-Stone:* Pennsylvania. 85. *falchion:* sword. 127. *And Kansas helped:* See Rogers, *The Repeal of the Missouri Compromise Considered* and note. 141, 143. *Thor:* In Scandinavian mythology Thor is god of thunder, and *Odin* is king of the gods and god of war. Among foreign allies of the Union, notable are: 147. Gauseppe *Garibaldi* (1807–82), Italian patriot and general who led the final, unsuccessful battle for Rome's freedom (see Whitfield's "How Long" [59]); and 155. Carl *Schurz,* the German American who later became President Hayes's secretary of the interior and a prominent Republican statesman. 175. *Abraham:,* Lincoln, (1809–65), sixteenth president, viewed by his contemporaries as the Great Emancipator of the slaves. Later in the poem, he is called *Our real Moses* (201) in contrast to his successor, President Andrew Johnson, called *The self-styled Moses* (195) (see Bell's "Modern Moses" and note).

DANIEL ALEXANDER PAYNE

Daniel Alexander Payne (1811–93) gained international prominence as a clergyman, author, and educator. Born in Charleston, South Carolina, to free parents, Martha and London Payne, he eagerly pursued learning as a youth and soon built a school in which he taught slaves. When the legislature made such teaching illegal, Payne left South Carolina to study for the ministry in Pennsylvania (1835). He was ordained by the Lutheran church (1839) and joined the African Methodist Episcopal church in 1841. As an A.M.E. preacher and bishop, Payne held pulpits in Washington, D.C. and Baltimore, and he traveled widely in America—to preach and organize schools and societies for preachers and laymen—and abroad to represent the church at conferences. In 1863 Payne purchased Wilberforce University in Xenia, Ohio, and, as president for thirteen years, led it to educational excellence. In these years, and while remaining active at Wilberforce until his death, Payne published an invaluable history of the A.M.E. church, an autobiography, and several other volumes of sermons, treatises, and history.

Payne's poetry reflects his lifelong devotion to teaching pious and moral living. His verse is formal, classical in structure, diction, and allusions; it is practical and sincere in celebration of virtue and God's will.

The Pleasures and Other Miscellaneous Poems (Baltimore: Sherwood & Co., 1850).

from The Pleasures

Long hast thou slumber'd, O my sounding Lyre!
Now Muses wake thee, now thy song inspire;
Now will they tune each soft melodious string,
And in thy lay their sweetest numbers fling.
O lift thy voice on high, and start the soul!   5
From sinful *Pleasure's* dark and foul control,
Point her to *those* whose holy breath imparts
The life of joy to men of virtuous hearts.
Paint thou, the *One* in colors dark and dire,
Against her charms, the youthful mind inspire   10
With holy hate; the *Other* then portray
In robes celestial, such as Prophets say
The angels wore when from the courts above,
They came to men with messages of Love.

Wilt thou my thoughts dictate, O holy One!   15
Who tun'd the harp of Jesse's royal son:
Him didst thou teach in melting strains to pour
His sacred songs o'er Zion's hallowed shore.
O that, like his, my humble notes may rise,
With sweet acceptance to the list'ning skies!   20
Show how the paths of Vice in ruin end,
While Virtue's footsteps up to glory tend.
Pleasures of Vice are those which most pursue,
Regarding all their promis'd joys as true;
Nor will they heed the warning voice that cries,   25
The soul which sins, that soul in mis'ry lies.
But, like the headlong horse or stubborn mule,
Despise all truth, contemn all righteous rule,
Delight in sin as swine delight in mire,
Till hell itself entomb their souls in fire!   30
Thus does the Drunkard, in the sparkling bowl,
Pursue the joys which charm his brutish soul;
But soon he feels the serpent's fang is there,

The gall of wo, the demon's awful stare:
For in the visions of his crazied soul,   35
The furies dance and horrid monsters roll.

Some find their pleasure in tobacco wads,
Delight in them as goats in chewing cuds;
Others believe they find it quite enough,
In smoking cigars, or in taking snuff.   40
The glutton and the greasy epicure,
Believe they have it—for they tell us so—
In eating venison, turtle-soup and clams,
Beef a la mode and lobsters, ducks and hams;
In puddings, pound-cakes, pies and cold ice cream;   45
In black-strap, brandy, claret, and champagne.
O who could think that men, to whom is given
Such souls as will outlive the stars of heaven,
Could hope to find in such a low employ,
The sweet pulsations of a real joy!   50

But dandies find it in their curled hair,
Greas'd with pomatum or the oil of bear;
In fine mustaches, breast-pins, golden chains;
In brass-capt boot-heels, or in walking canes.
Some ladies find it in their boas and muffs,   55
In silks and satins, laces, muslin-stuffs
Made into dresses, pointed, long and wide,
With flounces deep, and bran-bustles beside,
All neat and flowing in Parisian grace;
With small sunshades to screen their smiling face;   60
Then up the streets, like pea-fowls bright and gay,
They promenade on every sunny day.
Some seek for pleasure in the giddy dance,
Where Fashion smiles, and Beauty's siren glance
The soul delights and fills light bounding hearts   65
With dreams of love,—such dreams as sin imparts;
Not the pure streams that flow, my God, from thee:
The streams of bliss—the love of purity.
In cock-fights others find it; some, in dice;

Some in the chambers of lascivious vice.   70
The vile blasphemer seeks it in his shame,
Who sport like devils with the Holy Name.
O hapless wretches! fool'd and self deceiv'd!
Angel's weep o'er you! God himself is griev'd!
Ye act more silly than the man at noon,   75
Who should mistake a razor for a spoon!

. . . .

Immortal man, be wise! and know thou this:
Pleasure in God alone, is perfect bliss;
'Tis Virtue—holy Virtue! Child of Love!
With the pure spirit of the peaceful dove—   80
That nymph of light! in whose bright face divine,
All the sweet graces of God's Spirit shine.
'Tis she who can a charm of joy bestow
On all the pleasures man can find below;
Her potent fiat, from the womb of night,   85
Starts into being the beauteous forms of light;
Turns ill to good, and anguish into joy;
With god-like thoughts the mind of man employ;
In earth's dark vale, by angry thunders riven,
Creates the fruits, and sheds the light of heaven!   90

. . . .

I sing of Pleasure flowing now from God,
Pleasure derived from all his works abroad;
Streaming thro' earth, and air, thro' boundless skies;
In birds and beasts, and flowers of softest dies.
'Tis felt whene'er the eyes survey the fields,   95
In verdant Spring, or when bright summer yields
Her fragrant flowers, and her shady groves
Are vocal with the moans of turtle-doves,
The notes of soaring larks or mimic jays—
The mocking bird's inimitable lays.   100
Sweetest of songsters! O, whene'er she sings,
The heart of man doth bound—the welkin rings
With bliss,—the feather'd minstrels, mute with joy,

Feel that deep silence is their best employ.
E'en Philomel herself must yield the palm,   105
In silent homage to superior charm.

'Tis felt in scenes where hills and mountains rise,
Like rugged columns, to the bending skies,
While murm'ring fountains gushing from their sides
Roll towards the seas, in deep'ning, wid'ning tides,   110
Or rushing on o'er beds of jutting rocks,
Dash down the abyss in thund'ring cataracts —
With glitt'ring sprays impregn the humid air,
And paint the bow of smiling heaven there.

. . . .

When Music pours her dulcet strains around,   115
And woman's voice commingles with the sound,
Sweet as the notes that did the Orphean lyre,
With tenderness, the cruel brutes inspire;
And mountains, vales and rocks, and radiant plains,
Were vocal with the minstrel's melting strains.   120
O then we feel a pleasure quite divine,
Pour'd in the heart, by each harmonious line.
Wrapt in a flame of pure desire, we burn,
Like holy incense in a golden urn;
And sigh and wish, with feelings keen and strong,   125
To hear the sonnets of an angel's tongue!

Men talk of Love! But few do ever feel
The speechless raptures which its joys reveal.
They mistake Love, that pure celestial thing,
Whose end is God, and in Him has its spring,   130
For grovelling lust, that vile, that filthy dame,
Whose bosom ne'er can feel the sacred flame —
Hence when they look'd for peace, fierce strife arose
And for the loving kiss, gave cruel blows.
The hearth domestic is the field of blood —   135
The smile of joy, dark sorrow's bitter flood.

But they who seek the nymph that came from heav'n —
Which only can to chasten'd hearts be given —
Shall find in her embrace a fount of joy,
Like heaven's pure nectar, free from each alloy;   140
Thought meeting thought, and love returning love,
As the sweet fondlings of the peaceful dove;
In smiling children, like the roses sweet,
The virtuous wife her husband's wishes meet,
And from the altars of their sacred home,   145
Their sweet devotions scale the starry dome.

. . . .

Here Science brings her treasures, more than gold;
Here Hist'ry tells her mighty deeds of old,
And Poetry, that child of love and song,
Whose angel-mind to worlds of light belong,   150
Attunes his harp — and with his tongue of fire,
The youthful ones, with wisdom does inspire.
Religion, too, that goddess from the skies,
From whose bright visage every evil flies,
She sheds her hallowing influence all around,   155
And makes each heart with pure emotions bound.

Here love is seen in forms divinely sweet;
Here husband, wife, and brothers, sisters, meet
As angels do, to bless each one, and guide
Where saving Faith and holy Love preside.   160
O! where's the scene below which pictures heav'n?
A bright oasis in Earth's desert giv'n,
Where angels, looking from the skies, descend
And with man's joy, heav'n's sacred raptures blend?
'Tis here! 'tis here! a family whose love   165
Are the sweet fetters of the world above!

O save me from the home whence Christ is driv'n!
Where the bright bonds of peace are spurn'd and riv'n!
The Holy Ghost despis'd, the Bible scorn'd,
And pure Religion into laughter turn'd,   170

Nor less from that where Fashion is the god,
The Wife, her joy and solace find abroad—
The children's morals, like a barren field,
No luscious fruits nor flow'rs of virtue yield,
Where novels, romance, gossip, hold their sway,   175
And vile theatres close the sinful day.
The fell miasma which from fens arise,
Like fumes of vengeance 'neath the torrid skies,
I dread far less than such a home as this,
Where prayer is banish'd and each form of bliss.   180
O save me from the wife whose pleasures tell
Her final doom must be the flames of hell!

. . . .

O holy Virtue! such thy Pleasures are!
They banish sorrow and they banish fear.
Thy gifts are crowns! Thy palaces are gold!   185
Rising in grandeur, glorious to behold;
Thy gates are precious stones! thy rivers, love!
Thy fruits, the glories of the climes above.
No fang of asp—no scorpion's sting is there—
No breath of sin pollutes the limpid air.   190
There is not heard the voice of stormy strife,
And Death ne'er treads that land of endless Life!

Thy paths are paths of peace, whose tow'ring height
Leads up to regions of unclouded light!
Beyond the stars that gild the realms above,   195
In the bright Eden of eternal love!
There the sweet voices of the Cherubim,
In notes melodious, chant the immortal hymn;
There life-crown'd Saints attune their golden lyres
To such sweet songs as God himself inspires,   200
And in thy grace, O Saviour of mankind!
Their life—their love—their sinless pleasures find!

Notes

1. *Lyre:* a small harplike instrument. 16. *Jesse's royal son:* David, king of Israel
in ca. 1010–970 B.C., a musician and poet traditionally credited with authorship

of many Psalms. 18. *Zion's hallowed shore:* biblical Palestine, the Hebrews' home-land. 94. dyes. 105. *Philomel:* see Horton's "On Summer" (15). 117. *Orphean lyre:* Orpheus, in Greek legend, could charm wild beasts with the music of his lyre. 177. *fell miasma . . . fens:* deadly vapor from swamps. 197. *Cherubim:* the second order of angels (seraphim being the first order). As linked here to "the immortal hymn," cherubim may designate the church choir that enters singing the Cherubic Hymn.

ALFRED GIBBS CAMPBELL

Alfred Gibbs Campbell (1826?–?), as publisher, editor, and writer, devoted his monthly newspaper, *The Alarm Bell,* to campaigns for temperance, abolitionism, women's rights, and the supremacy of individual conscience over religious and secular authorities. His newspaper appeared for about fifteen months from 1851 to 1852 in Paterson, New Jersey. Campbell married Anne Hutchinson of Trenton (1852) and was a vice president of the American Anti-Slavery Society (1857). A man of strong convictions, he had the courage and talent to express his beliefs well in prose and poetry. The primary subjects of his poems are religion and abolitionism, which he often treats in novel and imaginative ways with spirited imagery, metrical variety, and fervid commitment. His unique whimsical tale of the old decanter may be the first American "concrete" poem.

Poems (Newark, N.J.: Advertiser Printing House, 1883).

Warning

SUGGESTED BY THE CHRISTIANA (PA.) TREASON TRIALS.

Treason? yes, make it treason, if ye will;
Build up your gallows, and your victims bring
Forth from their gloomy dungeon; bind their hands;
Tie, with your pious fingers, round their necks,
The consecrated rope; touch then the spring   5
And let the traitors drop! there let them hang,
A solemn sacrifice unto *your* god;
Call in your priests. Let Stuart, Dewey, Lord,
Spencer and Spring, and all their train attend
To join your holy sacrament, and chant,   10
In pleasing concord, praise unto the great
And most puissant deity whose throne
Is built on human souls, and laved with seas
Of human blood. Aye! let their thankful songs
With Hell's hoarse shouts of diabolic joy   15
Ascend in unison, — precious indeed
To Modern Moloch as the agony
Of the fond mother when her child is snatched
From her maternal grasp, to be no more
Clasped lovingly upon her bosom, or   20
The piercing shriek of the poor hunted slave
Torn piecemeal by his bloodhounds.
       But take heed!
Know that a day of reckoning is at hand,
For God is just! His Justice will not sleep   25
Forever! Even now behold how shakes
This guilty nation from its centre round
Unto its broad circumference. In wrong
Were its foundations laid, and crime inwrought
Into its structure. It must fall! The slave   30
Shall o'er its ruins make his exodus
From cursed bondage: and as Israel's hosts
Saw their oppressors utterly destroyed,
(When God had wrought deliverance from their foes,)
And sang His great salvation, — so the bound   35

And stricken millions of our land shall stand
Freed from their shackles, and the arm of God,
Made bare in their deliverance, they shall see
Strike sorely their oppressors.

                  Then shall they   40
Exult and sing—"God is our strength and song!
In glory hath He triumphed o'er our foes,
And led us forth in mercy and redeemed!"

                            (1851; 1883)

Notes

Christiana (Pa.) Treason Trials: Author's Footnote: "In 1851 several colored men were indicted for treason because of their resistance to the Fugitive Slave Law." (See Subject Index, Slavery and Abolitionism: Laws.) In Christiana, thirty-six blacks and two whites were charged in 1851 with treason for their armed resistance to a Maryland slave-owner, Edward Gorsuch, and his party of slave-catchers who were trying to recover fugitive slaves in Pennsylvania. The fugitives who actually killed Gorsuch escaped to Canada, and the indicted Christiana prisoners were freed before trial. 8–9. *Stuart . . . Spring:* proponents of slavery and/or the innate inferiority of African Americans. 12. *puissant:* powerful. 17. *Modern Moloch:* Molech, in the Bible, was a pagan deity to whom children were sacrificed; the modern child-devourer is slavery. 31–43. *exodus . . . redeemed:* Allusion is to the biblical account of Israel's Egyptian captivity and redemption. The same allusion appears in Campbell's "The Divine Mission" (37), where Jesus replaces the God of the Old Testament as the hoped-for redeemer of American slaves. (See Subject Index, Religion: Moses.)

Song of the Decanter

There was an old decan-
ter, and its mouth was
gaping wide; the
rosy wine had
ebbed away
and left
its crys-
tal side;
and the wind
went humming
humming,
up and
down the
sides it flew,
and through the
reed like
hollow neck
the wildest notes it
blew. I placed it in the
window where the blast was
blowing free, and fancied that its
pale mouth sang the queerest strains to
me. "They tell me—puny conquerors! the
Plague has slain his ten, and War his hundred
thousand of the very best of men; but I"—'twas
thus the Bottle spake—"but I have conquered
more than all your famous conquerors, so
feared and famed of yore. Then come, ye
youths and maidens all, come drink from
out my cup, the beverage that dulls the
brain and burns the spirits up; that puts
to shame your conquerors that slay their
scores below; for this has deluged millions with the lava tide of woe. Tho'
in the path of battle darkest waves
of blood may roll; yet while I killed the body, I have damn'd the very soul. The cholera, the plagues,
the sword, such ruin never wro't,
as I, in mirth or malice, on the
innocent have brought. And
still I breathe upon them, and
they shrink before my breath;
and year by year my thousands
tread the dismal road of Death."

The Alarm Bell, 1:5 (June 1852)

The Divine Mission

When on the earth had settled moral night,
And darkness reigned where once shone Sinai's light;
When superstitious rites usurped the place
Where beamed Religion once with holy grace;
When Justice, Truth and Mercy far had fled   5
From Church and State, and hollow forms instead—
Tithings of "anise, mint and cummin," made
For sanctimonious priests a thriving trade,
Who, like our modern priests, gain-seeking men,
God's holy temple made a robbers' den;—   10
At such a time, long centuries ago,
From Heaven's high mansions to the earth below
An angel band, on gladsome errand bound,
Sped to the plains where, seated on the ground,
The humble shepherds through the solemn night   15
Watched their loved flocks, and gathered pure delight
And holy wisdom, which each glowing star
Rained on them with its radiance from afar.
Around the shepherds shone celestial light,
(Each gem eclipsing in the crown of night,)   20
Making them quake with apprehensive dread,
But momentary, for God's angel said,
"Fear not, I bring glad tidings unto all
People who dwell on this terrestrial ball."
Then Heaven's high dome with sounds harmonic rang   25
As the angelic host in concert sang
"Glory to God! Good-will and peace on earth!"
Most fitting song to usher in the birth
Of Heaven's divinest Son, whose mission grand
Eternal Love had from eternal planned!   30

* * * * * * * * * * * * *

Lo! in a manger where the oxen fed,
The Son of God made His first lowly bed;

He who, on high, with glory erst was crowned,
No prouder birth-place than a stable found.
As in our time the North-star's steady ray   35
Guides weary pilgrims on their toilsome way
From bondage worse than that of Pharaoh's reign,
So there appeared, among the shining train,
One flaming star which like a beacon shone,
And from the East-land led the sages on,   40
Who, finding Jesus, worshiped him, and rolled
Full at His feet their gifts of precious gold,
And incense-breathing gums, whose odors rare
Symboled the fragrance of their praise and prayer.

When unto manhood had the Christ-child grown,   45
Sunlike, but spotless, His example shone,
Teaching the world great truths which long had been
Hid by traditions false and priestly din.
He trampled on the vain and hollow rites
Practiced by vainer, hollower hypocrites,   50
Who hoped by them to bring the heavens in debt,
Or blind the omniscient eye of God, while yet
They daily added to their ill-got store
By stealing bread from God's afflicted poor,
And still contrived how they might still steal more!   55
The poor, the blind, the outcast and the slave,
The victims of the rich, proud Pharisee,
These were the sharers of His sympathy,
These were the ones He loved to bless and save.

Oh! Holy Christ, Thy mission is not done;   60
Still on oppression shines the noon-day sun;
Thy children still are trampled in the dust,
'Neath the remorseless hell of power crushed.
Dost Thou not hear their grief-extorted cry?
Look'st Thou not on them still with pitying eye?   65
Behold, the Oppressor waxes yet more bold,
And grasps them with a tighter, sterner hold,
While, as of old, the Church and priesthood stand
Leagued with Thy foes, and claiming Heaven's command

For all their deeds of villainy and crime   70
Which stain with human blood the page of time.

But as unto the least of Thine 'tis done,
'Neath night's dark cover, or the blazing sun,
So is it done to Thee, and Thou wilt yet
Thy majesty and power vindicate!   75

(1852; 1883)

Notes

2. *Sinai's light:* the Ten Commandments and other laws given by God to Moses on Mount Sinai (Exod. 19 ff.). 7. *Tithings . . . :* offerings of herbs. 8. *sanctimonious:* pretending to be very holy. 57. *Pharisee:* member of a religious sect in the time of Jesus, characterized in the New Testament as self-righteous and hypocritical.

Lines

Wake not again the cannon's thundrous voice,
Nor to the breeze throw out the stars and stripes;
'Tis not the time to revel and rejoice
Beneath the shadow of our nation's types —
Types of her ancient glory, present shame.   5
The stars have faded of her old renown,
For Liberty is but an empty name,
While Slavery wields the sceptre, wears the crown.

Why should we to the lie, persistent, cling,
And falsely boast our freedom on this day?   10
What though we are not governed by a king?
A sterner tyrant o'er our land holds sway,
And tramples on the dearest rights of man; —
Transforms God's image into merchandise;
Places free speech beneath his impious ban,   15
And all our God-given liberties denies.

Each foot of land within our wide domain
He claims as hunting-ground, whereon to chase
The hero-fugitive who breaks his chain,
And earns his freedom by advent'rous race.   20
On *our* limbs, too, the shackles he would bind;
Pluck out our hearts, or change them into stone;
Crush all our sympathies for human kind,
And bid us God and manhood to disown.

Give but a crust of bread to one of these   25
God's weary wanderers in search of rest,
Point out to him the North-star as he flees,
Or make him but an hour your welcome guest; —
And on your head the Robber Despot lays
With violence his unrelenting hand,   30
And with imprisonment and fine repays
Simple obedience to God's clear command.

We are not free! In every Southern State
Speech and the Press are fettered; — and for him
Who dares speak out, the martyr-fires await,   35
Or hangman's rope from tallest pine-tree's limb.
We are not free! One man in every seven,
Throughout our false Republic, groans beneath
The vilest despotism under heaven,
Which leaves no hope of freedom but in death.   40

Nearly four millions in our land in chains!
One-half our country slave-land! and the whole
Man-hunting ground! And Kansas' virgin plains,
(Once pledged to Freedom,) under the control
Of the Slave Power! Say, Boaster, are we free?   45
See if the huge lie blister not your lips:
Where Slavery reigns, there Freedom cannot be!
Light vanishes beneath the sun's eclipse.

                                    (July 4, 1855; 1883)

Note

As in "Warning," Campbell here denounces the Fugitive Slave Act and also the
Kansas-Nebraska Act (see Subject Index, Slavery and Abolitionism, Laws).

Cry "Infidel!"

If you find a man who does not receive
The doctrines you have been taught to believe,
   Spare him not! Cry "Infidel!"
If he worships not at the shrines you raise,
Joins not in your feasts on your holy days,   5
    Cry "Infidel!"

What though his heart with love overflow
To the victims of sin and want and woe,
   Spare him not! Cry "Infidel!"
What though, in the long-waged fearful fight, 10
He is ever found on the side of Right,
    Cry "Infidel!"

What though in each fellow-man he see
An image of Him of Calvary,
   Spare him not! Cry "Infidel!"   15
What though he endeavor each soul to win
From the fearful paths of folly and sin,
    Cry "Infidel!"

What right has he to think other than you?
To judge for himself what is false or true? 20
   Spare him not! Cry "Infidel!"
Wherefore have you been commissioned to preach,
If any may question the dogmas you teach?
    Cry "Infidel!"

Make him acknowledge you only are right, 25
That you hold the keys of the portals of light;
   Spare him not! Cry "Infidel!"
Until he consent your fetters to wear,
And conscience and reason both to forswear,
    Cry "Infidel!" 30

Note
Infidel: one who does not believe in the prevailing religion or creed.

FRANCES ELLEN WATKINS HARPER

Frances Ellen Watkins Harper (1824–1911) devoted her life's work to abolitionism, race advancement and equality, women's and children's rights, Christian morality, and temperance. She achieved financial independence and nationwide acclaim through her eloquent lectures and poetry readings and the sale of her poems. Born of free parents in Baltimore, Watkins attended an academy run by her uncle and in the 1840s, while working as a maid to a bookseller, she continued her education in his library and published poems and articles. From 1850 to 1853 Watkins taught school in Ohio and Pennsylvania before moving to Philadelphia, where she lived at a station of the Underground Railroad and pledged herself to the antislavery cause. From 1854 to 1860 she lectured to enthusiastic audiences in eight Northern states. After a short break in 1860 to marry Fenton Harper and have a daughter, Mary, she traveled from 1864 to 1871 in thirteen Southern states at her own expense, living with the freedmen and speaking in their churches, schools, and homes. Philadelphia became Harper's permanent home after 1872. For the next forty years she lectured on social and moral issues, worked with a dozen national and racial organizations on behalf of education, civil rights, and temperance, and continued to write and publish prose and poetry. Harper was the first black woman to publish a short story ("The Two Offers," 1859) and the second to publish a novel (*Iola Leroy,* 1892). Her essays, speeches, and poems appeared regularly in prominent African-American periodicals, and she collected some 120 poems in eleven slim volumes (1854–1901). Harper died of heart disease and was buried in Eden Cemetery, Philadelphia. Her celebrity as an author, lecturer, and reformer was unsurpassed in her time, and her contributions to literature and human welfare are widely honored in our time.

Harper believed in art for humanity's sake, and to be fully effective her frankly propagandistic poetry on religion, race, and social reform requires dramatic recitation by a charismatic crusader like Harper. On the page, many verses, varying little in mechanical forms, trite diction and rhymes, and generalized sentiments, seem superficial stock pieces. But in her better poems, Harper's unique passionate voice is heard invoking a militant redeemer God's vengeance on a sinful nation, or chastizing the "land of slaves," or projecting her own moral and spiritual strength into biblical heroines. Her most notable artistic successes are the blank verse allegory *Moses,* told in reverent tones with harmonious blending of elevated diction, vibrant concrete imagery, and formal meter; and the innovative monologs of wise Aunt Chloe (1872), with their earthy humor, irony, and colloquialisms. Much of Harper's poetry, by its focus on nineteenth-century black experience and its roots in African-American oral and literary traditions, is valuable for affirming the strength of racial identity and culture. Significant, too, is her social consciousness, particularly concerning the status of women. Overall, Harper offers the most complete single poetic record of the minds and hearts of her people in the last fifty years of the century.

Harper's volumes were reissued many times, some with new poems, several with reprinted poems; only the first-known editions of major collections are listed here. *Poems on Miscellaneous Subjects,* 2d ed. (Boston: J. B. Yerrington & Son, 1854); *Moses: A Story of the Nile,* 2d ed. (Philadelphia: Merrihew & Son, 1869, retitled *Idylls of the Bible,* 1901); *Poems* (Philadelphia: Merrihew & Son, 1871); *Sketches of Southern Life* (Philadelphia: Merrihew & Son, 1872); *Atlanta Offering* (Philadelphia: Author, 1895).

Eliza Harris

Like a fawn from the arrow, startled and wild,
A woman swept by us, bearing a child;
In her eye was the night of a settled despair,
And her brow was o'ershaded with anguish and care.

She was nearing the river — in reaching the brink,   5
She heeded no danger, she paused not to think!
For she is a mother — her child is a slave —
And she'll give him his freedom, or find him a grave!

'Twas a vision to haunt us, that innocent face —
So pale in its aspect, so fair in its grace;   10
As the tramp of the horse and the bay of the hound,
With the fetters that gall, were trailing the ground!

She was nerved by despair, and strengthen'd by woe,
As she leap'd o'er the chasms that yawn'd from below;
Death howl'd in the tempest, and rav'd in the blast,   15
But she heard not the sound till the danger was past.

Oh! how shall I speak of my proud country's shame?
Of the stains on her glory, how give them their name?
How say that her banner in mockery waves —
Her "star-spangled banner" — o'er millions of slaves?   20

How say that the lawless may torture and chase
A woman whose crime is the hue of her face?
How the depths of the forest may echo around
With the shrieks of despair, and the bay of the hound?

With her step on the ice, and her arm on her child,   25
The danger was fearful, the pathway was wild;
But, aided by Heaven, she gained a free shore,
Where the friends of humanity open'd their door.

So fragile and lovely, so fearfully pale,
Like a lily that bends to the breath of the gale,   30
Save the heave of her breast, and the sway of her hair,
You'd have thought her a statue of fear and despair.

In agony close to her bosom she press'd
The life of her heart, the child of her breast: —
Oh! love from its tenderness gathering might,   35
Had strengthen'd her soul for the dangers of flight.

But she's free! — yes, free from the land where the slave
From the hand of oppression must rest in the grave;
Where bondage and torture, where scourges and chains
Have plac'd on our banner indelible stains.   40

The bloodhounds have miss'd the scent of her way;
The hunter is rifled and foil'd of his prey;
Fierce jargon and cursing, with clanking of chains,
Make sounds of strange discord on Liberty's plains.

With the rapture of love and fullness of bliss,   45
She plac'd on his brow a mother's fond kiss: —
Oh! poverty, danger and death she can brave,
For the child of her love is no longer a slave!

                            (1853; 1854)

Note

Eliza Harris was the mulatto woman in *Uncle Tom's Cabin* (1852) who escaped
from slavery with her child across the frozen Ohio River. Harriet Beecher Stowe's
novel was a powerful antislavery force. Based on many actual events and documents
of slavery, the book aggravated the tensions between North and South that led
to the Civil War; indeed, Abraham Lincoln purportedly told Mrs. Stowe it was
"the book that made this great war." The novel had spectacular success in America
and abroad, and in many dramatic versions it became the world's most popular
play. Mrs. Stowe (1811–96) defended the accuracy of her novel with the factual
work *A Key to Uncle Tom's Cabin* (1853); in 1856 she wrote a second antislavery
novel, *Dred, A Tale of the Great Dismal Swamp,* and throughout the century
African Americans paid homage to her (see Subject Index, Literature; see also
Slavery and Abolitionism: Laws).

Bury Me in a Free Land

Make me a grave where'er you will,
In a lowly plain, or a lofty hill,
Make it among earth's humblest graves,
But not in a land where men are slaves.

I could not rest if around my grave   5
I heard the steps of a trembling slave:
His shadow above my silent tomb
Would make it a place of fearful gloom.

I could not rest if I heard the tread
Of a coffle gang to the shambles led,   10
And the mother's shriek of wild despair
Rise like a curse on the trembling air.

I could not sleep if I saw the lash
Drinking her blood at each fearful gash,
And I saw her babes torn from her breast,   15
Like trembling doves from their parent nest.

I'd shudder and start if I heard the bay
Of blood-hounds seizing their human prey,
And I heard the captive plead in vain
As they bound afresh his galling chain.   20

If I saw young girls from their mother's arms
Bartered and sold for their youthful charms,
My eye would flash with a mournful flame,
My death-paled cheek grow red with shame.

I would sleep, dear friends, where bloated might   25
Can rob no man of his dearest right;
My rest shall be calm in any grave
Where none can call his brother a slave.

I ask no monument, proud and high,
To arrest the gaze of the passers by;   30
All that my yearning spirit craves,
Is bury me not in a land of slaves.

                    (1858; 1864; 1871)

To the Union Savers of Cleveland

Men of Cleveland, had a vulture
   Sought a timid dove for prey,
Would you not, with human pity,
   Drive the gory bird away?

Had you seen a feeble lambkin,   5
   Shrinking from a wolf so bold,
Would ye not to shield the trembler,
   In your arms have made its fold?

But when she, a hunted sister,
   Stretched her hands that ye might save,   10
Colder far than Zembla's regions
   Was the answer that ye gave.

On the Union's bloody altar,
   Was your hapless victim laid;
Mercy, truth and justice shuddered,   15
   But your hands would give no aid.

And ye sent her back to torture,
   Robbed of freedom and of right.
Thrust the wretched, captive stranger,
   Back to slavery's gloomy night.   20

Back where brutal men may trample,
   On her honor and her fame;
And unto her lips so dusky,
   Press the cup of woe and shame.

There is blood upon your city,   25
   Dark and dismal is the stain;
And your hands would fail to cleanse it,
   Though Lake Erie ye should drain.

There's a curse upon your Union,
   Fearful sounds are in the air;   30
As if thunderbolts were framing,
   Answers to the bondsman's prayer.

Ye may offer human victims,
   Like the heathen priests of old;
And may barter manly honor   35
   For the Union and for gold.

But ye can not stay the whirlwind,
   When the storm begins to break;
And our God doth rise in judgment,
   For the poor and needy's sake.   40

And, your sin-cursed, guilty Union,
   Shall be shaken to its base,
Till ye learn that simple justice,
   Is the right of every race.

                (1860; 1861)

from Moses: A Story of the Nile

Flight into Midian — Chapter III

The love of Moses for his race soon found
A stern expression. Pharaoh was building
A pyramid; ambitious, cold and proud,
He scrupled not at means to gain his ends.
When he feared the growing power of Israel   5
He stained his hands in children's blood, and held
A carnival of death in Goshen; but now
He wished to hand his name and memory
Down unto the distant ages, and instead
Of lading that memory with the precious   10
Fragrance of the kindest deeds and words, he
Essayed to write it out in stone, as cold
And hard, and heartless as himself.
                              And Israel was
The fated race to whom the cruel tasks   15
Were given. Day after day a cry of wrong
And anguish, some dark deed of woe and crime,
Came to the ear of Moses, and he said,
"These reports are ever harrowing my soul;
I will go unto the fields where Pharaoh's   20
Officers exact their labors, and see
If these things be so — if they smite the feeble
At their tasks, and goad the aged on to toils
Beyond their strength — if neither age nor sex
Is spared the cruel smiting of their rods."   25
And Moses went to see his brethren.
                              'Twas eventide,
And the laborers were wending their way
Unto their lowly huts. 'Twas a sad sight, —
The young girls walked without the bounding steps   30
Of youth, with faces prematurely old,
As if the rosy hopes and sunny promises
Of life had never flushed their cheeks with girlish

Joy; and there were men whose faces seemed to say
We bear our lot in hopeless pain, we've bent unto   35
Our burdens until our shoulders fit them,
And as slaves we crouch beneath our servitude
And toil. But there were men whose souls were cast
In firmer moulds, men with dark secretive eyes,
Which seemed to say, to-day we bide our time,   40
And hide our wrath in every nerve, and only
Wait a fitting hour to strike the hands that press
Us down. Then came the officers of Pharaoh;
They trod as lords, their faces flushed with pride
And insolence, watching the laborers   45
Sadly wending their way from toil to rest.
And Moses' heart swelled with a mighty pain; sadly
Musing, he sought a path that led him
From the busy haunts of men. But even there
The cruel wrong trod in his footsteps; he heard   50
A heavy groan, then harsh and bitter words,
And, looking back, he saw an officer
Of Pharaoh smiting with rough and cruel hand
An aged man. Then Moses' wrath o'erflowed
His lips, and every nerve did tremble   55
With a sense of wrong, and bounding forth he
Cried unto the smiter, "Stay thy hand; seest thou
That aged man? His head is whiter than our
Desert sands; his limbs refuse to do thy
Bidding because the cruel tasks have drained   60
Away their strength." The Egyptian raised his eyes
With sudden wonder; who was this that dared dispute
His power? Only a Hebrew youth. His
Proud lip curved in scornful anger, and he
Waved a menace with his hand, saying, "Back   65
To the task base slave, nor dare resist the will
Of Pharaoh." Then Moses' wrath o'erleaped the bounds
Of prudence, and with a heavy blow he felled
The smiter to the earth, and Israel had
One tyrant less. Moses saw the mortal paleness   70
Chase the flushes from the Egyptian's face,
The whitening lips that breathed no more defiance,

And the relaxing tension of the well knit limbs;
And when he knew that he was dead, he hid
Him in the sand and left him to his rest.   75
                      Another day Moses walked
Abroad, and saw two brethren striving
For mastery; and then his heart grew full
Of tender pity. They were brethren, sharers
Of a common wrong: should not their wrongs more   80
Closely bind their hearts, and union, not division,
Be their strength? And feeling thus, he said, "ye
Are brethren, wherefore do ye strive together?"
But they threw back his words in angry tones
And asked if he had come to judge them, and would   85
Mete to them the fate of the Egyptian?
Then Moses knew the sand had failed to keep
His secret, that his life no more was safe
In Goshen, and he fled unto the deserts
Of Arabia and became a shepherd   90
For the priest of Midian.

Chapter IV

    Men grow strong in action, but in solitude
Their thoughts are ripened. Like one who cuts away
The bridge on which he has walked in safety
To the other side, so Moses cut off all retreat   95
To Pharaoh's throne, and did choose the calling
Most hateful to an Egyptian; he became
A shepherd, and led his flocks and herds amid
The solitude and wilds of Midian, where he
Nursed in silent loneliness his earnest faith   100
In God and a constant love for kindred, tribe
And race. Years stole o'er him, but they took
No atom from his strength, nor laid one heavy weight
Upon his shoulders. The down upon his face
Had ripened to a heavy beard; the fire   105
That glowed within his youthful eye had deepened

To a calm and steady light, and yet his heart
Was just as faithful to his race as when he had
Stood in Pharaoh's courts and bade farewell
Unto his daughter.   110
There was a look of patient waiting on his face,
A calm, grand patience, like one who had lifted
Up his eyes to God and seen, with meekened face,
The wings of some great destiny o'ershadowing
All his life with strange and solemn glory.   115
But the hour came when he must pass from thought
To action,—when the hope of many years
Must reach its grand fruition, and Israel's
Great deliverance dawn. It happened thus:
One day, as Moses led his flocks, he saw   120
A fertile spot skirted by desert sands,—
A pleasant place for flocks and herds to nip
The tender grass and rest within its shady nooks;
And as he paused and turned, he saw a bush with fire
Aglow; from root to stem a lambent flame   125
Sent up its jets and sprays of purest light,
And yet the bush, with leaves uncrisped, uncurled,
Was just as green and fresh as if the breath
Of early spring were kissing every leaf.
Then Moses said I'll turn aside to see   130
This sight and as he turned he heard a voice
Bidding him lay his sandals by, for Lo! he
Stood on holy ground. Then Moses bowed his head
Upon his staff and spread his mantle o'er
His face, lest he should see the dreadful majesty   135
Of God; and there, upon that lonely spot,
By Horeb's mount, his shrinking hands received
The burden of his God, which bade him go
To Egypt's guilty king, and bid him let
The oppressed go free.   140

. . . .

Chapter V

. . . .

Moses sought again the presence of the king;
And Pharaoh's brow grew dark with wrath,
And rising up in angry haste, he said,
Defiantly, "If thy God be great, show
Us some sign or token of his power."   145
Then Moses threw his rod upon the floor,
And it trembled with a sign of life;
The dark wood glowed, then changed into a thing
Of glistening scales and golden rings, and green,
And brown and purple stripes; a hissing, hateful   150
Thing, that glared its fiery eye, and darting forth
From Moses' side, lay coiled and panting
At the monarch's feet. With wonder open-eyed
The king gazed on the changed rod, then called
For his magicians—wily men, well versed   155
In sinful lore—and bade them do the same.
And they, leagued with the powers of night, did
Also change their rods to serpents; then Moses'
Serpent darted forth, and with a startling hiss
And angry gulp, he swallowed the living things   160
That coiled along his path. And thus did Moses
Show that Israel's God had greater power
Than those dark sons of night.
                           But not by this alone
Did God his mighty power reveal: He changed   165
Their waters; every fountain, well and pool
Was red with blood, and lips, all parched with thirst,
Shrank back in horror from the crimson draughts.
And then the worshiped Nile grew full of life;
Millions of frogs swarmed from the stream—they clogged   170
The pathway of the priests and filled the sacred
Fanes, and crowded into Pharaoh's bed, and hopped
Into his trays of bread, and slumbered in his
Ovens and his pans.

There came another plague, of loathsome vermin;   175
They were gray and creeping things, that made
Their very clothes alive with dark and sombre
Spots—things so loathsome in the land they did
Suspend the service of the temple; for no priest
Dared to lift his hand to any god with one   180
Of these upon him. And then the sky grew
Dark, as if a cloud were passing o'er its
Changeless blue; a buzzing sound broke o'er
The city, and the land was swarmed with flies.
The murrain laid their cattle low; the hail   185
Cut off the first fruits of the Nile; the locusts,
With their hungry jaws, destroyed the later crops,
And left the ground as brown and bare as if a fire
Had scorched it through.
               Then angry blains   190
And fiery boils did blur the flesh of man
And beast; and then for three long days, nor saffron
Tint, nor crimson flush, nor soft and silvery light
Divided day from morn, nor told the passage
Of the hours; men rose not from their seats, but sat   195
In silent awe. That lengthened night lay like a burden
On the air,—a darkness one might almost gather
In his hand, it was so gross and thick. Then came
The last dread plague—the death of the first born.
               'Twas midnight,   200
And a startling shriek rose from each palace,
Home and hut of Egypt, save the blood-besprinkled homes
Of Goshen; the midnight seemed to shiver with a sense
Of dread, as if the mystic angel's wing
Had chilled the very air with horror.   205
Death! Death! was everywhere—in every home
A corpse—in every heart a bitter woe.
There were anxious fingerings for the pulse
That ne'er would throb again, and eager listenings
For some sound of life—a hurrying to and fro—   210
Then burning kisses on the cold lips
Of the dead, bitter partings, sad farewells,
And mournful sobs and piercing shrieks,

And deep and heavy groans throughout the length
And breadth of Egypt. 'Twas the last dread plague,   215
But it had snapped in twain the chains on which
The rust of ages lay, and Israel was freed;
Not only freed, but thrust in eager haste
From the land. Trembling men stood by, and longed
To see them gather up their flocks and herds,   220
And household goods, and leave the land; because they felt
That death stood at their doors as long as Israel
Lingered there; and they went forth in haste,
To tread the paths of freedom.

Chapter VI

But Pharaoh was strangely blind, and turning   225
From his first-born and his dead, with Egypt's wail
Scarce still upon his ear, he asked which way had
Israel gone? They told him that they journeyed
Towards the mighty sea, and were encamped
Near Baalzephen.   230
Then Pharaoh said, "the wilderness will hem them in,
The mighty sea will roll its barriers in front,
And with my chariots and my warlike men
I'll bring them back, or mete them out their graves."
                              Then Pharaoh's officers arose   235
And gathered up the armies of the king,
And made his chariots ready for pursuit.
With proud escutcheons blazoned to the sun,
In his chariot of ivory, pearl and gold,
Pharaoh rolled out of Egypt; and with him   240
Rode his mighty men, their banners floating
On the breeze, their spears and armor glittering
In the morning light; and Israel saw,
With fainting hearts, their old oppressors on their
Track: then women wept in hopeless terror;   245
Children hid their faces in their mothers' robes,
And strong men bowed their heads in agony and dread;
And then a bitter, angry murmur rose,—

"Were there no graves in Egypt, that thou hast
Brought us here to die?"   250
Then Moses lifted up his face, aglow
With earnest faith in God, and bade their fainting hearts
Be strong and they should his salvation see.
"Stand still," said Moses to the fearful throng
Whose hearts were fainting in the wild, "Stand still."   255
Ah, that was Moses' word, but higher and greater
Came God's watchword for the hour, and not for that
Alone, but all the coming hours of time.
"Speak ye unto the people and bid them
Forward go; stretch thy hand across the waters   260
And smite them with thy rod." And Moses smote
The restless sea; the waves stood up in heaps,
Then lay as calm and still as lips that just
Had tasted death. The secret-loving sea
Laid bare her coral caves and iris-tinted   265
Floor; that wall of flood which lined the people's
Way was God's own wondrous masonry;
The signal pillar sent to guide them through the wild
Moved its dark shadow till it fronted Egypt's
Camp, but hung in fiery splendor, a light   270
To Israel's path. Madly rushed the hosts
Of Pharaoh upon the people's track, when
The solemn truth broke on them—that God
For Israel fought. With cheeks in terror
Blenching, and eyes astart with fear, "let   275
Us flee," they cried, "from Israel, for their God
Doth fight against us; he is battling on their side."
They had trusted in their chariots, but now
That hope was vain; God had loosened every
Axle and unfastened every wheel, and each   280
Face did gather blackness and each heart stood still
With fear, as the livid lightnings glittered
And the thunder roared and muttered on the air,
And they saw the dreadful ruin that shuddered
O'er their heads, for the waves began to tremble   285
And the wall of flood to bend. Then arose
A cry of terror, baffled hate and hopeless dread,

A gurgling sound of horror, as "the waves
Came madly dashing, wildly crashing, seeking
Out their place again," and the flower and pride   290
Of Egypt sank as lead within the sea
Till the waves threw back their corpses cold and stark
Upon the shore, and the song of Israel's
Triumph was the requiem of their foes.

. . . .

The Death of Moses — Chapter IX

His work was done; his blessing lay   295
Like precious ointment on his people's head,
And god's great peace was resting on his soul.
His life had been a lengthened sacrifice,
A thing of deep devotion to his race,
Since first he turned his eyes on Egypt's gild   300
And glow, and clasped their fortunes in his hand
And held them with a firm and constant grasp.
But now his work was done; his charge was laid
In Joshua's hand, and men of younger blood
Were destined to possess the land and pass   305
Through Jordan to the other side. He too
Had hoped to enter there — to tread the soil
Made sacred by the memories of his
Kindred dead, and rest till life's calm close beneath
The sheltering vines and stately palms of that   310
Fair land; that hope had colored all his life's
Young dreams and sent its mellowed flushes o'er
His later years; but God's decree was otherwise.
And so he bowed his meekened soul in calm
Submission to the word, which bade him climb   315
To Nebo's highest peak, and view the pleasant land
From Jordan's swells unto the calmer ripples
Of the tideless sea, then die with all its
Loveliness in sight.

. . . .

He stood upon the highest peak of Nebo,   320
And saw the Jordan chafing through its gorges,
Its banks made bright by scarlet blooms
And purple blossoms. The placid lakes
And emerald meadows, the snowy crest
Of distant mountains, the ancient rocks   325
That dripped with honey, the hills all bathed
In light and beauty, the shady groves
And peaceful vistas, the vines opprest
With purple riches, the fig trees fruit-crowned
Green and golden, the pomegranates with crimson   330
Blushes, the olives with their darker clusters,
Rose before him like a vision, full of beauty
And delight. Gazed he on the lovely landscape
Till it faded from his view, and the wing
Of death's sweet angel hovered o'er the mountain's   335
Crest, and he heard his garments rustle through
The watches of the night.
      Then another, fairer, vision
Broke upon his longing gaze; 'twas the land
Of crystal fountains, love and beauty, joy   340
And light, for the pearly gates flew open,
And his ransomed soul went in. And when morning
O'er the mountain fringed each crag and peak with light,
Cold and lifeless lay the leader. God had touched
His eyes with slumber, giving his beloved sleep.   345

  Oh never on that mountain
  Was seen a lovelier sight
  Than the troupe of fair young angels
  That gathered 'round the dead.
  With gentle hands they bore him   350
  That bright and shining train,
  From Nebo's lonely mountain
  To sleep in Moab's vale.
  But they sang no mournful dirges,
  No solemn requiems said,   355

And the soft wave of their pinions
Made music as they trod.
But no one heard them passing,
None saw their chosen grave;
It was the angels secret   360
Where Moses should be laid.
And when the grave was finished,
They trod with golden sandals
Above the sacred spot,
And the brightest, fairest flower   365
Sprang up beneath their tread.
Nor broken turf, nor hillock
Did e'er reveal that grave,
And truthful lips have never said
We know where he is laid.   370

(1869)

Notes

Harper versifies the biblical account of Moses's birth, early life, career as leader
and law-giver of the Israelites, and his death (Exodus, Numbers, Deuteronomy).
The following parts of Harper's forty-page poem have been omitted from the
text: *Chapter I:* A dramatic dialog between Moses and Princess Charmian, daughter
of the pharaoh, reveals how Charmian found the infant Moses floating in a basket
on the Nile, gave him to his natural (Hebrew) mother to nurse, and protected
him until this moment of their parting, when Moses leaves "to share the fortune
of his race." *Chapter II:* Young Moses returns to his family and recounts the
history of the Hebrews and his rejection of the "pomp and pride of Egypt." *End
of Chapter IV and beginning of Chapter V:* Moses and his family leave Midian,
and in the desert he meets his brother Aaron with whom he plans Israel's deliverance. Pharaoh rejects their plea; instead, he increases the Hebrew slaves' burdensome labors so they will have no time to plot "sedition and revolt." *End of
Chapter VI, Chapters VII and VIII:* The Hebrews celebrate their triumph with
"music, dance and song." God proclaims his Oneness, and the poet hymns the
brotherhood of all people with God and Christ. Moses suffers to see Israel revert
to heathen rites and desire former pleasures of Egypt; the Hebrews' souls, the
poet notes, have been corrupted by slavery. *Part of Chapter IX:* The people bid
farewell to Moses as he climbs Mount Nebo and stands alone except for "God's
great presence." (See Whitfield's "How Long" [141–60] and Subject Index, Religion: Moses.)

7. *Goshen:* fertile land assigned to the Israelites in Egypt. 91, 99. *Midian:* a

son of Abraham and Keturah (Gen. 25:1–4), whose descendants, Midianites, lived in deserts of northwestern Arabia. 137. *Horeb's mount:* Mount Sinai. 172. *Fanes:* temples. 185. *murrain:* infectious disease. 190. *blains:* blisters. 192. *saffron:* yellow-orange color. 238. *escutcheons:* shields. 304. *Joshua's:* Joshua, successor to Moses and leader of the Israelites into the Promised Land. 316, 320, 352. *Nebo's:* Mount Nebo, summit of the mountain ridge Pisgah. 353. *Moab's:* Moab, an ancient kingdom east of the Dead Sea in what is now Jordan.

"Sir, We Would See Jesus"

We would see Jesus; earth is grand,
Flowing out from her Creator's hand.
Like one who tracks his steps with light,
His footsteps ever greet our sight;
The earth below, the sky above,   5
Are full of tokens of his love;
But 'mid the fairest scenes we've sighed—
Our hearts are still unsatisfied.

We would see Jesus; proud and high
Temples and domes have met our eye.   10
We've gazed upon the glorious thought,
By earnest hands in marble wrought,
And listened where the flying feet
Beat time to music, soft and sweet;
But bow'rs of ease, and halls of pride,   15
Our yearning hearts ne'er satisfied.

We would see Jesus; we have heard
Tidings our inmost souls have stirred,
How, from their chambers full of night,
The darkened eyes receive the light;   20
How, at the music of his voice,
The lame do leap, the dumb rejoice.
Anxious we'll wait until we've seen
The good and gracious Nazarene.

(1871)

Vashti

She leaned her head upon her hand
   And heard the king's decree—
"My lords are feasting in my halls,
   Bid Vashti come to me.

"I've shown the treasures of my house,   5
   My costly jewels rare,
But with the glory of her eyes
   No rubies can compare.

"Adorn'd and crown'd I'd have her come,
   With all her queenly grace,   10
And, 'mid my lords and mighty men,
   Unveil her lovely face.

"Each gem that sparkles in my crown,
   Or glitters on my throne,
Grows poor and pale when she appears,   15
   My beautiful, my own!"

All waiting stood the chamberlains
   To hear the Queen's reply,
They saw her cheek grow deathly pale,
   But light flash'd to her eye: 20

"Go, tell the King," she proudly said,
   "That I am Persia's Queen,
And by his crowds of merry men
   I never will be seen.

"I'll take the crown from off my head   25
   And tread it 'neath my feet
Before their rude and careless gaze
   My shrinking eyes shall meet.

"A queen unveil'd before the crowd!—
   Upon each lip my name!—   30
Why, Persia's women all would blush
   And weep for Vashti's shame!

"Go back!" she cried, and waived her hand,
   And grief was in her eye:
"Go, tell the King," she sadly said,   35
   "That I would rather die."

They brought her message to the King,
   Dark flash'd his angry eye;
'Twas as the lightning ere the storm
   Hath swept in fury by.   40

Then bitterly outspoke the King,
   Through purple lips of wrath—
"What shall be done to her who dares
   To cross your monarch's path?"

Then spake his wily counsellors—   45
   "O King of this fair land!
From distant Ind to Ethiop,
   All bow to thy command.

"But if, before thy servants' eyes,
   This thing they plainly see,   50
That Vashti doth not heed thy will
   Nor yield herself to thee,

"The women, restive 'neath our rule,
   Would learn to scorn our name,
And from her deed to us would come   55
   Reproach and burning shame.

"Then, gracious King, sign with thy hand
   This stern but just decree,
That Vashti lay aside her crown,
   Thy Queen no more to be."   60

She heard again the King's command,
　　And left her high estate,
Strong in her earnest womanhood,
　　She calmly met her fate,

And left the palace of the King,　　　　　65
　　Proud of her spotless name—
A woman who could bend to grief,
　　But would not bow to shame.

　　　　　　　　　　(1871)

Notes

Vashti was queen of Ahasuerus, king of Persia (Xerxes to the Greeks), who banished her for refusing to show the king's guests her beauty (Esth. 1). 33. Waved. 47. *Ind to Ethiop:* boundaries (India to Ethiopia) of ancient Persia (Esth. 1:1).

Learning to Read

Very soon the Yankee teachers
   Came down and set up school;
But, oh! how the Rebs did hate it,—
   It was agin' their rule.

Our masters always tried to hide   5
   Book learning from our eyes;
Knowledge did'nt agree with slavery—
   'Twould make us all too wise.

But some of us would try to steal
   A little from the book.   10
And put the words together,
   And learn by hook or crook.

I remember Uncle Caldwell,
   Who took pot liquor fat
And greased the pages of his book,   15
   And hid it in his hat.

And had his master ever seen
   The leaves upon his head,
He'd have thought them greasy papers,
   But nothing to be read.   20

And there was Mr. Turner's Ben,
   Who heard the children spell,
And picked the words right up by heart,
   And learned to read 'em well.

Well, the Northern folks kept sending   25
   The Yankee teachers down;
And they stood right up and helped us,
   Though Rebs did sneer and frown.

And I longed to read my Bible,
   For precious words it said;   30
But when I begun to learn it,
   Folks just shook their heads,

And said there is no use trying,
   Oh! Chloe, you're too late;
But as I was rising sixty,   35
   I had no time to wait.

So I got a pair of glasses,
   And straight to work I went,
And never stopped till I could read
   The hymns and Testament.   40

Then I got a little cabin
   A place to call my own—
And I felt as independent
   As the queen upon her throne.

              (1872)

Save the Boys

Like Dives in the deeps of Hell
I cannot break this fearful spell,
Nor quench the fires I've madly nursed,
Nor cool this dreadful raging thirst.
Take back your pledge—ye come too late!   5
Ye cannot save me from my fate,
Nor bring me back departed joys;
But ye can try to save the boys.

Ye bid me break my fiery chain,
Arise and be a man again,   10
When every street with snares is spread,
And nets of sin where'er I tread.
No; I must reap as I did sow.
The seeds of sin bring crops of woe;
But with my latest breath I'll crave   15
That ye will try the boys to save.

These bloodshot eyes were once so bright;
This sin-crushed heart was glad and light;
But by the wine-cup's ruddy glow
I traced a path to shame and woe.   20
A captive to my galling chain,
I've tried to rise, but tried in vain—
The cup allures and then destroys.
Oh! from its thraldom save the boys.

Take from your streets those traps of hell   25
Into whose gilded snares I fell.
Oh! freemen, from these foul decoys
Arise, and vote to save the boys.
Oh! ye who license men to trade
In draughts that charm and then degrade,   30

Before ye hear the cry, Too late,
Oh, save the boys from my sad fate.

(1887; 1895)

Note

1. *Dives:* the rich man punished in hell who begged for water while the beggar Lazarus was comforted in heaven (Luke 16:19–31).

The Present Age

Say not the age is hard and cold—
   I think it brave and grand;
When men of diverse sects and creeds
   Are clasping hand in hand.

The Parsee from his sacred fires   5
   Beside the Christian kneels;
And clearer light to Islam's eyes
   The word of Christ reveals.

The Brahmin from his distant home
   Brings thoughts of ancient lore;   10
The Bhuddist breaking bonds of caste
   Divides mankind no more.

The meek-eyed sons of far Cathay
   Are welcome round the board;
Not greed, nor malice drives away   15
   These children of our Lord.

And Judah from whose trusted hands
   Came oracles divine;
Now sits with those around whose hearts
   The light of God doth shine.   20

Japan unbars her long sealed gates
   From islands far away;
Her sons are lifting up their eyes
   To greet the coming day.

The Indian child from forests wild   25
   Has learned to read and pray;
The tomahawk and scalping knife
   From him have passed away.

From centuries of servile toil
   The Negro finds release,   30
And builds the fanes of prayer and praise
   Unto the God of Peace.

England and Russia face to face
   With Central Asia meet;
And on the far Pacific coast,   35
   Chinese and natives greet.

Crusaders once with sword and shield
   The Holy Land to save;
From Moslem hands did strive to clutch
   The dear Redeemer's grave.   40

A battle greater, grander far
   Is for the present age;
A crusade for the rights of man
   To brighten history's page.

Where labor faints and bows her head,   45
   And want consorts with crime;
Or men grown faithless sadly say
   That evil is the time.

There is the field, the vantage ground
   For every earnest heart;   50
To side with justice, truth and right
   And act a noble part.

To save from ignorance and vice
   The poorest, humblest child;
To make our age the fairest one   55
   On which the sun has smiled;

To plant the roots of coming years
   In mercy, love and truth;
And bid our weary, saddened earth
   Again renew her youth.   60

Oh! earnest hearts! toil on in hope,
  'Till darkness shrinks from light;
To fill the earth with peace and joy,
  Let youth and age unite;

To stay the floods of sin and shame   65
  That sweep from shore to shore;
And furl the banners stained with blood,
  'Till war shall be no more.

Blame not the age, nor think it full
  Of evil and unrest;   70
But say of every other age,
  "This one shall be the best."

The age to brighten every path
  By sin and sorrow trod;
For loving hearts to usher in   75
  The commonwealth of God.
      (1890; 1895)

Notes

Among *diverse sects and creeds* (3) are: 5. *Parsee:* Persian Zoroastrianism; 7. *Islam* and 39. *Moslem:* Muslimism; 9. *Brahmin:* Hinduism; 11. *Bhuddist:* Buddhism of India and Asia; 13. *Cathay:* a literary term for China; 17. *Judah:* Judaism, Judah being the biblical kingdom of the Hebrews.

Songs for the People

Let me make the songs for the people,
   Songs for the old and young;
Songs to stir like a battle-cry
   Wherever they are sung.

Not for the clashing of sabres, 5
   For carnage nor for strife;
But songs to thrill the hearts of men
   With more abundant life.

Let me make the songs for the weary,
   Amid life's fever and fret, 10
Till hearts shall relax their tension,
   And careworn brows forget.

Let me sing for little children,
   Before their footsteps stray,
Sweet anthems of love and duty, 15
   To float o'er life's highway.

I would sing for the poor and aged,
   When shadows dim their sight;
Of the bright and restful mansions,
   Where there shall be no night. 20

Our world, so worn and weary,
   Needs music, pure and strong,
To hush the jangle and discords
   Of sorrow, pain, and wrong.

Music to soothe all its sorrow, 25
   Till war and crime shall cease;
And the hearts of men grown tender
   Girdle the world with peace.
               (1894; 1895)

A Double Standard

Do you blame me that I loved him?
  If when standing all alone
I cried for bread a careless world
  Pressed to my lips a stone.

Do you blame me that I loved him,   5
  That my heart beat glad and free,
When he told me in the sweetest tones
  He loved but only me?

Can you blame me that I did not see
  Beneath his burning kiss   10
The serpent's wiles, nor even hear
  The deadly adder hiss?

Can you blame me that my heart grew cold
  That the tempted, tempter turned;
When he was feted and caressed   15
  And I was coldly spurned?

Would you blame him, when you draw from me
  Your dainty robes aside.
If he with gilded baits should claim
  Your fairest as his bride?   20

Would you blame the world if it should press
  On him a civic crown;
And see me struggling in the depth
  Then harshly press me down?

Crime has no sex and yet to-day   25
  I wear the brand of shame;
Whilst he amid the gay and proud
  Still bears an honored name.

Can you blame me if I've learned to think
  Your hate of vice a sham,   30
When you so coldly crushed me down
  And then excused the man?

Would you blame me if to-morrow
  The coroner should say,
A wretched girl, outcast, forlorn,   35
  Has thrown her life away?

Yes, blame me for my downward course,
  But oh! remember well,
Within your homes you press the hand
  That led me down to hell.   40

I'm glad God's ways are not our ways,
  He does not see as man,
Within His love I know there's room
  For those whom others ban.

I think before His great white throne,   45
  His throne of spotless light,
That whited sepulchres shall wear
  The hue of endless night.

That I who fell, and he who sinned,
  Shall reap as we have sown;   50
That each the burden of his loss
  Must bear and bear alone.

No golden weights can turn the scale
  Of justice in His sight;
And what is wrong in woman's life   55
  In man's cannot be right.

                  (1895)

JOSEPH CEPHAS HOLLY

Joseph Cephas Holly (1825–55) worked as a bootmaker in Brooklyn, New York, and Burlington, Vermont, before settling in Rochester in 1852. He was the older brother of James Theodore Holly, a renowned abolitionist, colonizationist, and the Bishop of Haiti. From 1841, Joseph was active in antislavery work, but he opposed colonization, and conflict over this issue may have been the cause of the brothers' estrangement in the 1850s. Holly was married and had a son who died in infancy in 1852. Ill and destitute in the last years of his life, Holly died of consumption in Rochester.

Holly's verse passionately champions his race, demanding freedom, vengeance, and justice from man and God. These militant poems, like his songs for temperance, tributes to race heroes, and pleas for poetic power suffer from hackneyed diction, irregular metrics, and choppy thought, but their sincerity and anger are palpable.

Freedom's Offering, A Collection of Poems (Rochester, N.Y.: Chas. H. McDonnell, 1853).

A Wreath of Holly

I long to spread my tiny wings,
    And soar away on fancy bright;
Or stopping at Parnassus' springs,
    Drink in his streams of liquid light.
I long—Oh pray forgive the folly—   5
    Tho' sable hue bedeck my brow;
To wear like Burns, a wreath of holly:—
    The inspired muse of Mossgiel's plow.
Or wildly at my touch, the Lyre
    Its tones in vivid transport yield;   10
The crashing sound, the lightning fire
    Of Afric's favor'd bard Whitfield.
Perchance my muse by perseverance,
    Soul crushing bars, and doubts may brave:
And soar on eagle's wings like Terrance,   15
    The chainless hearted Roman slave.
Not that I would be wafted light,
    Upon the breath of transient fame;
But strong in cause of GOD and right,
    Would win like them a deathless name.   20
May sing of wrongs by man inflicted,
    On brothers of a common blood;
The crimes by pen ne'er half depicted,
    Of children of one brotherhood.
Of war, of pillage, artful knavery,   25
    And last and blackest of the train;
Thou foul man-scourge! soul crushing slavery,
    Who feed on hearts, and feasts on brain.
Oh man! thou living marble statue;
    What tho' thy brothers cast in bronze?   30
He's not disowned of loving nature;
    God loves whom thou poor earthworm scorns.
Think ye that power, arts or treasure,
    Can shield thee from impending wrath,

If ye invoke God's stern displeasure   35
   By walking iniquity's path?
Oh hear ye not the direful warning,
   Of freedom's poet, bold Whittier;
Of earthquakes underneath ye yawning?
   'Hear ye no warnings in the air'?   40
Or feel ye not the burning satire, —
   When gazing on your pile of glory —
Which streams from Lowell's pen of fire,
   And lives in his poetic story;
The mockery of cloud-capped spires,   45
   To celebrate your sire's graves;
While smothering freedom's altar-fires,
   Which burns in hearts of trampled slaves.
But freedom's morn is faintly dawning,
   In love and peace; or as of yore, —   50
Oh list to Monticello's warning —
   'Twill come if't must in floods of gore.

Notes

3. *Parnassus' springs:* Parnassus, a mountain in Greece, was in classical mythology home of the Muses (goddesses of various arts) and thus the source of poetry. 7–8. *Burns . . . Mossgiel's plow:* Robert Burns (1759–96), a Scottish poet who leased and worked a farm at Mossgiel; he was called the "ploughman poet." 12. *Whitfield:* James Monroe Whitfield (see pp. 71–93). 15. *Terence:* Publius Terentius Afer (ca. 186–159? B.C.), a slave, freed by his Roman master, who became a major comic dramatist. 28. *feeds.* 38. *Whittier:* John Greenleaf Whittier (1807–92), a Quaker from Massachusetts, the most prolific and ardent abolitionist poet of his time. 43. *Lowell's:* James Russell Lowell (1819–91), from a prominent Massachusetts family, a Harvard professor, editor, and distinguished writer. He contributed abolitionist essays and verse to the *National Anti-Slavery Standard,* which he also edited in 1848–49, and to the *Pennsylvania Freeman.* 51. *Monticello's warning:* Thomas Jefferson (1743–1826), third president of the United States (1801–9), resided at Monticello in Virginia. His writings of the late eighteenth century deplored the institution of slavery and warned that it would end only in bloodshed.

The Patriot's Lament

Oh, weep for Columbia! oh, weep for the time!
When slavery dark, and degrading crime,
First poluted thy shores, oh glorious nation!
In spite of thy great, and thy true declaration,
Which proclaims that all men are both equal and free,   5
Whether rich and exalted, or humble they be,
And this is endowed by the mighty creator—
The King of the world, and the great legislator.
Bewildered Columbia! I weep for thy fate,
For the years thou hast borne thy inglorious weight;   10
But the cloud of thy burden is passing away,
'Fore Appollo refulgent, the bright star of day.
Shall Maryland, where the brave Donaldson fell,
Be cursed by this foul scourge of hell?
Shall the land of our WASHINGTON, the glorious, and brave,   15
Be disgraced by the fettered feet of the slave?
Shall Carolina, the birth place of New Orleans' hero,
Stern JACKSON the sage, the American Nero,
Be a land for despots, and tyrants to meet,
And be trod by bondmen's inglorious feet?   20
Shall Georgia, where brave Green our rights did maintain,
Bear the disgrace, the niggardly stain,
Of a cruel, and treacherous barbarous knavery,
Of a base, and a brutal, and degraded slavery?
Shall men, women and children, by freemen be bought,   25
In Louisiana, where the brave Jackson fought,
In market under auctioneer's hammers be sold
For ungrateful tyrant's ill-gotten gold?
Columbia, awake! from thy lethargic sleep,
No more let thy desolate children weep!   30
No more let cruel tyrants angry eyes flash!
Whilst human flesh quake under the torturing lash.
No more let female shrieks impart!
Anguishing arrows to the christian heart;
No more tare asunder the husband and wife!   35

Who have vowed to each other as long as lasts life.
No more from fond parents their children separate!
Entirely ignorant of each others fate;
No more let freemen for slavery's curse moan!
But throw off the yoke, and as christians atone. 40
Then I'll hail the Columbia, the happy and free!
"The home of the brave," and pray so let it be;
Wipe out the deep blot of thy foul degradation!
And prove to the world that thou art a free nation.
Then no more wilt thou be the foot-stool of the slave, 45
But the "land of the free and the home of the brave!"
Thy genius commands thee to wipe out the stain,
And forever the glorious, and happy to reign.

Notes

1, 9, 29, 41. *Columbia:* America. 3. *polluted.* 12. *Apollo:* the Roman and Greek god of light, with the sun as his chariot; also the god of poetry, prophecy, and music, among other areas; *refulgent:* shining. 15. *Washington:* George Washington (1732–99), commander-in-chief of the Continental armies during the Revolutionary War and first president of the United States. 18, 26. *Jackson* and *brave Jackson:* Andrew Jackson (1767–1845), the general who defeated the British in the Battle of New Orleans (Louisiana) during the War of 1812, and seventh president of the United States (1829–37). 18. *Nero:* emperor of Rome (A.D. 54–68), infamous for his cruel murders and for persecution of Christians. Holly seems unaware of Nero's reputation when he calls Andrew Jackson "the American Nero." 21. *Green:* probably General Nathanael Greene (1742–86), commander of the Southern Department of Washington's Continental Army in the Revolutionary War. 32. *quakes.* 35. *tear.* 41. *thee.*

Our Family Tree

ON THE DEATH OF MY SISTER CECILIA—THE LAST OF FIVE
MEMBERS OF THE FAMILY, WHO DIED SUCCESSIVELY.

Our family tree is in the sear
   And yellow leaf of life;
Branch after branch, year after year,
   Yields to death's pruning knife.
First, youngest born, as if 'twere meet,   5
   The sacrifice should be,
"The last of earth," the first to meet
   Th' unknown eternity.
'Twas God who gave, 'twas He who took,
   His voice let us obey,   10
So that in his eternal book,
   Our names shine bright as day.

This Is a Fatherland to Me

Oh! tell me not of fatherland
  Far, far beyond the deep blue sea;
Of fruitful soil — of golden sand;
  Of orange groves, and cocoa tree —
My mother breathed the inspiring air,   5
  That sweeps along our craft-filled sea;
And here my father lisped his prayer;
  This is a fatherland to me.
Oh! tell me not that God appoints,
  The sable man Afric too free;   10
Whom he selects — whom he annoints
  He'll make the path of duty see:
Oh! tell me not of power, and place,
  Of wealth, of pomp, and luxury —
Of the improvement of my race,   15
  When transplanted beyond the sea.
God ne'er but one race made to dwell,
  Beneath the broad o'erarching sky;
There's but one heaven — but one hell,
  And but one vast eternity;   20
And whereso'er he warms the soul
  Into our mortal bodies, — there
Without intrusion or control,
  We may abide if anywhere.

Note

See note to Simpson's "Old Liberia Is Not the Place for Me"; (see also Subject
Index, African-American Race: Colonization).

GEORGE BOYER VASHON

George Boyer Vashon (1824–78), a brilliant teacher, attorney, and author, was the first African American to graduate from Oberlin College and the first to become a lawyer in New York state. He was born in Carlisle, Pennsylvania, the son of the eminent abolitionist John Bethume Vashon. George went to school in Pittsburgh and there served as secretary of the first Juvenile Anti-Slavery Society in the United States (1838). After earning his B.A. from Oberlin in 1844, Vashon studied law in Pittsburgh but was denied admittance to the bar because of his race. He left the country for a thirty-month exile in Haiti, stopping on the way in New York, where he was admitted to the bar in 1848. Vashon taught at College Faustin in Port-au-Prince; he then practiced law in Syracuse, New York, from 1850 to 1854 and for the next three years was professor of belles lettres and mathematics at New York Central College in McGrawville. Returning to Pittsburgh, Vashon married Susan Paul Smith in 1857, and the couple had seven children. He served as a principal and teacher in Pittsburgh until 1867. During his remaining years, Vashon held government posts in Washington, D.C., worked for race advancement with the Colored Men of America, and published learned essays, poems, and letters in periodicals. It is commonly thought that he died of yellow fever in Mississippi.

Vashon's epic on the Haitian insurrection is surely the most imaginative poem by an African American of his century. The slaves' revolt becomes not only a metaphor for universal racial conflict and resistance to tyranny, but also a symbol of disequilibrium, of a world in perpetual chaotic motion. Within a finely structured, dramatic whole, Vashon sustains an ambience of instability through an image pattern of flickering light, storms, blood, and warfare; by shifts from classical to prosaic to metaphorical diction; by abrupt changes in metrical and stanzaic form; by intermittent use of descriptive, narrative, and subjective voices; by movement in temporal and spatial scene; and by direct statement of theme. The artistry and passion of this poem insure Vashon's stature among his contemporaries.

"Vincent Ogé" in *Autographs for Freedom*, edited by Julia Griffiths (Auburn, N.Y.: Alden, Beardsley & Co., 1854).

Vincent Ogé

[Fragments of a poem hitherto unpublished, upon a
revolt of the free persons of color, in the island of
St. Domingo (now Hayti), in the years 1790-1.]

There is, at times, an evening sky —
　　The twilight's gift — of sombre hue,
All checkered wild and gorgeously
　　With streaks of crimson, gold and blue; —
A sky that strikes the soul with awe,　　　　　　　5
　　And, though not brilliant as the sheen,
Which in the east at morn we saw,
　　Is far more glorious, I ween; —
So glorious that, when night hath come
And shrouded it in deepest gloom,　　　　　　　　10
We turn aside with inward pain
And pray to see that sky again.
Such sight is like the struggle made
When freedom bids unbare the blade,
And calls from every mountain-glen —　　　　　　15
　　From every hill — from every plain,
Her chosen ones to stand like men,
　　And cleanse their souls from every stain
Which wretches, steeped in crime and blood,
Have cast upon the form of God.　　　　　　　　　20
Though peace like morning's golden hue,
　　With blooming groves and waving fields,
Is mildly pleasing to the view,
　　And all the blessings that it yields
Are fondly welcomed by the breast　　　　　　　　25
　　Which finds delight in passion's rest,
That breast with joy foregoes them all,
While listening to Freedom's call.
Though red the carnage, — though the strife
Be filled with groans of parting life, —　　　　　　30
Though battle's dark, ensanguined skies
Give echo but to agonies —
　　To shrieks of wild despairing, —

We willingly repress a sigh—
Nay, gaze with rapture in our eye,   35
Whilst "FREEDOM!" is the rally-cry
    That calls to deeds of daring.

* * * * * * * * * * * * *

The waves dash brightly on thy shore,
    Fair island of the southern seas!
As bright in joy as when of yore   40
    They gladly hailed the Genoese,—
That daring soul who gave to Spain
A world—last trophy of her reign!
Basking in beauty, thou dost seem
A vision in a poet's dream!   45
Thou look'st as though thou claim'st not birth
With sea and sky and other earth,
That smile around thee but to show
Thy beauty in a brighter glow,—
That are unto thee as the foil   50
    Artistic hands have featly set
Around Golconda's radiant spoil,
    To grace some lofty coronet,—
A foil which serves to make the gem
The glory of that diadem!   55

* * * * * * * * * * * * *

If Eden claimed a favored haunt,
    Most hallowed of that blessed ground,
Where tempting fiend with guileful taunt
    A resting place would ne'er have found,—
As shadowing it well might seek   60
    The loveliest home in that fair isle,
Which in its radiance seemed to speak
    As to the charmed doth Beauty's smile,
That whispers of a thousand things
For which words find no picturings.   65
Like to the gifted Greek who strove
    To paint a crowning work of art,

And form his ideal Queen of Love,
　By choosing from each grace a part,
Blending them in one beauteous whole,　　　　　70
To charm the eye, transfix the soul,
And hold it in enraptured fires,
Such as a dream of heaven inspires,—
So seem the glad waves to have sought
　From every place its richest treasure,　　　　75
And borne it to that lovely spot,
　To found thereon a home of pleasure;—
A home where balmy airs might float
　Through spicy bower and orange grove;
Where bright-winged birds might turn the note　　80
　Which tells of pure and constant love;
Where earthquake stay its demon force,
And hurricane its wrathful course;
Where nymph and fairy find a home,
And foot of spoiler never come.　　　　　　　85

*　*　*　*　*　*　*　*　*　*　*　*　*

And Ogé stands mid this array
　Of matchless beauty, but his brow
Is brightened not by pleasure's play;
　He stands unmoved—nay, saddened now,
As doth the lorn and mateless bird　　　　　90
That constant mourns, whilst all unheard,
The breezes freighted with the strains
Of other songsters sweep the plain,—
That ne'er breathes forth a joyous note,
Though odors on the zephyrs float—　　　　　95
The tribute of a thousand bowers,
Rich in their store of fragrant flowers.
Yet Ogé's was a mind that joyed
　With nature in her every mood,
Whether in sunshine unalloyed　　　　　　100
　With darkness, or in tempest rude;
And, by the dashing waterfall,
　Or by the gently flowing river,

Or listening to the thunder's call,
  He'd joy away his life forever. 105
But ah! life is a changeful thing,
  And pleasures swiftly pass away,
And we may turn, with shuddering,
  From what we sighed for yesterday.
The guest, at banquet-table spread 110
With choicest viands, shakes with dread,
Nor heeds the goblet bright and fair,
Nor tastes the dainties rich and rare,
Nor bids his eye with pleasure trace
The wreathed flowers that deck the place, 115
If he but knows there is a draught
Among the cordials, that, if quaffed,
Will send swift poison through his veins.
  So Ogé seems; nor does his eye
With pleasure view the flowery plains, 120
  The bounding sea, the spangled sky,
As, in the short and soft twilight,
  The stars peep brightly forth in heaven,
And hasten to the realms of night,
  As handmaids of the Even. 125

*   *   *   *   *   *   *   *   *   *   *   *   *

The loud shouts from the distant town,
  Joined in with nature's gladsome lay;
The lights went glancing up and down,
  Riv'ling the stars—nay, seemed as they
    Could stoop to claim, in their high home, 130
     A sympathy with things of earth,
    And had from their bright mansions come,
     To join them in their festal mirth.
For the land of the Gaul had arose in its might,
And swept by as the wind of a wild, wintry night; 135
And the dreamings of greatness—the phantoms of power,
Had passed in its breath like the things of an hour.
Like the violet vapors that brilliantly play
Round the glass of the chemist, then vanish away,

The visions of grandeur which dazzlingly shone,   140
Had gleamed for a time, and all suddenly gone.
And the fabric of ages—the glory of kings,
Accounted most sacred mid sanctified things,
Reared up by the hero, preserved by the sage,
And drawn out in rich hues on the chronicler's page,   145
Had sunk in the blast, and in ruins lay spread,
While the altar of freedom was reared in its stead.
And a spark from that shrine in the free-roving breeze,
Had crossed from fair France to that isle of the seas;
And a flame was there kindled which fitfully shone   150
Mid the shout of the free, and the dark captive's groan;
As, mid contrary breezes, a torch-light will play,
Now streaming up brightly—now dying away.

     *   *   *   *   *   *   *   *   *   *   *   *

The reptile slumbers in the stone,
    Nor dream we of his pent abode;   155
The heart conceals the anguished groan,
    With all the poignant griefs that goad
            The brain to madness;
Within the hushed volcano's breast,
    The molten fires of ruin lie;—
Thus human passions seem at rest,   160
    And on the brow serene and high,
            Appears no sadness.
But still the fires are raging there,
Of vengeance, hatred, and despair;
And when they burst, they wildly pour   165
    Their lava flood of woe and fear,
And in one short—one little hour,
    Avenge the wrongs of many a year.

     *   *   *   *   *   *   *   *   *   *   *   *

And Ogé standeth in his hall;
    But now he standeth not alone;—   170
A brother's there, and friends; and all
    Are kindred spirits with his own;

For mind will join with kindred mind,
As matter's with its like combined.
They speak of wrongs they had received—   175
Of freemen, of their rights bereaved;
And as they pondered o'er the thought
Which in their minds so madly wrought,
Their eyes gleamed as the lightning's flash,
Their words seemed as the torrent's dash   180
That falleth, with a low, deep sound,
Into some dark abyss profound,—
A sullen sound that threatens more
Than other torrents' louder roar.
Ah! they had borne well as they might,   185
    Such wrongs as freemen ill can bear;
And they had urged both day and night,
    In fitting words, a freeman's prayer;
And when the heart is filled with grief,
    For wrongs of all true souls accurst,   190
In action it must seek relief,
    Or else, o'ercharged, it can but burst.
Why blame we them, if they oft spake
Words that were fitted to awake
The soul's high hopes—its noblest parts—   195
The slumbering passions of brave hearts
And send them as the simoom's breath,
Upon a work of woe and death?
And woman's voice is heard amid
    The accents of that warrior train;   200
And when has woman's voice e'er bid,
    And man could from its hest refrain?
Hers is the power o'er his soul
    That's never wielded by another,
And she doth claim this soft control   205
    As sister, mistress, wife, or mother.
So sweetly doth her soft voice float
    O'er hearts by guilt or anguish riven,
It seemeth as a magic note
    Struck from earth's harps by hands of heaven.   210

And there's the mother of Ogé,
  Who with firm voice, and steady heart,
And look unaltered, well can play
  The Spartan mother's hardy part;
And send her sons to battle-fields,   215
  And bid them come in triumph home,
Or stretched upon their bloody shields,
  Rather than bear the bondman's doom.
"Go forth," she said, "to victory;
Or else, go bravely forth to die!   220
Go forth to fields where glory floats
In every trumpet's cheering notes!
Go forth, to where a freeman's death
Glares in each cannon's fiery breath!
Go forth and triumph o'er the foe;   225
Or failing that, with pleasure go
To molder on the battle-plain,
Freed ever from the tyrant's chain!
But if your hearts should craven prove,
Forgetful of your zeal—your love   230
For rights and franchises of men,
My heart will break; but even then,
Whilst bidding life and earth adieu,
This be the prayer I'll breathe for you:
'Passing from guilt to misery,   235
May this for aye your portion be,—
A life, dragged out beneath the rod—
An end, abhorred of man and God—
As monument, the chains you nurse—
As epitaph, your mother's curse!' "   240

*   *   *   *   *   *   *   *   *   *   *   *

A thousand hearts are breathing high,
And voices shouting "Victory!"
    Which soon will hush in death;
    The trumpet clang of joy that speaks,
    Will soon be drowned in the shrieks   245
      Of the wounded's stifling breath,

The tyrant's plume in dust lies low —
Th' oppressed has triumphed o'er his foe.
But ah! the lull in the furious blast
May whisper not of ruin past;   250
It may tell of the tempest hurrying on,
To complete the work the blast begun.
With the voice of a Syren, it may whisp'ringly tell
Of a moment of hope in the deluge of rain;
And the shout of the free heart may rapt'rously swell,   255
    While the tyrant is gath'ring his power again.
Though the balm of the leech may soften the smart,
    It never can turn the swift barb from its aim;
And thus the resolve of the true freeman's heart
    May not keep back his fall, though it free it from shame. 260
Though the hearts of those heroes all well could accord
With freedom's most noble and loftiest word;
Their virtuous strength availeth them nought
With the power and skill that the tyrant brought.
Gray veterans trained in many a field   265
Where the fate of nations with blood was sealed,
In Italia's vales — on the shores of the Rhine —
Where the plains of fair France give birth to the vine —
Where the Tagus, the Ebro, go dancing along,
Made glad in their course by the Muleteer's song —   270
All these were poured down in the pride of their might,
On the land of Ogé, in that terrible fight.
Ah! dire was the conflict, and many the slain,
Who slept the last sleep on that red battle-plain!
The flash of the cannon o'er valley and height   275
Danced like the swift fires of a northern night,
Or the quivering glare which leaps forth as a token
That the King of the Storm from his cloud-throne has spoken.
And oh! to those heroes how welcome the fate
Of Sparta's brave sons in Thermopylae's strait;   280
With what ardor of soul they then would have given
Their last look at earth for a long glance at heaven!
Their lives to their country — their backs to the sod —
Their heart's blood to the sword, and their souls to their God!

But alas! although many lie silent and slain,   285
More blest are they far than those clanking the chain,
In the hold of the tyrant, debarred from the day; —
And among these sad captives is Vincent Ogé!

*   *   *   *   *   *   *   *   *   *   *

Another day's bright sun has risen,
And shines upon the insurgent's prison;   290
Another night has slowly passed,
And Ogé smiles, for 'tis the last
He'll droop beneath the tyrant's power—
The galling chains! Another hour,
And answering to the jailor's call,   295
He stands within the Judgment Hall.
They've gathered there;—they who have pressed
Their fangs into the soul distressed,
To pain its passage to the tomb
With mock'ry of a legal doom.   300
They've gathered there;—they who have stood
Firmly and fast in hour of blood,—
Who've seen the lights of hope all die,
As stars fade from a morning sky,—
They've gathered there, in that dark hour—   305
The latest of the tyrant's power,—
An hour that speaketh of the day
Which never more shall pass away,—
The glorious day beyond the grave,
Which knows no master—owns no slave.   310
And there, too, are the rack—the wheel—
The torturing screw—the piercing steel,—
Grim powers of death all crusted o'er
With other victims' clotted gore.
Frowning they stand, and in their cold,   315
Silent solemnity, unfold
The strong one's triumph o'er the weak—
The awful groan—the anguished shriek—
The unconscious mutt'rings of despair—
The strained eyeball's idiot stare—   320

The hopeless clench — the quiv'ring frame —
The martyr's death — the despot's shame.
The rack — the tyrant — victim, — all
Are gathered in that Judgment Hall.
Draw we the veil, for 'tis a sight   325
But friends can gaze on with delight.
The sunbeams on the rack that play,
For sudden terror flit away
From this dread work of war and death,
As angels do with quickened breath,   330
From some dark deed of deepest sin,
Ere they have drunk its spirit in.

*   *   *   *   *   *   *   *   *   *   *   *   *

No mighty host with banners flying,
   Seems fiercer to a conquered foe,
Than did those gallant heroes dying,   335
   To those who gloated o'er their woe; —
Grim tigers, who have seized their prey,
Then turn and shrink abashed away;
And, coming back and crouching nigh,
Quail 'neath the flashing of the eye,   340
Which tells that though the life has started,
The will to strike has not departed.

*   *   *   *   *   *   *   *   *   *   *   *   *

Sad was your fate, heroic band!
Yet mourn we not, for yours' the stand
Which will secure to you a fame,   345
That never dieth, and a name
That will, in coming ages, be
A signal word for Liberty.
Upon the slave's o'erclouded sky,
   Your gallant actions traced the bow,   350
Which whispered of deliv'rance nigh —
   The meed of one decisive blow.
Thy coming fame, Ogé! is sure;

Thy name with that of L'Ouverture,
And all the noble souls that stood   355
With both of you, in times of blood,
Will live to be the tyrant's fear—
Will live, the sinking soul to cheer!

Syracuse, N.Y., August 31st, 1853

Notes

Asterisks separating "fragments" are Vashon's own; the text here is complete. Ogé was a Haitian mulatto executed by the French at Cap-Francais in March 1791 for his part in the rebellion (see Reason's "Freedom" (58) and Rowe's "Toussaint L'Overture" and notes). 31. *ensanguined:* stained with blood. 41. *the Genoese:* Christopher Columbus, discoverer of the West Indian island of Hispaniola, now occupied by the nations of Haiti and the Dominican Republic. 52. *Golconda's radiant spoil:* ruins of a royal city near Hyderabad, India. 134–49. *land of the Gaul . . . isle of the seas:* France and the French Revolution, begun in 1789, which inspired revolutionaries of other nations. 197. *simoom's breath:* a hot, violent desert wind. 214, 280. *Spartan:* Sparta, a city in ancient Greece, famous for its rigorously trained, strictly disciplined soldiers; by extension, its civilians (mothers) were equally "spartan." 253. *Syren* (or Siren): a mythological sea nymph whose seductive singing lured men to destruction. 267–69. *In Italia's vales:* Italy, France, and Spain, where the *Rhine, Tagus,* and *Ebro* rivers flow, sent troops to subdue Haiti and reinstitute slavery. 280. *Thermopylae's:* a pass in Greece where the Persians defeated the Spartans (480 B.C.).

ELYMAS PAYSON ROGERS

Elymas Payson Rogers (1815–61) was a third-generation African American, descended from a slave who survived a shipwreck off the coast of Connecticut in the early eighteenth century. Rogers, born to Chloe (Ladue) and Abel Rogers in Madison, Connecticut, grew up in poverty. In the early 1830s he attended school in Hartford then supported himself in New York by teaching in Rochester while he studied for the ministry, first in Peterboro, then at Oneida Institute in Whitesboro (1835–41). With a degree from Oneida in 1841, Rogers moved to Trenton, New Jersey, where he married Harriet E. Sherman and began his nineteen-year career as an educator and ordained minister in Trenton, Princeton, and Newark. In 1860, having labored for the African Civilization Society for many years, he sailed to Sierra Leone to fulfill a lifelong dream of becoming a missionary; but Rogers died of heart disease just fifty days after he stepped on African soil.

Rogers's political arguments in octosyllabic couplets are unique and effective topical satires that were courageous ventures for a black poet in the 1850s. The verse is precise and attractive, the whole well-structured and rich with historical and erudite references. Rogers's moral indignation, neatly balanced by astute humor and logical reasoning, gives power to these potent attacks against two major restrictive bills.

A Poem on the Fugitive Slave Law (Newark, N.J.: A. Stephen Holbrook, 1855); *The Repeal of the Missouri Compromise Considered* (Newark, N.J.: A. Stephen Holbrook, 1856).

from *A Poem on the Fugitive Slave Law*

Law! what is law? The wise and sage,
Of every clime and every age,
In this most cordially unite,
That 'tis a rule for doing right.

Great Blackstone, that illustrious sire,   5
Whose commentaries all admire,
And Witherspoon, and Cicero,
And all distinguished jurists show
That law is but the power supreme
To shield, to nurture, or redeem   10
Those rights so sacred, which belong
To man; and to prohibit wrong.
But definitions more concise,
Than any framed by man's device,
The conscientious patriot draws   15
From the Eternal code of laws;
From which he clearly understands
That God's immutable commands
Are law throughout the universe,
Which human edicts can't reverse.   20
All human laws must therefore be,
Founded alone on God's decree:
Which firm decree in every case
Must constitute their only base.
God's laws are suns supremely bright;   25
Man's laws should but reflect their light.

. . . .

In fifty, Congress passed a Bill,
Which proved a crude and bitter pill
At least in many a northern mouth,
Though sweet as honey at the South.   30

It was the object of this Act
(By priests and politicians backed)
That masters might with ease retake
The wretched slaves who chanced to break
Away from servitude thenceforth,   35
And sought a refuge at the North.

It was the purpose of this Act
To make the Northern States, in fact,
The brutal master's hunting grounds,
To be explored by human hounds   40
Who would, for shining gold, again
Bind on the bleeding captive's chain.
This Bill most clearly was designed
To prejudice the public mind
In favor of the master's claim,   45
Howe'er circuitous or lame.

From officers of baser sort,
The Bill sought sanction and support:
And lawyers bought of no repute
And bribed the dough-faced judge to boot,   50
It gave encouragement to knaves,
It mocked the suff'rings of the slaves
By giving, if the slave went free,
The judge five dollars as his fee.
But if the judge bound on his chains,   55
He won ten dollars for his pains.

Go to yon Capitol and look
On this free nation's statute book,
And there you'll find the monstrous Bill
Upon the nation's records still.   60
And dough-faced politicians now
Their rev'rence for the Act avow,
And hundreds impudently say
That all should peacefully obey
The Act, and yield to its demands,   65

And give back to the master's hands
The poor, dejected, bleeding slave,
This great Confederacy to save.
We scarce can quench our indignation,
Aroused by such an intimation,   70
For government should man befit,
And not man sacrifice to it.
And if the Union long has stood
Cemented with the bondsman's blood;
If human hearts and human bone   75
Are truly its chief corner stone;
If State from State would soon divide
If not with negro sinews tied;
Then let th' accursed Union go,
And let her drift, or, sink below,   80
Or, let her quick in sunder break
And so become a shattered wreck.

And is that vile requirement just
Which tramples manhood in the dust?
Shall we arrest escaping slaves   85
At every beck of Southern knaves?
Shall Northern freemen heed a few
Of that untoward apostate crew,
And, let them hunt upon their soil
And drag to unrequited toil   90
A man, however rude or raw,
Because of that nefarious law
Which causes liberty to bleed,
And gravely sanctions such a deed?

. . . .

That Bill a law? some call it so,   95
But One above us answers, "No:
It conflicts with my firm decree;
A law therefore it cannot be.
I tell this nation, as I told

My servants in the days of old,   100
That none the wand'ring shall perplex,
Or e'er the honest stranger vex:
Deliver not the refugee
Who from his master flees to thee;
He who escapes his master's hand   105
Shall dwell among you in the land,
And to him ye shall not refuse
The dwelling place which he shall choose.
He shall dwell where he likes it best,
And neither shall he be oppressed."   110

. . . .

Is that Bill law? hark! from below
The voice of Lucifer cries, "No!
That Bill is a complete gewgaw,
Unworthy of the name of law,
And certainly I ought to know,   115
'Twas manufactured here below,
And then to leading statesmen sent
Who urged it 'to the full extent.'
Some think it binding to the letter;
But here in Tophet we know better,   120
For, we are better lawyers far,
Than half the Philadelphia bar:
The meanest devil can explain
Law more correctly than Judge Kane;
We like the Act, it suits us well;   125
For, 'tis a measure fresh from hell."

That Bill a law? the South say so,
But Northern freemen answer, No!
It overthrows our sacred rights,
And sympathetic feeling blights;   130
It cools the zeal of every heart
That feign would act a generous part
To God's outraged and injured poor,
Or harbor them within the door.

. . . .

That Bill is law, doughfaces say;   135
But black men everywhere cry, Nay:
We'll never yield to its control
While life shall animate one soul.
That Bill we ever shall ignore,
And, as we've often done before,   140
Will tread the measure in the dust,
And ask the world if 'tis not just.

. . . .

But whence that voice, so soft, so clear,
So musical within my ear?
It says "We'll every power defy   145
Beneath which helpless women sigh,
And seek to mitigate their grief,
And toil and pray for their relief.
We will for fugitives provide,
We will the trembling outcast hide: 150
This will we do while we have breath,
Fearless of prisons, chains, or death."
This voice is from the female band
Who are united heart and hand
With all the truly good and brave,   155
To aid the poor absconding slave.
Those earthly angels ever hold
An office which appears two-fold.
For they not only act their part
But, like sweet music, cheer the heart   160
Of those who labor by their side,
If faith, or hope, or zeal, subside.

. . . .

Will any then the Act obey?
Both male and female answer, Nay;
For he who heeds it must withdraw   165

His reverence for the Higher Law.
Whatever human laws may say
God's law we dare not disobey.

Philanthropists, you've nought to fear;
Take courage, be ye of good cheer: 170
Advancing onward is your cause
In spite of all oppressive laws.
Ten thousands speak out for the dumb
And thousands more are yet to come,
Until the whole united North   175
In all her majesty stands forth,
With banners waving o'er her head,
On which their motto may be read,
No more slave laws or territory
To soil our Nation's rising glory.   180

We've leaders of the royal pith,
Like Seward, Hale, and Gerrit Smith,
Sumner and Wilson, who've no lack
Of bony substance in the back.
Led on by such a fearless band   185
Securely trusting in God's hand,
Soon slave laws will be obsolete,
And victory will be complete.

Notes

The Fugitive Slave Act, passed by Congress in 1850, was designed to strengthen a previous law of 1793. The act created a body of federal commissioners who were paid to issue warrants for the arrest and return to the South of fugitive slaves who had escaped to the North. 5. *Blackstone:* Sir William Blackstone (1723–80), an English judge and writer of famous commentaries on law. 7. *Witherspoon:* John Witherspoon (1723–94), a Scottish-born Presbyterian minister, active in American educational reform and theological and political affairs. 7. *Cicero:* see Reason's "The Spirit Voice" (31). 50, 61, 135. *dough-faced:* applied to a Northerner who sided with the South on slavery issues. 68. *Confederacy:* the eleven States that seceded from the "Union" and fought the North in the Civil War (1861–65); these Confederate States were: Alabama, Arkansas, Florida, Georgia, Louisiana, Mississippi, North Carolina, South Carolina, Tennessee, Texas, and

Virginia. *92. nefarious:* unspeakably wicked. *112, 120. Lucifer... Tophet:* names for the devil, or satan, and hell. *113. geegaw:* a showy but valueless trinket. *182–83.* William Henry *Seward* (1801–72), activist for abolition and black civil rights, governor of New York, a senator, and secretary of state under presidents Lincoln and Johnson (1861–69); John P. *Hale* (1806–73), abolitionist and politician of New Hampshire, a congressman and senator; *Gerrit Smith* (1797–1874), philanthropist and abolitionist, president of the New York State Vigilance Committee that aided fugitive slaves, and a congressman; Charles *Sumner* (1811–74), Massachusetts abolitionist, reformer, scholar, writer, and an impassioned orator for black rights in the U.S. Senate; Henry *Wilson* (1812–75), antislavery senator from Massachusetts and later vice president under Grant (1873–75).

from The Repeal of the Missouri Compromise Considered

. . . .

The covetous Nebraskaites
Have near extinguished Freedom's lights,
Have thrown her altars to the ground
And hurled the hallowed parts around.
And then, their treason to complete,   5
They've leaped with their unhallowed feet
Upon the fragments on the sand,
(Still both magnificent and grand,)
And in their wild delirium swore
That liberty should be no more.   10
The dignified and lofty tree,
Of heaven-descending liberty,
No longer tow'ring upward stands,
But, prostrate by Vandalic hands,
Lies where the faithless act was done,   15
And withers in the noon-tide sun.

. . . .

"I want the land," was Freedom's cry;
And Slavery answered, "So do I!
By all that's sacred, I declare
I'll have my just and lawful share.   20
The Northern cheek should glow with shame
To think to rob me of my claim:
And if my claim you dare deny,
I'll knock the Union into pi."
The Northern faces did not glow,   25
Because they were composed of dough:
But such a tall and horrid threat
Their equilibrium upset.
"O gracious heavens!" the patriot said,
As nervously he shook his head,   30
And quickly moved his tangled hair

To feel the bump of firmness there:
But how distracted was his mind,
When searching long he could not find
This stately organ of the brain,   35
Nor could the mystery explain,
Or make a fit apology
For this freak of phrenology.
The reason why the bump was low
Was it was fashioned out of dough;   40
And Slavery's bold and fearless threat
Had crushed the lofty organ flat.

This horrid threat from Southern men,
In Congress was all powerful then;
And when the North opposed the South,   45
This remedy sealed up their mouth,
And made them quickly toe the mark
And sanction schemes however dark.
The Union breaking threat prevailed,
When every other measure failed.   50

But recently the North drove back
The Southern tyrants from the track,
And put to flight their boasting ranks,
And gave the speaker's chair to BANKS.

In twenty tyranny prevailed,   55
And Northern men before it quailed
And bowed to Slavery — sad mistake —
But all was for the Union's sake.
The glorious Union, they declared,
Must never, never be impaired!   60
It is, said they, a sacred thing,
And to it we will ever cling;
The Union is above all price.
'Tis wisdom to convey a slice
Of territory, thus to save   65
The Union from a dismal grave.
And if God's righteous law we break,

'Twill all be for the Union's sake!
We must support the Constitution
And if we sin seek absolution.   70

A few, of never-dying fame,
Would never yield to Slavery's claim,
Would have no fellowship with it,
And now their wisdom we admit.
But these were a minority,   75
The others a majority;
And hence the Compromise was made,
And Slavery's claim was duly paid.

And, after gaining his desire,
He scarce was willing to retire,   80
And, as he turned to take his leave,
He laughed immoderate in his sleeve,
And said he'd surely call for more
In eighteen hundred fifty-four.
"The rest," quoth he, "I cannot get,   85
I am not strong enough as yet;
But when I am maturely strong,
I'll seize the balance, right or wrong."

But Freedom cried, "Wo worth the day
When such a treacherous game you play;   90
And such a treacherous game to win
Would be a most atrocious sin.
The act would gracious heaven defy,
And tempt the Majesty on high;
And then would ruin most complete   95
Accompany your sad defeat."

"But hold!" said Slavery; "you're too fast;
I judge the future by the past.
I always have high heaven defied,
And man's authority denied;   100
I always have securely seized

And borne away whate'er I pleased,
And, if my numerous games be sin,
Whene'er I play, I always win:
And I control the legislation   105
Of this great democratic nation,
And to my tried and cordial friends
My lib'ral patronage extends;
I raise them up to seats of power,
Although unworthy, base, and poor.   110
O'er each department I preside,
And all official actions guide;
I send ambassadors afar,
And, when I please, provoke a war
Ostensibly for public weal,   115
But 'tis in fact my burning zeal
To multiply my territory,
Instead of for the nation's glory.
And presidents I nominate
For confirmation by each State,   120
And no Chief-Magistrate is made
Without my all-sufficient aid.
Of politics, I am the pope
To whom each candidate must stoop,
And there devoutly kneeling low   125
Do homage to my sacred toe.
All these are facts which I defy
My sanguine scoffers to deny.

. . . .

"Some Northern men despise me much
And fear pollution from my touch,   130
And cry to heaven both night and day
To smite me dead without delay;
Then from their altars turn away,
The painted hypocrite to play,
And to my filthy garments cling   135
And seek to crown me as their king.
If I but gain their votes at last,

I care not how they pray and fast;
Their prayers are but the merest hoax—
But daring and blasphemous jokes.   140
When I am privileged to see
Their words and actions *both* agree,
I then may tremble, not before,
Upon my lofty seat of power.

. . . .

"And now," said Slavery, "I must go;   145
I've business down in Mexico;
But purpose to return this way
Upon the first auspicious day,
And with no acts preparatory
Enlarge my spacious territory."   150

Then Freedom gave a mournful sigh,
But made no audible reply.

And who can truthfully allege
That Slavery's not redeemed his pledge.
He has returned, increased in might,   155
And put his strongest foes to flight.
The Compromise, as we've supposed,
Which was by prudent men proposed,
Was clearly all the measure then
Which would unite our Congressmen.   160
And some constituents confessed
The measure was by far the best
To cause fierce jealousies to cease,
And to establish public peace;
And, as the loaf could not be won,   165
The half was preferable to none.
And thus united did they fix
The parallel of thirty-six
And thirty minutes, to divide
The land, and ever to decide   170
The bounds of Slavery's dismal night.

. . . .

For thirty years the Compromise
Has met with favor in the eyes
Of Unionists throughout the nation,
Of every party, creed and station.   175
And when the venerable act
Was first by ruthless hands attacked,
The wise and good of every creed
Repudiated such a deed.
The country's noble Constitution,   180
The parent of each institution,
Was no more sacred in their eyes
Than the Missouri Compromise.
But now the precious Compromise
In wild and reckless ruin lies,   185
Plucked like a jewel from a crown,
And ruthlessly is trodden down.

And why this wild and daring deed
For which our land must surely bleed?
Why is the landmark now removed,   190
The landmark which the sires approved?
Why are the fathers' works erased,
Their early monuments defaced?
Why is their wisdom cast aside
Which thirty years have sanctified?   195

It is, indeed, O, sad to tell!
For 'tis a measure fresh from hell,
It is that Slavery may expand
O'er all our new and fertile land;
That its black flag may be unfurled,   200
And wave o'er all the western world;
That tyrants may the helpless spoil,
And thrive on unrequited toil;
May bury hope in deep despair,
And traffic in God's image there: 205
That they may there exert their sway

And more securely hold their prey,
And pass this scheme of degradation
To the succeeding generation;

. . . .

But all the blind Nebraskaites   210
Who have invaded human rights,
Will at the North in every case
Be overwhelmed in deep disgrace.
The President and Cabinet,
Together with his lordly set,   215
Will all undoubtedly retire
As fast as legal terms expire.
Their steps they cannot now retrace,
They're sinking deeper in disgrace,
And stormy vengeance waits to shed   220
Her bitterness on every head.
When their eventful life is o'er,
No one their loss will much deplore;
And when their kindred call their name,
Their cheeks will mantle o'er with shame;   225
But soon their names will be forgot,
The memory of them all shall rot.
And let their burying places be
Upon the coast beside the sea;
And let the ever-rolling surge   230
Perform a constant funeral dirge.
And when the stranger shall demand
Why these are buried in the sand,
Let him be told without disguise
They trod upon the Compromise!   235

But o'er us reigns the Holy One:
He does but speak and it is done:
He has declared that truth shall roll
Until it reaches either pole.
And though her enemies may be   240

Like pebbles round the rolling sea,
They all will ultimately fail:
For God's predictions must prevail.

Notes

When the Missouri Territory applied for statehood as a slave state in 1819, slave and free states were equally represented in the U.S. Senate. After bitter debates, this political equilibrium was maintained by passage of the Missouri Compromise in 1820, which admitted Missouri as a slave state and Maine as a free state while prohibiting slavery in future states north of latitude 36°30'. In 1854, the Kansas-Nebraska Act repealed the Missouri Compromise's prohibition of slavery's expansion and allowed people who lived in Kansas and Nebraska to determine whether these territories would be slave or free. Violent political upheavals followed this act as proslavery and free-soil forces raced to colonize "Bleeding Kansas" (see Subject Index, Slavery and Abolitionism: Laws). 14. *Vandalic hands:* Vandals were Germanic people who ravaged Gaul (now France and Belgium), Spain, and Rome in the fifth century. 54. *Banks:* Nathaniel Prentiss Banks (1816–94), a general in the Union army during the Civil War and speaker of the House of Representatives in 1856–57. 146. *Mexico:* From the 1820s, Mexico's antislavery legislation conflicted with proslavery sentiments of Texans and Southerners. The issue of slavery as well as President Polk's expansionist program led to America's war with Mexico (1846–48).

ADAH ISAACS MENKEN

Adah Isaacs Menken (1839?–68) achieved fame and infamy as the world's highest-paid actress, a celebrated writer and lecturer, and mistress of famous men. Although her parentage remains in doubt, she probably was born Philomène Croi Théodore in New Orleans to Auguste Theodore, a mulatto, and his wife, Magdaleine Jean Louis Janneaux. At the age of fifteen, in Texas, Adah gave readings of Shakespeare, published a few poems, and married Alexander Isaac Menken, a wealthy businessman whose Judaism she adopted as her own heritage. She soon left Menken and subsequently married John C. Heenan (1859), Robert Henry Newell (1862), and James Paul Barkley (1866). Adah's acting career began in New Orleans in 1856 and continued until her death. Billed as "The World's Delight," she earned riches and acclaim on international stages, particularly in Byron's *Mazeppa*. During her brief life, Adah published many poems and articles in periodicals; she enjoyed the friendship of famous writers on both sides of the Atlantic and scandalized Victorian society by her rebellious free-living and love affairs. Despite her great theatrical success, Adah longed for appreciation as a poet, and in the last year of her life she collected about half her poems for the slim volume she designed and published.

Menken's major subject is her own suffering, and her verse most often shrieks with hysterical breast-beating lamentations, shrill with bitterness, disillusionment, anguish, and self-denigration. The poetic art is smothered by rhetorical questions, histrionic exclamations, and incoherencies. Menken's poetry, however, is never dully conventional but rather dramatically modern in its intense self-awareness, defiant confessional personas, and its condemnation of a male-dominated world that oppresses, mocks, and dooms creative women. Some of her poems, stylistically imitating Walt Whitman whom she admired, employ free verse, significant repetitions, and incantatory rhythms. Her simplest poems, short and sincere, may be her best.

Infelicia (New York, 1868; London, 1868).

Aspiration

Poor, impious Soul! that fixes its high hopes
   In the dim distance, on a throne of clouds,
And from the morning's mist would make the ropes
   To draw it up amid acclaim of crowds—
Beware! That soaring path is lined with shrouds;   5
   And he who braves it, though of sturdy breath,
May meet, half way, the avalanche and death!

O poor young Soul!—whose year-devouring glance
   Fixes in ecstasy upon a star,
Whose feverish brilliance looks a part of earth,   10
   Yet quivers where the feet of angels are,
And seems the future crown in realms afar—
   Beware! A spark *thou* art, and dost but see
Thine own reflection in Eternity!

My Heritage

"My heritage!" It is to live within
The marts of Pleasure and of Gain, yet be
No willing worshiper at either shrine;
To think, and speak, and act, not for my pleasure,
But others'. The veriest slave of time   5
And circumstances. Fortune's toy!
To hear of fraud, injustice, and oppression,
And feel who is the unshielded victim.
      Cold friends and causeless foes!
      Proud thoughts that rise to fall.   10
Bright stars that set in seas of blood;
Affections, which are passions, lava-like
Destroying what they rest upon. Love's
Fond and fervid tide preparing icebergs
That fragile bark, this loving human heart.   15
      O'ermastering Pride!
      Ruler of the Soul!
Life, with all its changes, cannot bow ye.
      Soul-subduing Poverty!
That lays his iron, cold grasp upon the high   20
Free spirit: strength, sorrow-born, that bends
But breaks not in his clasp—all, all
These are "my heritage!"
And mine to know a reckless human love, all passion
and intensity, and see a mist come o'er the scene, a dim-
ness steal o'er the soul!
    Mine to dream of joy and wake to wretchedness!   25
Mine to stand on the brink of life
One little moment where the fresh'ning breeze
Steals o'er the languid lip and brow, telling
Of forest leaf, and ocean wave, and happy
Homes, and cheerful toil; and bringing gently   30
To this wearied heart its long-forgotten

Dreams of gladness.

But turning the fevered cheek to meet the soft kiss of
the winds, my eyes look to the sky, where I send up my
soul in thanks. The sky is clouded — no stars — no music
— the heavens are hushed.

My poor soul comes back to me, weary and disap-
pointed.

The very breath of heaven, that comes to all, comes not   35
to me.

Bound in iron gyves of unremitting toil, my vital air is
wretchedness — what need I any other?

"My heritage!" The shrouded eye, the trampled leaf,
wind-driven and soiled with dust — these tell the tale.

Mine to watch
The glorious light of intellect
Burn dimly, and expire; and mark the soul,   40
Though born in Heaven, pause in its high career,
Wave in its course, and fall to grovel in
The darkness of earth's contamination, till
Even Death shall scorn to give a thing
So low his welcome greeting!   45
Who would be that pale,
Blue mist, that hangs so low in air, like Hope
That has abandoned earth, yet reacheth
Not the stars in their proud homes?
A dying eagle, striving to reach the sun?   50
A little child talking to the gay clouds as they flaunt
past in their purple and crimson robes?
A timid little flower singing to the grand old trees?
Foolish waves, leaping up and trying to kiss the moon?
A little bird mocking the stars?
Yet this is what men call Genius.   55

Hear, O Israel!

(*From the Hebrew.*)
"And they shall be my people, and I will be their God."
—JEREMIAH xxxii. 38.

I

Hear, O Israel! and plead my cause against the
ungodly nation!
'Midst the terrible conflict of Love and Peace, I departed from thee, my people, and spread my tent of many
colors in the land of Egypt.
In their crimson and fine linen I girded my white form.
Sapphires gleamed their purple light from out the darkness of my hair.
The silver folds of their temple foot-cloth was spread   5
beneath my sandaled feet.
Thus I slumbered through the daylight.
    Slumbered 'midst the vapor of sin,
    Slumbered 'midst the battle and din,
    Wakened 'midst the strangle of breath,
    Wakened 'midst the struggle of death!   10

II

Hear, O Israel! my people—to thy goodly tents do I
return with unstained hands.
Like as the harts for the water-brooks, in thirst, do pant
and bray, so pants and cries my longing soul for the house
of Jacob.
My tears have unto me been meat, both in night and
day:
And the crimson and fine linen moulders in the dark
tents of the enemy.
With bare feet and covered head do I return to thee, O   15
Israel!
With sackcloth have I bound the hem of my garments.

With olive leaves have I trimmed the border of my
bosom.

The breaking waves did pass o'er me; yea, were mighty
in their strength—

      Strength of the foe's oppression.

My soul was cast out upon the waters of Sin: but it has   20
come back to me.

My transgressions have vanished like a cloud.

The curse of Balaam hath turned to a blessing;

And the doors of Jacob turn not on their hinges against
me.

Rise up, O Israel! for it is I who passed through the
fiery furnace seven times, and come forth unscathed, to redeem thee from slavery, O my nation! and lead thee back
to God.

III

Brothers mine, fling out your white banners over this   25
Red Sea of wrath!

Hear ye not the Death-cry of a thousand burning,
bleeding wrongs?

Against the enemy lift thy sword of fire, even thou, O
Israel! whose prophet I am.

For I, of all thy race, with these tear-blinded eyes, still
see the watch-fire leaping up its blood-red flame from the
ramparts of our Jerusalem!

And my heart alone beats and palpitates, rises and falls
with the glimmering and the gleaming of the golden beacon
flame, by whose light I shall lead thee, O my people!
back to freedom!

Give me time—oh give me time to strike from your   30
brows the shadow-crowns of Wrong!

On the anvil of my heart will I rend the chains that
bind ye.

Look upon me—oh look upon me, as I turn from the
world—from love, and passion, to lead thee, thou Chosen
of God, back to the pastures of Right and Life!

Fear me not; for the best blood that heaves this heart
now runs for thee, thou Lonely Nation!

Why wear ye not the crown of eternal royalty, that God
set down upon your heads?

Back, tyrants of the red hands!   35

Slouch back to your ungodly tents, and hide the Cain-
brand on your foreheads!

Life for life, blood for blood, is the lesson ye teach
us.

We, the Children of Israel, will not creep to the kennel
graves ye are scooping out with iron hands, like scourged
hounds!

Israel! rouse ye from the slumber of ages, and, though
Hell welters at your feet, carve a road through these
tyrants!

The promised dawn-light is here; and God—O the God   40
of our nation is calling!

       Press on—press on!

IV

Ye, who are kings, princes, priests, and prophets. Ye
men of Judah and bards of Jerusalem, hearken unto my
voice, and I will speak thy name, O Israel!

Fear not; for God hath at last let loose His thinkers,
and their voices now tremble in the mighty depths of this
old world!

Rise up from thy blood-stained pillows!

Cast down to dust the hideous, galling chains that bind   45
thy strong hearts down to silence!

       Wear ye the badge of slaves?

       See ye not the watch-fire?

Look aloft, from thy wilderness of thought!

Come forth with the signs and wonders, and thy strong
hands, and stretched-out arms, even as thou didst from
Egypt!

Courage, courage! trampled hearts!   50

Look at these pale hands and frail arms, that have rent
asunder the welded chains that an army of the Philistines
bound about me!

But the God of all Israel set His seal of fire on my
breast, and lighted up, with inspiration, the soul that pants
for the Freedom of a nation!

With eager wings she fluttered above the blood-stained
bayonet-points of the millions, who are trampling upon
the strong throats of God's people.

   Rise up, brave hearts!
The sentry cries: "All's well!" from Hope's tower!   55
Fling out your banners of Right!
The watch fire grows brighter!
   All's well! All's well!
   Courage! Courage!
The Lord of Hosts is in the field,   60
The God of Jacob is our shield!

Notes

The speaker adopts the persona of a prophet of Israel (incorporating several
biblical heroes) who Moses-like will lead the slaves to freedom (see Subject Index,
Religion: Moses, and see notes to these poems). 12. *harts:* deer. 12, 23, 61. *house
(doors) (God) of Jacob:* Jacob, younger son of Isaac, fathered the twelve patriarchs
of the Hebrews (Gen. 25:24–34). The name *Jacob* means the ancient nation Israel.
16. *sackcloth:* coarse cloth, worn as a symbol of mourning. 22. *curse of Balaam:*
Balaam the prophet, his eyes opened by an angel, refused the Moabite king's
request to curse the Israelites; rather, Balaam praised them as God's chosen people
who would become a great nation (Num. 22–24). 24. *fiery furnace seven times:*
Nebuchadnezzar, king of Babylon, threw the Jews Shadrach, Meshach, and Abed-
nego into a seven-times-heated fiery furnace because they refused to worship his
golden image. An angel of God saved them (Dan. 3). 51. *Philistines:* inhabitants
of ancient Philistia, neighbor and enemy of the Israelites.

Infelix

Where is the promise of my years;
    Once written on my brow?
Ere errors, agonies and fears
Brought with them all that speaks in tears,
Ere I had sunk beneath my peers;   5
    Where sleeps that promise now?

Naught lingers to redeem those hours,
    Still, still to memory sweet!
The flowers that bloomed in sunny bowers
Are withered all; and Evil towers   10
Supreme above her sister powers
    Of Sorrow and Deceit.

I look along the columned years,
    And see Life's riven fane,
Just where it fell, amid the jeers   15
Of scornful lips, whose mocking sneers,
For ever hiss within mine ears
    To break the sleep of pain.

I can but own my life is vain
    A desert void of peace;   20
I missed the goal I sought to gain,
I missed the measure of the strain
That lulls Fame's fever in the brain,
    And bids Earth's tumult cease.

Myself! alas for theme so poor   25
    A theme but rich in Fear;
I stand a wreck on Error's shore,
A spectre not within the door,
A houseless shadow evermore,
    An exile lingering here.   30

Note

Coined from the Latin, the word *infelix* means "not happy" or "unhappiness," like the title of Menken's volume, *Infelicia*.

JAMES MADISON BELL

James Madison Bell (1826–1902), the "Bard of the Maumee," was a native of Gallipolis, Ohio, where he spent his first sixteen years. He worked as a plasterer in Cincinnati (1842–53) and there married Louisiana Sanderlin with whom he had several children. From 1854 to 1860, Bell plied the plasterer's trade in Canada West, Ontario (where he became a friend, ally, and fundraiser for John Brown), then in San Francisco from 1860 to 1865 and in several other cities, North and South. He returned to Toledo about 1890. During all these years, Bell wrote, published, and gave public readings of his poetry; he lectured nationwide for abolitionism and black educational and legal rights; he served as a prominent lay worker for the A.M.E. church; and in the 1870s he was briefly active in Republican politics. All in all, Bell was one of the century's most articulate witnesses to racial oppression and to the African-American struggle for equality.

For forty years, Bell's orations in verse surveyed slavery, the Civil War, emancipation, and Reconstruction. These long poems (750–950 lines each) require the spirited dramatic recitals Bell offered on his reading tours, for their abstractions, clichés, and monotonously regular iambic tetrameter and rhymes smother both emotional force and intellectual conviction. Occasionally, specific references to historical persons and events or variations in stanza length do occur, but the orations remain almost identical and dull. A dozen shorter poems in *Works,* most on racial themes, are commonplace, but Bell triumphs with his daring, vigorous satire of President Andrew Johnson. Shrewd humor and irony, concrete topicality, and personal emotion combine to make "Modern Moses" Bell's most inventive and readable work.

Bell's long poems include *A Poem* (1862); *A Poem Entitled the Day and the War* (1864); *An Anniversary Poem Entitled the Progress of Liberty* (1866); and *A Poem, Entitled the Triumph of Liberty* (1870). They were published separately and later included in *The Poetical Works* (Lansing, Mich.: Wynkoop Hallenbeck Crawford Co., 1901).

JAMES MADISON BELL

---

from A Poem Entitled the Day and the War

Though Tennyson, the poet king,
  Has sung of Balaklava's charge,
Until his thund'ring cannons ring
  From England's center to her marge,
The pleasing duty still remains   5
To sing a people from their chains—
To sing what none have yet assay'd,
The wonders of the Black Brigade.
The war had raged some twenty moons,
Ere they in columns or platoons,   10
To win them censure or applause,
Were marshal'd in the Union cause—
Prejudged of slavish cowardice,
While many a taunt and foul device
Came weekly forth with Harper's sheet,   15
To feed that base, infernal cheat.

    But how they would themselves demean,
Has since most gloriously been seen.
'Twas seen at Milliken's dread bend!
Where e'en the Furies seemed to lend   20
To dark Secession all their aid,
To crush the Union Black Brigade.

The war waxed hot, and bullets flew
  Like San Francisco's summer sand,
But they were there to dare and do,   25
  E'en to the last, to save the land.
And when the leaders of their corps
  Grew wild with fear, and quit the field,
The dark remembrance of their scars
  Before them rose, they could not yield: 30
And, sounding o'er the battle din,
  They heard their standard-bearer cry—

"Rally! and prove that ye are men!
   Rally! and let us do or die!
For war, nor death, shall boast a shade   35
   To daunt the Union Black Brigade!"

And thus he played the hero's part,
   Till on the ramparts of the foe
A score of bullets pierced his heart,
   He sank within the trench below.   40
His comrades saw, and fired with rage,
Each sought his man, him to engage
In single combat. Ah! 'twas then
The Black Brigade proved they were men!
For ne'er did Swiss! or Russ! or knight!   45
   Against such fearful odds arrayed,
With more persistent valor fight,
   Than did the Union Black Brigade!

As five to one, so stood their foes,
When that defiant shout arose,   50
And 'long their closing columns ran,
Commanding each to choose his man!
And ere the sound had died away,
Full many a ranting rebel lay
Gasping piteously for breath—   55
Struggling with the pangs of death,
From bayonet thrust or shining blade,
Plunged to the hilt by the Black Brigade.
   And thus they fought, and won a name—
None brighter on the scroll of Fame;   60
For out of one full corps of men,
But one remained unwounded, when
The dreadful fray had fully past—
All killed or wounded but the last!

   And though they fell, as has been seen,   65
Each slept his lifeless foes between,
And marked the course and paved the way

To ushering in a better day.
Let Balaklava's cannons roar,
   And Tennyson his hosts parade,   70
But ne'er was seen and never more
   The equals of the Black Brigade!

Then nerve thy heart, gird on thy sword,
For dark Oppression's ruthless horde
And thy tried friends are in the field—   75
Say which shall triumph, which shall yield?
Shall they that heed not man nor God—
Vile monsters of the *gory rod*—
Dark forgers of the *rack* and *chain:*
Shall *they* prevail—and Thraldom's reign,   80
With all his dark unnumber'd ills,
Become eternal as the hills?
No! by the blood of freemen slain,
On hot-contested field and main,
And by the mingled sweat and tears,   85
Extorted through these many years
From Afric's patient sons of toil—
Weak victims of a braggart's spoil—
This bastard plant, the Upas tree,
Shall not supplant our liberty!   90

Notes

Bell composed and recited *The Day and the War* for the first anniversary celebration of the Emancipation Proclamation and *The Progress of Liberty* for the third anniversary. The former, a poem of 750 lines, takes the reader from slavery days, through the Civil War to Emancipation; the latter, in 850 lines, reviews four years of war and peace (1862–66), liberty's triumph, and Lincoln's martyrdom. 1–2, 69. *Tennyson . . . Balaklava's charge:* In his poem, "The Charge of the Light Brigade," Alfred, Lord Tennyson (1809–92) celebrated the allied victory at the Battle of Balaclava, fought in 1854 during the Crimean War. 8, ff. *Black Brigade:* Civil War recruitment of black soldiers by the federal government began officially only in 1863. Black brigades were raised in the South and North, originally as state regiments with fanciful titles; later the regiments were renumbered as U.S. Colored Troops. By the end of the war, 12 percent of the Union Army was African American. 19. *Millikin's:* Millikin's Bend, the site of a major battle in June 1863 in which black troops fought valiantly. 20. *Furies:* in Greek myth, three fierce female divinities who punished criminals. 89. *the Upas tree:* literally, a tree of Java whose milky sap is poisonous. Metaphorically, the upas tree represents discriminatory laws and actions against blacks. Bell is referring to the Kansas-Nebraska Act. A later black poet, Charles Douglas Clem (1876–1934), published an essay *The Upas Tree of Kansas* (1917); Clem's upas tree was Kansas's policy of hiring only white teachers.

from *An Anniversary Poem Entitled the Progress of Liberty*

The bondsman's gloomy night has passed;
   The slavery of this land is dead;
No tyrant's power, however vast,
   Can wake it from its gory bed.
For in the order of events,   5
   And after an ignoble reign,
It died. None mourned its going hence,
   Nor followed in its funeral train;
Ignoble birth, ignoble life,
   Ignoble death, ignoble doom!   10
Conceived by fiends in deadly strife,
   And cast into a nameless tomb.

Though slavery's dead, yet there remains
A work for those from whom the chains
Today are falling one by one;   15
Nor should they deem their labor done,
Nor shrink the task, however hard,
While it insures a great reward,
And bids them on its might depend
For perfect freedom in the end.   20

Commend yourselves through self-respect;
   Let self-respect become your guide:
Then will consistency reflect
   Your rightful claims to manhood's pride.
But while you cringe and basely cower,   25
   And while you ostracise your class,
Heaven will ne'er assume the power
   To elevate you as a mass.

In this yourselves must take the lead;
   You must yourselves first elevate;   30
Till then the world will ne'er concede
   Your claims to manhood's high estate.

Respect yourself; this forms the base
    Of manhood's claim to man's regard.
Next to yourself, respect your race,   35
    Whose care should be your constant ward;
Remember that you are a class
    Distinct and separate in this land,
And all the wealth you may amass,
    Or skill, or learning, won't command   40
That high respect you vainly seek,
    Until you practice what you claim —
Until the acts and words you speak
    Shall, in the concrete, be the same.

Screen not behind a pallid brow;   45
    Paint lends no virtue to the face;
Until the Black's respected, thou,
    With all the branches of his race,
Must bow beneath the cruel ban
    And often feel the wrinkled brow   50
Bent on you by a fellow-man
    Not half so worthy, oft, as thou.

Away with caste, and let us fight
    As men, the battles of the free,
And Heaven will arm you with the might   55
    And power of man's divinity.
There may be causes for distrust,
And many an act that seems unjust;
But who, when taking all in all,
    And summing up our present state,   60
Would find no objects to extol,
    No worthy deeds to emulate?

Modern Moses, or "My Policy" Man

There is a tide in men's affairs,
Leading to fame not wholly theirs—
Leading to high positions, won
Through noble deeds by others done.
And crowns there are, and not a few,   5
And royal robes and sceptres, too,
That have, in every age and land,
Been at the option and command
Of men as much unfit to rule,
As apes and monkeys are for school.   10

For seldom an assassin's blow
Has laid a benefactor low
Of any nation, age or clime,
In all the lengthened march of time,
That has not raised to power and might,   15
Some braggart knave or brainless wight,
Whose acts unseemly and unwise,
Have caused the people to despise
And curse the hours of his reign,
And brand him with the marks of Cain.   20
And yet to crown the mystery,
All these have had a *Policy.*

Though Cain was treach'rous and unjust,
And smote a brother to the dust—
'Tis not of him we wish to speak,   25
Nor of the wife he went to seek;
Nor of the blood his Nimrod spilt,
Or famous city which he built.

But choose we rather to discant,
On one whose swaggish boast and rant,   30
And vulgar jest, and pot-house slang,

Has grown the pest of every gang
Of debauchees wherever found,
From Baffin's Bay to Puget Sound.
And yet he occupies a sphere   35
And fills a more exalted chair,
(With arrogant unworthiness,
To his disgrace, I must confess),
Than any officer of State,
Or king, or princely magistrate   40
Of royal blood or noble birth,
Throughout the kingdoms of the earth.

But how he chance attain'd that hight,
Amid the splendor and the light,
The effulgent glory and the ray   45
Of this the nineteenth century,
May, to the superficial mind,
Seem much complexed and undefined;
But when the dark and shameless truth,
Is properly ascribed to Booth,   50
The strangeness vanishes in haste,
And we through murder stand disgraced.
Disgraced! Perhaps some other word,
Or milder term should be preferred;
And if preferred, that term might be   55
Exposed to *My Policy.*

But there's a legend much in vogue,
The act of some *knave, wit* or *rogue,*
A sort of fabled heresy,
Clothed in the garb of prophecy;   60
In which 'tis said that "in the day,
When kith and kindred shall array,
Their hostile armies and engage
In deadly contest, youth and age,
Lo! from the people shall arise,   65
One of the people in disguise;
A man loquacious in his way,

And greatly given to display;
A self-wrought garment he shall wear,
And *beverage* be his constant fare;   70
Akin his normal state shall be,
To a ship unballas'd and at sea.

And he shall favor all that's mean,
Or low, or vicious and obscene;
And pay to neither age nor youth,   75
A due regard, nor e'en to truth—
And he shall by his subtle vows,
Induce the people to arouse,
And bear him in their confidence,
Toward a lofty eminence.   80
Just here occurs a short hiatus,
And then concludes the legend thus—
And he shall owe to tragedy,
His zenith of felicity;
And unto gross apostacy,   85
The basis of *My Policy.*"

. . . .

But as for *Mose,* he has been
And is to-day as free from sin
As that fond friend who kissed his Lord,
In presence of a Roman horde.   90
'Tis true he did somewhat disguise
His real intentions, and surprise
The loyal voters of the North,
By feigning hatred to the South;
Through which he gained their confidence,   95
And won that lofty eminence.

'Tis said, and yet I know not why,
His fingers wear a crimson dye,
The which retraced, would likely lead
Aback to some unlawful deed,   100
And only back perhaps, alas,

To constant pressure of the glass—
Or to his deep intensity,
Of interest in *My Policy.*

. . . .

Sumner he claims is much at fault,   105
And Stevens plotting a revolt
Of Congress 'gainst the President,
And 'gainst his noble sentiment—
With which e'en Davis doth agree,
And all his learned constituency;   110
Hence, Sumner must not there remain,
And Stevens' might we ought restrain,
And Phillips should not be allowed
To exercise before the crowd,
His foul bombastic heresy,   115
In variance to *My Policy.*

His life he deems quite insecure,
And such a thought long to endure,
Is torturous in the extreme,
And breeds full many a fitful dream.   120
He fears some hireling knave may prove
Recreant to pretended love,
And give for *brandy,* water instead,
And thus consign him to the dead,
With all his virtue on his head.   125

His friends have counseled 'gainst alarm,
And 'gainst all apprehended harm,
And well they might, since few are more
From hurt and violence secure.
For those who practice lawless deed,   130
And on the life of virtue feed,
Are not accounted with his foes,
But now and e'er have been of those
Who would through nameless years protract

His office and his life intact— 135
The dauntless sons of chivalry,
Who glory in *My Policy.*

'Tis said, that in the days agone,
He pledged himself to the forlorn;
He pledged himself the bondsman's friend, 140
And one on whom they might depend
For counsel, succor or redress,
In all their hours of wretchedness,
And swore that he would be their guide,
And lead them past the crimson tide, 145
And through the wilderness that lay
Between their night and that blest day
That shines forever on the rest
Of all the worthy, free and blest;
That he their *Moses* would become, 150
And lead them to a freeman's home
And swore that he would ne'er forsake
Them, nor his pledge or promise break,
Till every bondsman in the land
Should on the plains of freedom stand. 155

Pledged to the sacred cause of truth;
Pledged in the early days of youth;
Pledged by the summer, winter, spring,
And pledged by all the truth may bring;
With all these pledges on his soul, 160
And clothed with power to control
The future destiny of those,
His wards by all his recent oaths.

Mark well his action when for aid
Their suppliant prayer to him was made? 165
Witness an instance of his love,
And all your former doubts remove.
Mark when that bill for the supply
Of starving millions met his eye;
A breadless, clotheless, houseless throng, 170

Thus rendered by his nation's wrong.
Does he the bill in haste receive
And sign, their suff'rings to relieve?

Yes, if withholding of the cup
From parched lips, whereof one sup   175
Would quite allay an inward pain,
And quite restore to health again
A prostrate mortal, doomed to die,
Unless his needs met swift supply,
Can be accounted as relief—   180
Then he in their deep hour of grief,
Did them relieve and kept his vow;
When with a dark and wrinkled brow,
He stamped his veto on their prayer,
And doomed the suppliants to despair.   185

O, what a "Moses" he has been!
How strenuously against the sin
Of his fathers he has fought;
And how ingeniously besought
The nation in this trying hour,   190
To invest with all their wonted power
Our late rebellious, loving foes,
To whom for all our recent woes,
Our wasted treasure, wasted lives,
Our orphaned children, widowed wives,   195
Our prostrate cities, deserted farms,
And all the joys of wars alarms,
We are most deeply debtors all,
And in meek gratitude should fall
Prostrate before them in the dust,   200
And yield the nation to their trust:
And to enforce the reason why,
That we should not this boon deny,
Propounds with matchless dignity,
His ineffable—*My Policy.*   205

School'd in his childhood to regard
Foul treason worthiest of reward,
And loyalty an empty name,
Meriting dark reproach and shame;
Therefore, he deems the rebels more   210
Worthy positions than before;
Before their nameless deeds of horror
Spread o'er our land the veil of sorrow;
And fain would from the very scurf,
E'en as from the rising surf   215
Of rebeldom, at once create
Grand officers of high estate,
And bring them to the nation's court,
His grave *My Policy* to support.

'Tis said the clergy everywhere,   220
Have held up holy hands in prayer
For his redemption from the thrall,
And pit of his apostate fall;
But recently by dream or word,
Have been most signally assured,   225
That there are no blest agencies
Of grace, outside the promises,
And in that almost boundless plan,
Salvation offered unto man,
Are no provisions that embrace   230
A proffered pardon in his case;
That it were madness to bewail,
Since all their efforts can but fail;
For he, to use a term uncivil,
Has long been mortgaged to the Devil;   235
But the fact which no one knows,
Is why the deuce he don't foreclose.
Perhaps he entertains a doubt,
And fears that Mose might turn him out;
Hence, *His Satanic* Majesty's   240
Endorsement of *My Policy.*

He claims that suffrage, if applied
To Negroes, should be qualified;
That they diplomacied, should hail
From Dartmouth, Harvard or from Yale,   245
Before entrusted for an hour
With manhood's great elective power.

But every rebel in the land,
From Maine to Georgia's distant strand;
Though dark their minds as rayless night,   250
Should exercise this manly right,
Though destitute of reason's force
As Balaam's ancient riding horse:
On these the boon he would confer,
Without a scruple or demur,   255
Because these *gentlemen, quoth he,*
Are members of *My Policy.*

His vetoes—gracious! what a list!
Never in time did there exist
Such an array of negative,   260
Bombastic and explanative;
'Tis said their reasons are profound,
Their logic almost passing sound;
And that such lucid rays they shed,
They're understood before they're read.   265

The Bureau Bill is deemed the first
Of numerous acts, by him reversed;
The power that bill sought to confer
On him, provoked his just demur,
And for this strange, unlikely fault,   270
His meekness rose in fierce revolt,
And flamed with wrath and power to kill,
He hurled his veto at the bill;
For actions of humanity,
Accord not with *My Policy.*   275

He next reversed the bill of rights,
Lest all the girls — that is the whites —
Should Desdemonia's become,
And fly each one her cherished home,
And take to heart some sooty moor,   280
As Fathers did in days before.
If but the legal right were given,
He fears that six in every seven
Of all the maids in all the land,
Would give the matrimonial hand   285
Unto some swarthy son or other,
And some, perhaps, might wed a *brother.*

This horrid thought his wrath excites,
And swearing 'gainst all "woman's rights,"
He grasped the veto in his ire,   290
And doomed the *bill* to endless fire;
For all such reciprocity,
Was foreign to *My Policy.*
This ghost-like thought preyed on his soul,
And robbed him of all self control,   295
Till from his fears, lest they obtain,
He got the veto on the brain;
The inflated type, the very worst,
With which a mortal e'er was cursed.

And hence, when e'er an act is brought,   300
For which is signature is sought,
How plain soever the device,
He fancies that he "smells a mice,"
And forthwith runs the trap to bring
My Policy, and sets the spring,   305
And waits with pain-suspended cough,
To see the curious thing go off.

. . . .

The little giant of the West —
His labor done, was laid to rest,

And to eternalize his fame,   310
And thus immortalize his name,
Moses, with vassals of renown,
Comes swinging past from town to town;
And makes a quite imposing tour,
Save that he proves himself a boor   315
At divers times in divers ways,
All through his eagerness for praise,
For e'en despite the peerless Grant,
And monument he came to plant,
All those that were not wholly blind,   320
Could see he had an axe to grind;

The monument was but a ruse,
A subtle means to introduce
My liege of graceless dignity,
The author of *My Policy.*   325
'Tis said that he at times would come
To cities which were not "to home,"
From which long ere the pageant closed.
The peerless Grant grew indisposed,
And to the banks of Erie's Lake,   330
Repaired for reputation's sake.

But be this statement false or true,
It has the smallest part to do
With the matter of fact at hand,
Which is this, when through the land   335
He'd gone and played the *knave and clown,*
In every city, village, town,
And felt *My Policy* was sure
To win by virtue of the tour,
The people rise in mass and vote,   340
And thus must signally denote
By their vote and by their voice,
And by the subjects of their choice,
That they had blindly failed to see
The beauties of *My Policy.*   345

. . . .

O, were I but a dramatist,
What stores of thought I would enlist,
What telling words I would indite,
And what a play my pen should write;
I'd hie me to the nation's dome;   350
Amid its splendors I would roam,
Discant on palace, hall and court,
And on the nation's grave support,
Until I placed upon the stage
The grandest burlesque of the age;   355

"Moses! *Moses!*" should be my theme;
Not He that through the crimson stream
Led out from Egypt Israel's host;
But "our Mose" of rant and boast,
Who from the nation's balcony,   360
Cajoled a drunken revelry,
In telling words of pothouse lore,
The which had ne'er been heard before,
Since Kidd, the terror of the wave,
Placed men's life-chart within the grave.   365

Oh, Demosthenes! in silence rest,
Henceforth "our Mose" shall be the test
Of all oratorical display,
And for a sample, by the way,
Witness his chaste and classic art,   370
In his description of sweetheart,
And Penny nibbling at his heels,
And then how graphic he reveals
His wond'rous buncombe, and his pluck,
In that grave story of the duck.   375
And when you have read, O think of the stage,
And the wonderful *star* of a wonderful age!
                                        (ca. 1867; 1901)

Notes

This satire denounces the character and "Policy" of President Andrew Johnson (1865–69), successor to Lincoln. Bell compares Johnson to the biblical Cain (20, 23), who murdered his brother and denied responsibility for the crime, and to Judas, the betrayer of Jesus (89–90). Bell ridicules Johnson's personal flaws (vulgarity and drinking) and his broken pledges and treacherous political acts, including vetoes of the Freedman's Bureau Bill (164–85, 266–75) and the Civil Rights Bill (276–99). Both bills were passed by Congress in 1866 over Johnson's vetoes. The poet also vilifies Johnson for granting pardons to Southern rebels and restoring their civil rights and confiscated lands, lands promised to the freed slaves (186 ff.), as well as for his vindictive and vituperative behavior on a political tour of the Midwest in 1866, known as his "swing around the circle" (311–45). 27. *Nimrod:* great-grandson of Noah, noted as a great hunter. 34. *Baffin's Bay to Puget Sound:* the bay lies near Greenland and the Sound in Washington state; thus Bell includes all of North America from the Atlantic to the Pacific oceans. 43. height. 50. *Booth:* John Wilkes Booth (1838–65), an actor, assassin of President Lincoln. 81. *hiatus:* gap in a sequence. 105, 111. *Sumner:* see Rogers's *A Poem on the Fugitive Slave Law* (182). 106, 112. *Stevens:* Thaddeus Stevens (1792–1868), radical Republican congressman from Pennsylvania, a strong spokesman for Emancipation, black suffrage, and civil rights. 109. *Davis:* Jefferson Davis (1808–89) of Kentucky, a statesman and president of the Confederacy. 113. *Phillips:* Wendell Phillips (1811–84), Boston abolitionist, lecturer, and writer. 253. *Balaam's . . . horse:* see Menken's "Hear, O Israel!" (22); Balaam's eyes are opened to the angel of God by the actions and speech of the ass he rides (Num. 22–24); the biblical animal seems more capable of "reason" than Bell's horse. 278–80. *Desdemonia's:* Desdemona, a white Venetian woman, married the (black) Moor Othello in Shakespeare's play. 308. *little giant of the West:* Stephen A. Douglas (1813–61) of Illinois, a controversial Democratic senator, as well as Lincoln's rival in debates of 1858 and in the presidential election of 1860. The feisty Douglas stood only five feet tall. 364. *Kidd:* William Kidd (Captain Kidd, 1645?–1701), a pirate hanged for his crimes. 366. *Demosthenes:* (384?–322 B.C.), a statesman and great orator of Athens.

CHARLOTTE L. FORTEN GRIMKÉ

Charlotte L. Forten Grimké (1837–1914) was born into the leading African-American family of Philadelphia, a daughter of Mary Virginia (Woods) and Robert Bridges Forten. Educated by tutors at home, Forten lived for a time with her uncle, Robert Purvis, whose home was a refuge for radical abolitionists. In 1853, she settled in Salem, Massachusetts, and began to write her remarkable *Journals* (1854–64; 1885–92). Here, too, Forten participated in antislavery activities and enjoyed the friendship of outstanding orators, statesmen, and writers active in the abolitionist cause. After completing her formal education at the Higginson School in 1855 and Salem Normal School in 1856, Forten taught school for five years, sporadically because of poor health, and she further educated herself in world literature, art, music, and foreign languages. From 1862 to 1864 on St. Helena Island, South Carolina, she taught the freed slaves, set down their hymns and shouts, and recorded her experiences in eloquent letters and essays. Afterward, Forten lived mainly in Washington, D.C., where she married the Reverend Francis James Grimké in 1878; for thirty-six years, they worked together for racial equality and made their home a social and cultural center, although Mrs. Grimké was an invalid for the last thirteen years of her life.

Her fifteen poems and some fifteen essays appeared primarily in leading black periodicals from 1855 through the 1890s. Forten's subjects vary from a tribute to William Lloyd Garrison to a sensitive portrait of Charlotte Corday, murderer of Marat. Her poetic techniques and sentiments matured over the years, and her skills include admirable variation in emotional range and rhythms, sustained narrative lines, matched sound and sense, and apt topical and sensuous imagery.

"The Angel's Visit," in William Wells Brown, *The Black Man* (Boston: 1863); "Charles Sumner," "The Gathering of the Grand Army," and "Wordsworth," in Anna J. Cooper, *Life and Writings of the Grimké Family,* vol. 2 (N.p., 1951).

The Angel's Visit

'Twas on a glorious summer eve,—
  A lovely eve in June,—
Serenely from her home above
  Looked down the gentle moon;
And lovingly she smiled on me, 5
  And softly soothed the pain—
The aching, heavy pain that lay
  Upon my heart and brain.

And gently 'mid the murmuring leaves,
  Scarce by its light wings stirred, 10
Like spirit voices soft and clear,
  The night wind's song was heard;
In strains of music sweet and low
  It sang to me of peace;
It bade my weary, troubled soul 15
  Her sad complainings cease.

For bitter thoughts had filled my breast,
  And sad, and sick at heart,
I longed to lay me down and rest,
  From all the world apart. 20
"Outcast, oppressed on earth," I cried,
  "O Father, take me home;
O, take me to that peaceful land
  Beyond the moon-lit dome.

"On such a night as this," methought, 25
  "Angelic forms are near;
In beauty unrevealed to us
  They hover in the air.
O mother, loved and lost," I cried,
  "Methinks thou'rt near me now; 30
Methinks I feel thy cooling touch
  Upon my burning brow.

"O, guide and soothe thy sorrowing child;
  And if 'tis not His will
That thou shouldst take me home with thee,   35
  Protect and bless me still;
For dark and drear had been my life
  Without thy tender smile,
Without a mother's loving care,
  Each sorrow to beguile."   40

I ceased: then o'er my senses stole
  A soothing dreamy spell,
And gently to my ear were borne
  The tones I loved so well;
A sudden flood of rosy light   45
  Filled all the dusky wood,
And, clad in shining robes of white,
  My angel mother stood.

She gently drew me to her side,
  She pressed her lips to mine,   50
And softly said, "Grieve not, my child;
  A mother's love is thine.
I know the cruel wrongs that crush
  The young and ardent heart;
But falter not; keep bravely on,   55
  And nobly bear thy part.

"For thee a brighter day's in store;
  And every earnest soul
That presses on, with purpose high,
  Shall gain the wished-for goal.   60
And thou, beloved, faint not beneath
  The weary weight of care;
Daily before our Father's throne
  I breathe for thee a prayer.

"I pray that pure and holy thoughts   65
  May bless and guard thy way;

A noble and unselfish life
  For thee, my child, I pray."
She paused, and fondly bent on me
  One lingering look of love,   70
Then softly said,—and passed away,—
  "Farewell! we'll meet above."

I woke, and still the silver moon
  In quiet beauty shone;
And still I heard amid the leaves   75
  The night wind's murmuring tone;
But from my heart the weary pain
  Forevermore had flown;
I knew a mother's prayer for me
  Was breathed before the throne.   80

                (1858)

Charles Sumner

On seeing some pictures of the interior of his house,
Washington, D.C.

Only the casket left, the jewel gone
Whose noble presence filled these stately rooms,
And made this spot a shrine where pilgrims came—
Stranger and friend—to bend in reverence
Before the great, pure soul that knew no guile;   5
To listen to the wise and gracious words
That fell from lips whose rare, exquisite smile
Gave tender beauty to the grand, grave face.

Upon these pictured walls we see thy peers,—
Poet, and saint, and sage, painter, and king,—   10
A glorious band;—they shine upon us still;
Still gleam in marble the enchanting forms
Whereupon thy artist eye delighted dwelt;
Thy favorite Psyche droops her matchless face,
Listening, methinks, for the beloved voice   15
Which nevermore on earth shall sound her praise.

All these remain,—the beautiful, the brave,
The gifted, silent ones; but thou art gone!
Fair is the world that smiles upon us now;
Blue are the skies of June, balmy the air   20
That soothes with touches soft the weary brow;
And perfect days glide into perfect nights,—
Moonlit and calm; but still our grateful hearts
Are sad, and faint with fear,—for thou art gone!

Oh friend beloved, with longing, tear-filled eyes   25
We look up, up to the unclouded blue,
And seek in vain some answering sign from thee.
Look down upon us, guide and cheer us still
From the serene height where thou dwellest now;

Dark is the way without the beacon light   30
Which long and steadfastly thy hand upheld.
Oh, nerve with courage new the stricken hearts
Whose dearest hopes seem lost in losing thee
                    (June 1874, Columbia, S.C.)

Note

See Rogers's *A Poem on the Fugitive Slave Law* (182); Forten and Sumner were
friends in Salem.

The Gathering of the Grand Army

Through all the city's streets there poured a flood,
 A flood of human souls, eager, intent;
One thought, one purpose stirred the people's blood,
 And through their veins its quickening current sent.

The flags waved gayly in the summer air,   5
 O'er patient watchers 'neath the clouded skies;
Old age, and youth, and infancy were there,
 The glad light shining in expectant eyes.

And when at last our country's saviors came,—
 In proud procession down the crowded street,   10
Still brighter burned the patriotic flame,
 And loud acclaims leaped forth their steps to greet.

And now the veterans scarred and maimed appear,
 And now the tattered battle-flags uprise;
A silence deep one moment fills the air,   15
 Then shout on shout ascends unto the skies.

Oh, brothers, ye have borne the battle strain,
 And ye have felt it through the ling'ring years;
For all your valiant deeds, your hours of pain,
 We can but give to you our grateful tears!   20

And now, with heads bowed low, and tear-filled eyes
 We see a Silent Army passing slow;
For it no music swells, no shouts arise,
 But silent blessings from our full hearts flow.

The dead, the living,—All,—a glorious host,   25
 A "cloud of witnesses,"—around us press—
Shall we, like them, stand faithful at our post,
 Or weakly yield, unequal to the stress?

Shall it be said the land they fought to save,
　　Ungrateful now, proves faithless to her trust?　　　30
Shall it be said the sons of sires so brave
　　Now trail her sacred banner in the dust?

Ah, no! again shall rise the people's voice
　　As once it rose in accents clear and high—
"Oh, outraged brother, lift your head, rejoice!　　　35
　　Justice shall reign,—Insult and Wrong shall die!"

So shall this day the joyous promise be
　　Of golden days for our fair land in store;
When Freedom's flag shall float above the free,
　　And Love and Peace prevail from shore to shore.　　　40
　　　　　　　　　　(August 12, 1890, Boston)

Wordsworth

Poet of the serene and thoughful lay!
In youth's fair dawn, when the soul, still untried,
Longs for life's conflict, and seeks restlessly
Food for its cravings in the stirring songs,
The thrilling strains of more impassioned bards;   5
Or, eager for fresh joys, culls with delight
The flowers that bloom in fancy's fairy realm—
We may not prize the mild and steadfast ray
That streams from thy pure soul in tranquil song
But, in our riper years, when through the heat   10
And burden of the day we struggle on,
Breasting the stream upon whose shores we dreamed,
Weary of all the turmoil and the din
Which drowns the finer voices of the soul;
We turn to thee, true priest of Nature's fane,   15
And find the rest our fainting spirits need,—
The calm, more ardent singers cannot give;
As in the glare intense of tropic days,
Gladly we turn from the sun's radiant beams,
And grateful hail fair Luna's tender light.   20

(1890s)

Note

William Wordsworth (1770–1850), English poet, here admired for his tranquil evocations of the natural world.

ALFRED ISLAY WALDEN

(Alfred) Islay Walden (1847?–84) lived in slavery for eighteen years from his birth in Randolph County, North Carolina, until Emancipation. During his youth, Walden labored as a carpenter, hotel servant, and driver of oxen in a gold mine. Free, but illiterate and half-blind, he set out to become an educated citizen and a Christian minister in the winter of 1867–68, when he walked to Washington, D.C. For three years in the capital, Walden did manual labor, sold his political ballads on the street, and organized Sabbath schools for black children. He then worked his way to New Brunswick, New Jersey, by lecturing and selling his poetry; there the Second Reformed Church granted him a scholarship to study at Howard University. Walden graduated from Howard's normal school in 1876 and enrolled at the New Brunswick Theological Seminary. While a student, although he was destitute and handicapped by near-blindness, Walden established and ran a mission and school for poor African Americans in New Brunswick. He was ordained in 1879, and soon afterward the American Missionary Association sent him to Lassister's Mills, North Carolina. Walden had returned home, a certified teacher and minister, and he organized a Congregational church that he successfully led until his death.

Walden's verse resembles George Moses Horton's in its ingenuous and pious vision of life and its unsophisticated techniques. He, too, writes about religion and his heroes, but Walden never protests his previous enslavement. Like Horton, Walden is most original when he reflects on personal events and emotions of everyday life. His frankness, affectionate regard for people, naive waggish humor, and natural joy in living give special charm to verses on love and such homespun occasions as eating at school, ice skating, and needing a winter overcoat. Walden's hastily written "sacred" hymns, conventional in sentiments and techniques, seem uninspired and repetitious.

Miscellaneous Poems 2d ed. (Washington, D.C.: Author, 1873 [includes 1st ed. of 1872]); *Sacred Poems* (New Brunswick, N.J.: Terhune & Van Anglen's Press, 1877).

Introductory to Second Edition

My book is largely growing;
    Its leaves are multiplied;
Its pages are much longer,
    And nearly twice as wide.

At first I thought the reader   5
    Had not the time to spare,
To hail my little volume
    As it floated in the air.

I thought perhaps while floating
    Away through empty space,   10
Perchance would there discover
    Some long forgotten race.

I knew not it would mingle
    Among the great and wise,
Or that it would be subject   15
    Unto the critic's eyes.

I thought it was inferior,
    And of the minor class,
I knew not how the ladies
    Would read it as they pass.   20

But now I find it's useful,
    And laden every page,
For truly it must mingle
    With those of every age.

Therefore I should have measured;   25
    Should not have thought it vain
To make its little mysteries
    Unto the reader plain.

But surely there's no secret
  Where thought is not sublime,   30
That I have thus destroyed
  By keeping up my rhyme.

But if I should in future
  Find this to be the case,
I'd take my silver pencil   35
  And all these lines erase.

I'd rather use a license,
  Or grammar's laws dispense,
Than for to let my metre
  Or rhythm govern sense.   40

The reader will remember
  My chances are but slim,
Or else this little volume
  Would be in better trim.

Remember, too, in Dixie   45
  That I was born a slave.
And all my early genius
  Was locked within the grave.

Remember my condition —
  A mark within my eyes —   50
And all my inspirations
  Are showered from the skies.

I cannot read of authors,
  Nor those of noble fame,
For I'm just a learning   55
  The author, Milton's, name.

I cannot borrow subjects,
  Nor rob them of their style,
My book amid their volumes,
  Like me, is but a child.   60

Therefore, I bless this volume,
    And send with it my heart,
That it may to the critic
    My better thoughts impart.

Go forth, then, little volume,   65
    Much good from thee may spring,
If thou continueth pleading
    The merits of thy King.

And others yet may follow,
    All changed within their scale,   70
But thou, upon thy mission,
    I am sure can never fail.
                                    (1873)

Note

56. *Milton's name:* John Milton (1608–74), English poet. Walden was nearly blind (50), which may be why he was attracted to the blind poet Milton.

One to Love

Oh, where's the maid that I can love,
   With love which I have never told?
Where is the one that I would like
   To comfort me when I am old?

Do I not see before my face,   5
   A mate prepared for every one?
Then sure there's one prepared for me,
   Nor need I trudge the road alone.

Now who is he that speaks to me
   Of Mormons and of Mormonhood?   10
While this you know, the Lord has said,
   They twain shall be one flesh, one blood!

Come listen, then, to what I say
   Before this evening's work is done,
That you can do as you may please,   15
   But I'd be satisfied with one.
                 (1873)

Note

10. *Mormons and of Mormonhood:* Members of the Mormon Church (Church of Jesus Christ of Latter-day Saints), founded in 1830 in the United States, practiced polygamy, having more than one wife at a time.

The Nation's Friend

This nation has a faithful friend,
   In whom she may confide;
Whose influence is like a sea,
   Flowing both deep and wide.

Let us behold the sea, how calm —   5
   What ships her billows float,
Come let us hasten to the shore,
   And get on freedom's boat.

Upon her deck the nations meet;
   The white and colored there,   10
Where no first place nor second known,
   No difference in the fare.

I saw her raise her banner high,
   And cast it to the breeze,
While tempests raged and billows rolled   15
   She sailed through gulfs and seas.

Through smoke and fog she onward went
   This nation to defend,
When Dixie cried, "Take her last son,
   And her last dollar spend."   20

When hissing shot around her fell,
   From rebel cannon's mouth,
She stood the storm, the rain, the hail,
   And now can stand the drouth.

I heard her cry, while sailing on —   25
   And Justice is her name —
Grant equal rights to every man,
   And amnesty the same.

She soon will land her noble crew
  Within a city bright,   30
Where nations in one brotherhood
  Drink national delight.

Where we may have our public schools,
  With open doors displayed;
Where all may drink at wisdom's fount   35
  With none to make afraid.

Young friends, I know you will be there
  Bright, shining, as the sun;
With equal rights secured to all,
  When Sumner's work is done.   40

The nation's friend! still firm he stands,
  With neither sleep nor slumber,
Come every Freedman in this land
  And hail the name of Sumner.
                       (1873)

Note
40, 44. Charles *Sumner:* see Rogers's *A Poem on the Fugitive Slave Law* (182).

Dedicated to a Young Lady Representing the Indian Race at Howard University

While sitting in my room kind Miss,
  I thought I'd sing a praise,
But now I think I'll write a word,
  To lighten up thy days.

It's true I often write on Queens,   5
  And those of noble fame;
But now I seek to write a line
  Upon thy honored name.

What's in thy name moves me to write,
  This little verse on thee?   10
Perhaps it is thy pleasant ways,
  And cheering looks to me.

How oft I think of thee kind Miss,
  And oft admire thy grace,
Because I know that thou art of   15
  Another noble race!

When by the bells to meals we're called,
  Or round the table meet,
With anxious eye I look to see
  If thou art in thy seat.   20

And then I cast my eyes around,
  Through hall, though long and wide,
And then I quickly look to see
  Thy tea-mate by thy side.

But first of all the bell is rung,   25
  And each within his place,
In silence each one bows his head,
  'Till some one asks the grace.

Then each in seat with upturned plates,
   And scarce a word is said,   30
Until we have a full supply
   Of meats and baker's bread.

And dishes, too, are passing round
   About from you and me;
And Clara she looks up and asks—   35
   Pray, sir, what can it be?

It's pork, of course, or else it's beef;
   Perchance it may be ham—
Except the baker cooked a goose,
   And passed it off for lamb.   40

And if he has a cut will tell,
   If round about its swallow,
For surely it is not so dead,
   That it would fail to halloo.

While all of this is going on,   45
   There're other things in view;
For oft I catch myself, dear Miss,
   Exchanging looks with you.

But soon we're through, the bell does ring,
   We're called by duty's 'larms;   50
Nor can I longer sit and look
   Upon thy brilliant charms.

I'd speak of all my table mates
   Had I another pen,
For surely we're as happy guests   55
   As here have ever been.

          (1873)

Wish for an Overcoat

Oh! had I now an overcoat,
   For I am nearly freezing;
My head and lungs are stopped with cold,
   And often I am sneezing.

And, too, while passing through the street,   5
   Where merchants all are greeting,
They say, young man this is the coat
   That you should wear to meeting.

Then, looking down upon my feet,
   For there my boots are bursting,   10
With upturned heels and grinning toes,
   With tacks which long were rusting.

Ah! how they view my doeskin pants
   With long and crooked stitches,
They say, young man would you not like   15
   To have some other breeches?

My head is also hatless too,
   The wind is swiftly blowing,
They say, young man will you not freeze?
   See ye not how it's snowing?   20

And now they take me by the hand,
   And lead me toward the store,
And some are pulling down the coats
   Before I reach the door.

So walk I in, their goods to price,   25
   To quench a thirst that's burning,
And freely would I buy a coat,
   But nothing I am earning.

They say to me, I should have known,
   That winter time was coming,   30
When I was roaming through the park,
   With birds around me humming.

Their logic's true, I must confess,
   And all they say is pleasant;
But did I know that I would have   35
   No overcoat at present?

To satisfy these craving Jews,
   To buy I am not able,
For it is more than I can do
   To meet my wants at table.   40

Therefore my skin will toughly grow,
   Will grant to me this favor,
That I may learn to stand as much
   As little Jack, the sailor.

And if I live till winter's passed,   45
   Though nature's harps unstringing,
I then will fly to yon woodland
   To hear the oak trees singing.

Then I will not on hero's fame,
   Ride swiftly on to victory,   50
Although my saddle may be made
   Of cotton sacks or hickory.

But if I die, farewell to all,
   Oh! who will tell the story,
That I have lived a noble life.   55
   And now gone home to glory?

Yes, who will chant a song of praise
   For me—who will be weeping—
When I have yielded to the grave,
   And 'mid the dead am sleeping?   60

But some will ask, "how did he die?
  It was without my knowing;
Was it because he caught a cold,
  Last year when it was snowing?"

The answer now comes hurling back,   65
  In words I cannot utter,
It was not by a cold alone,
  But partly bread and butter.

[This poem is dedicated to my own necessities and wants.]
                     (1873)

The Transition—S.M.

The golden wings of time
  Are ever gliding by;
They bear my body to the tomb,
  My spirit to the sky.

This life is but a breath   5
  Which is and is no more.
'Tis like the struggle of a wave
  To reach some distant shore.

But tossed upon the deep,
  Strong billows o'er it surge;   10
Its drops are scattered far and wide
  Ere it can reach the verge.

Eternally 'tis lost,
  Nor will it more arise,
'Till nature shall its vapors bear   15
  To mingle in the skies.

And I, alas! I die!
  On earth I cannot stay!
My soul returns to God who gave,
  My body to the clay!   20

I'm like the fallen race
  Which pass from mortal sight,
To dwell in one eternal day,
  Or one eternal night.

But am I like the wave   25
  Whose parts can never meet,
Except it be by chance when they
  Shall mingle in the deep?

Ah! no, for I'll arise
    Upon the last great day;   30
My spirit from its God shall come,
    My body from the clay.

United, we shall stand
    Eternally in one.
Yes, in the likeness of my God   35
    The image of His son.
April 28, 1877.

                (1877)

Note

"S. M." means short meter, one of three standard hymn forms; the others are common meter and long meter.

ALBERY ALLSON WHITMAN

Albery Allson Whitman (1851–1901), who was born a slave and had only a year of schooling, became the finest African-American poet of his time. Orphaned at the age of twelve, Whitman labored on the farm of his birth near Mumfordville (Hart County), Kentucky. From 1864 to 1870, in Ohio and Kentucky, he worked in a plough shop, in railroad construction, and as a schoolteacher. At age nineteen, Whitman studied under Bishop Payne at Wilberforce University for six months and published the first of his seven volumes of poetry. In the 1870s, he was general financial agent for Wilberforce and pastor of an A.M.E. church in Springfield, Ohio; from 1879 to 1883, Whitman established churches and led congregations in Ohio, Kansas, Texas, and Georgia. During these years, his renown as "Poet Laureate of the Negro Race" grew as his remarkable books appeared, bringing him praise from other black poets and critics. Whitman died of pneumonia in Anniston, Alabama, and was survived by his widow, Caddie, and their three daughters, who gained international fame as an acclaimed vaudeville team, the Whitman Sisters, from 1910 to 1930.

For Whitman, poetry's "triumphs [are] the survival of the Beautiful, the True, and the Good." His art is not utilitarian or polemical like Frances Harper's, but rather art for art's sake and for the sake of showing the race's creative talent. Whitman attempts full-blown Romantic poetry. He looks back to legendary pastoral worlds (marred by race prejudice); sees the present as a sphere of unlimited human potentiality; and looks forward to an ideal earth perfected by human love and poetic genius. Thoroughly conversant with the century's great Romantic poets, English and American, Whitman naturally tried to emulate them but never had the opportunity to develop their disciplined craftsmanship. As a result, much of his poetry is technically weak and diffuse, marred by careless versification, awkward shifts in diction, overblown rhetoric, and homiletic digressions. Nevertheless, Whitman did supremely well with what he had: a sure dramatic sense; talent for suspenseful narration, romantic description, communication of pathos, irony, and lovers' emotions; a catholic range of subjects; and the courage to employ varied and difficult meters and rhyme schemes in epic-length poems, suiting his music to the shifting moods and meanings. To these poetic skills Whitman added a sense of honor, strong race pride, a code of manliness, and sensitive perception of universal issues, poignantly personalized. His finest lyrics lie within his longer poems, and Whitman's overall achievements tower over those of his contemporaries.

Not a Man, and Yet a Man (Springfield, Ohio: Republic Printing, 1877); *The Rape of Florida* (St. Louis, Mo.: Nixon-Jones, 1884, repr. as *Twasinta's Seminoles; or, Rape of Florida.* 1885, 1890); *An Idyl of the South: An Epic Poem in Two Parts* (New York: Metaphysical Publishing Co., 1901).

from *Not a Man and Yet a Man*

. . . .

THE OLD SAC VILLAGE

Ye who read in musty volumes
Pages worn of Backwoods Times,
Of the red man and the white man,
In the thrilling days of danger,
In the gall of border troubles,   5
In the wastes of deadly revenge,
And the ruffian hands of torture;
And of long and fierce death grapples,
With the bloody hands of combat,
On the yawning edge of famine;   10
Of adventure's rustling footsteps,
When the knees of stoutest valor
Smote together as they paused, where
Lynx-eyed strategy lay crouching,
On the bosom of still ambush,   15
Ready from his hands to let loose
A loud leash of swift cruelties;
Ye who read these musty volumes,
Till a strange sensation thrills you,
As of Indians skulking near you,   20
Lay aside your volume lightly,
Hear me sing of Nanawawa.

. . . .

Ye who shut up in warm houses,
Late on sombre Winter evenings,
Lulled by pleasant roaring grate fires,   25
And the cozy flap of curtains,
And the chirp of vacant childhood,

And the cheery streams of gaslight
Meekly stealing, that pause, bashful,
On the plushy lap of softness;   30
Ye who thus shut up in houses,
Dream of early life and hardships,
Shut in humble frontier cabins,
Far out on the unknown borders;
Dream of weariness o'ercoming   35
The lost traveler on his journey
Overtaken by the snow-storm;
Lone at night and his path dimming,
Sinking down to sleep his death sleep;
Chilly leagues from any dwelling,   40
And while loneliness bewails him,
Through the drear woods shrieks the gray blast,
Shrieks the eager flying North blast,
As a hungry eagle shrieketh;
Ye who shut up thus in houses,   45
Dream of these fell border hardships;
Hear me sing of Nanawawa.
Ah! ye shall behold a beauty!
On the lap of an old forest,
In the wigwam of her fathers,   50
By the cascades of her childhood
Ye shall see a sylvan maiden,
Meek as April's first fresh rose is,
Sweet as blushing light e'er looked on,
Brilliant as a melting dewdrop,   55
But in love pensively youthful.

. . . .

SAVILLE IN TROUBLE

. . . .

The hunters mount menacing as they go,
And thro' the village disappearing slow,
Betake them to the woods and brisker ride
Along the neighb'ring forest's eastern side.   60

There where a peaceful streamlet ambles by
Thro' dabbling ferns and gossips cheerfully
With shaggy roots that reach into the flood,
They spy a maid [Nanawawa] just bord'ring womanhood.
Now ranging feathers in her head-gear fair,   65
And with her fingers combing out her hair,
She on the prone bank stands, where smoothly flows
The liquid mirror, and her beauty shows.
Now grand old sylvans raise their solemn heads,
And make obesience as she lightly treads   70
Beneath their outstretched arms, and looks around
To gather nuts upon the leaf-spread ground.
The hunters see her, wayward, wild and sweet;
She sees them not, nor hears their horses' feet.
"Hold!" cries Sir Maxey, "What a lovely maid!   75
Ah! what a princess of this ancient shade!
Let me behold her! Quiet! Don't move!
Did admiration e'er see such a dove?
Young love no sweeter image ever drew
Upon imagination's tender view.   80
Her perfect form in idle movements seems
The fleeting creature of our youthful dreams."
A rougher comrade at his elbow growls,
"A purty good 'un o' the dusky fowls,
She's hard o' hearin', le'me try my gun;   85
Give her a skere, and see the red wench run."
His deadly eye directs, his rifle speaks,
The maiden throws her arms and runs and shrieks;
Towards the hunters pitiously flies,
The mournful wastes lamenting with her cries,   90
Till at their feet she sinks, and all is o'er,
Poor bleeding Nanawawa is no more.

. . . .

IN THE HOUSE OF THE AYLORS

. . . .

Brown Autumn came, and at her solemn close,
The swarthy hands of labor found repose.

Then sports set in, and harmless games began,   95
And through the livelong snowless winter ran.
What cares had slaves to mar their peace with dole,
And shut the light of mirth out from the soul,
When life-long labor made them richer none—
When nothing earned was theirs when work was done?   100
What reasons they to look back with remorse,
When careful conduct made their state the worse
Or better none? Their lives were not their own;
Hence past and future were to them unknown.
Hard labor's respite came, and as it neared,   105
Their burdens lightened and their hearts were cheered.
Religion, work and pastime, all in turn,
They had; but art and science must not learn.
And yet, contentment these vast wants supplied,
And loaned the pleasures caste had them denied.   110
The mind that never grasped hypotheses,
Nor wandered in the maze of theories;
Nor toil'd thro' demonstrations intricate,
Nor groaned beneath old histories' vast weight,
Can best afford in other paths *well* known,   115
To seek for pleasures not so over grown
The last day's labor was a day of feast,
And toil-earned freedom for both slave and beast.
The groaning barns were filled from floor to eaves,
And all the barnyard stacked around with sheaves.   120
Then, when the last full load of ripened corn
Was gathered in, the master took his horn,
And mounted high upon the rounded pile,
Rode homewards, sounding, followed by a file
Of empty wagons; while a lusty band   125
Of slaves came shouting on at either hand.
The shorn fields sank forsaken on their view,
And as they nearer to the barnyard drew,
Slave cabins emptied out a roaring crowd,
And gabbling hillsides answered them aloud.   130
Then shouts of triumph closed the boist'rous scene,
The master king, and mistress crowned a queen.
This edict then, thro' all *her* milder reign

Of hut-bound realms, awoke a glad refrain
In servitude's full heart: "Go waste the hours   135
As you may wish, good slaves; the time is yours
From now till blooming Spring shall come again,
And spread her painted sweets upon the plain."

They then set in with ev'ry setting sun,
And danced till they were tired of the fun.   140
Loud rang the fiddle on three strings or four,
But louder rang their feet upon the floor.
The music, started once, as well might cease,
For joy kept up the dance with lively ease.
Now all hands joined, their circling knew no bound,   145
Save that they paused to catch the music's sound;
And when caught, all hands joined around again,
They whirled away to overtake the strain.
Then, balanced all, they stood out pair and pair,
And trampled hugely down the flying air.   150
Thus on they strode till night's last watch had flown,
Or they had broke the smiling fiddler down;
Who, sweating like a hunter in the chase,
Dragged his bandanna o'er a hopeless face;
Sore puzzled, grinned, and chided, out of breath,   155
"Ah! darkies, will you dance a man to death?"

. . . .

Now thronged about by twenty men,
And savage bloodhounds, nine or ten,
That howl with rage, and gnaw and bay,
Like demons that from Tophet stray,   160
Thro' nether worlds to wing their way.
Rodney, with irons loaded, she [Leeona]
Must turn away, or bear to see.
But as she turns, the hounds appear,
And in their deep jaws Rodney tear.   165
Unarmed he falls, with pain he groans,
A gust of loud oaths mocks his moans,
While human monsters gather round,

And fierce dogs drag him o'er the ground,
Till he in cords of hemp is bound.   170
"Oh, save!" gasped Ona, as she, poor
Sweet child, sank swooning on the floor.
A moment there, a fair corpse seemed,
As in her face the sad moon beamed;
Then frantic rose, and down stairs flew,   175
And on her lover's bosom threw
Her wild sweet form, his stout neck drew
In her soft arms, and her cheeks fair
Nestled on his, and with her streaming hair,
Covered his bleeding shoulders that lay bare.   180

And this is Slav'ry! the wise faced creed,
That stretched a helping hand to Afric's need.
The holy Institution that was bound
To raise the heathen, tho' the Heavens frowned!
Ah! this was what a righteous Nation heard   185
Pray in her temples, and expound the Word.
This was Creation's good Samaritan,
And poor old Afric was the thief-torn man.
Oh, who has not the dear good shepherd seen,
Stand Moses-like, God and His hosts between,   190
Bless Slavery as a child from Heaven born,
Since Joseph was from poor old Jacob torn;
Watch ever sleepless, o'er his peaceful fold,
Unawed by dangers, uninduced by gold,
And weep if one poor lamb from shelter cries?   195
That is, one *white* lamb; if black, shut his eyes.
Ah! Young America, for God's sake, pause,
Hast thou such preachers, and hast thou such laws?

· ·

FLIGHT OF LEEONA

· ·

The chains are loosed, and at a smack,
Away fierce yelping fly the pack.   200

Their deep, loud throats in full chase break,
The darkling woods responsive speak,
And far off hills from slumbers wake.
The very night shades seem to fly,
And dance and flutter on the eye;   205
For dreadful sight is it to see,
A woman from swift bloodhounds flee.
Then like some lion, when loud dogs invade,
That flies ferocious from his roaring shade,
His bristling kindred scatters from his path,   210
And shakes the forests in his lordly wrath;
So now brave Rodney from his cover springs,
And right and left her loud pursuers flings.
These at him stare with trembling fears opprest,
He plucks a dagger from his heaving breast,   215
Displays the ghastly warning to their eyes,
And in pursuit of hounds and Creole flies.

Ah! ye whose eyes with pity doth run o'er,
When mournful tales come from a heathen shore,
Of babes by mothers thrown to crocodile;   220
The scaly terror of the languid Nile;
Of Brahma's car and Islam's wanton rites,
And bloody raids on Zion's sacred hights!
Ye who hear these and pray for God to come,
Behold yon mother fleeing from her home!   225
A master's child upon her frantic breast,
And by a master's savage bloodhounds prest;
And this, too, where in every steepled town,
The crucifix on human wrong looks down!
Think then no more of heathen lands to rave,   230
While in America there breathes a slave!

Rodney pursues, and where the sickened moon
Looks thro' the woods, comes on the Creole soon.
The angry hounds have overta'en their prey,
And round Leeona, madly mingling, bay.   235
Deep thro' the wastes their fiendish voices ring,

Fierce with their tongues, wood, plain and hillock sing;
And now they close upon her, thick around;
Ah! God, they seize and drag her to the ground!
Lo! Rodney nears, he hears his 'Ona's cries,   240
Right on the hounds with flashing steel he flies;
They on him furious turn, with eyes that glare
Like furies' fell, jaws gaping, and teeth bare;
This one and that he seizes as they lunge
Upon him, and their dread fangs in him plunge.   245
Deep thro' their reeking sides his blade he drives,
They reel away and empty out their lives;
Till with their warm blood dropping from his hands,
He master of the situation stands!

. . . .

THE RUNAWAY

. . . .

Thrice hail! proud land, whose genius boasts a Clay!   250
The Cicero of slavery's palmy day,
The gifted champion of Compromise,
Whose mien majestic filled a nation's eyes;
And on the eloquence of whose wise tongue
A learned Senate in rapt slience hung;   255
A Senate, too, whose fame no one impugns,
Of Websters, Randolphs, Marshals and Calhouns.
And could a land that boasts a mind like this —
That bord'ring on the clime of freedom is —
Suffer a harlot with her whorings vile   260
To peacefully pollute her gen'rous soil?
Yes, green Kentucky with her native pride,
Proclaiming trust in the great Crucified,
Flaunting her prestige in the world's wide face,
Boasting descent and precedence of race,   265
And by the greatest of all statesmen led,
Shared the pollutions of a slavish bed.
All o'er her fields, the blood-hound's savage bay

Pressed the poor sable trembling runaway,
And sometimes by the home of Henry Clay!   270

. . . .

I love Kentucky; tho' she merit scorn
I can't despise the land where I was born.
Her name I cherish, and expect to see
The day when all her sons will cherish me.
Her many sins have all in common been   275
With other sisters' who their sins have seen.
Yes, I will pray for that good time to come
When I can say: Kentucky is my *home*.
And this I now ask at my country's hand,
If I must die in some far distant land,   280
Then let my countrymen, when I am dead,
Where I was born, make my eternal bed.

. . . .

THE END OF THE WHOLE MATTER

. . . .

Hail dawning Peace! Speed on thy glorious rise!
And with thy beams unseal the nation's eyes.
Let Islam in the blaze of scimitar   285
Proclaim his rites, and gorge the fangs of war,
But peace be unto thee, land of our sires,
Whose sacred altar flames with holier fires!
Let lawlessness no longer stagger forth
With his destructive torch, nor South nor North;   290
And let the humblest tenant of the fields,
Secured of what his honest labor yields,
Pursue his calling, ply his daily care,
His home adorn and helpless children rear,
Assured that while our flag above him flies,   295
No lawless hand can dare molest his joys.

. . . .

Free schools, free press, free speech and equal laws,
A common country and a common cause,
Are only worthy of a freeman's boasts—
Are Freedom's *real* and intrinsic costs.   300
Without these, Freedom is an empty name,
And war-worn glory is a glaring shame.
Soon where yon happy future now appears,
Where learning now her glorious temple rears,
Our country's hosts shall round one interest meet,   305
And her free heart with one proud impulse beat,
One common blood thro' her life's channels flow,
While one great speech her loyal tongue shall know.
And soon, whoever to our bourne shall come,
Jew, Greek or Goth, he here shall be at home.   310
Then Ign'rance shall forsake her crooked ways,
And poor old Caste there end her feeble days.

Notes

Excerpts from this poem of more than five thousand lines can only suggest the
varied versification, moods, narrative action, and ideas that Whitman weaves into
a dramatic and ethically powerful whole. The main plot concerns the loves, trials,
and adventures of an octoroon (one-eighth part black) slave Rodney, a fearless
hunter, skilled woodsman, and paragon of all manly virtues, who flees from slavery
to ultimate freedom in Canada. A parallel Indian subplot, introduced in "The
Old Sac Village," concerns the Native Americans' quest for freedom from treacherous "civilized" whites such as Sir Maxey and his band, who murder Nanawawa,
the Sac chief's daughter. These narratives occasionally pause for Whitman's comments on life in slavery, the role of church and law in America, and his native
state, Kentucky. One of Rodney's many daring escapades as he travels through
North and South takes place in Florida, where he again escapes from chains of
slavery and rescues his beloved Leeona (Ona), a beautiful mixed-race slave, from
pursuing bloodhounds. Rodney and Leeona seek refuge in Kentucky and later
find happiness in Canada. At the poem's end, after the Civil War, in which Rodney
and his sons have fought with the Union army, the poem celebrates peace and a
free, classless society of the future. In "The Old Sac Village" Whitman uses
unrimed trochaic tetrameter for the Indian subplot, the meter of Longfellow's
Hiawatha (1855). He admired and wrote to Longfellow. 5. *gall:* irritation. 70.
obeisance: submission. 89. piteously. 187. *good Samaritan:* the man who aided

the dying traveler in Jesus' parable (Luke 10:25–37). 191. *Joseph . . . Jacob torn:* Jacob, son of Joseph, is sold into slavery by his jealous brothers (Gen. 37). 219–23, 230: *heathen:* originally, in the Old Testament, people not worshipping the God of Israel; here, non-Christians with cruel religious practices: child-sacrifice to the holy river *Nile;* rites to *Brahma,* supreme deity of Hinduism and to *Islam,* the Moslem religion; also, those who attack *Zion's sacred heights:* the hill in Jerusalem on which the temple was built, or here Jerusalem itself, or the holy land of Israel. 223. heights. 250, 270. *Clay . . . Henry Clay:* (1777–1852), born in Virginia but sent to Congress (House and Senate) from Kentucky; a leading statesman, orator, and force behind the passage of the Missouri *Compromise* (252) and other peace-preserving bills. It was Clay who said he'd "rather be right than be president"; he ran fourth in the election of 1824 and served under John Quincy Adams as secretary of state. 251. *Cicero:* see Reason's "The Spirit Voice" (31). 257. *Websters* [Daniel], *Randolphs* [John], *Marshals* [John Marshall] *and Calhouns* [John C.]: American statesmen and jurists prominent before the Civil War. Unlike the others, Calhoun defended slavery and Southern states' rights. 310. *Goth:* ancient Germanic conquerors of the Roman Empire; *Goth* came to mean a barbarian, an uncivilized person. Whitman's invitation to the Goth is unclear.

from *Twasinta's Seminoles; Or Rape of Florida*

CANTO I

INVOCATION

I

The poet hath a realm within, and throne,
And in his own soul singeth his lament.
A comer often in the world unknown —
A flaming minister to mortals sent;
In an apocalypse of sentiment   5
He shows in colors true the right or wrong,
And lights the soul of virtue with content;
Oh! could the world without him please us long?
What truth is there that lives and does not live in song?

II

"The stuff's in him of robust manliness,   10
He is a poet, singing more by ear
Than note." His great heart filled with tenderness,
Thus spoke the patriarch bard of Cedarmere
Of me, who dwelt in a most obscure sphere;
For I was in the tents of bondage when   15
The muse inspired, and ere my song grew clear,
The graceful Bryant called his fellow-men
To mark what in my lay seemed pleasing to him then.

III

O! shade of our departed Sire of song!
If what to us is dim be clear to thee,   20
Hear while my yet rude numbers flow along!
If spirit may a mortal's teacher be,
Stand thou near by and guidance offer me!
That, like thy verses, clear as summer blue, —
Bright mirrors of the peaceful and the free,   25
Reflecting e'er the good, the great and true, —
So mine may be, and *I* my pleasing task pursue.

IV

Say, then, of that too soon forgotten race
That flourished once, but long has been obscure
In Florida, and where the seas embrace   30
The Spanish isles; say if e'er lives more pure
Warmed veins, or patriots could more endure
Around the altars of their native bourne!
Say, when their flow'ry landscapes could allure,
What peaceful seasons did to them return,   35
And how requited labor filled his golden urn!

XVIII

Upon the shells by Carribea's wave
I've heard the anthems of the mighty sea;
Heard there the dark pines that their voices gave,
And heard a stream denote its minstrelsy—   40
How sweet, *all* lonely, was it there to be!
The stars were bright, the moon was up and clear;
But, when I thought of those who once were free,
And came at wonted times to worship there;
The sea's deep voice grew sad and claimed of me a tear!   45

XIX

Oh! sing it in the light of freedom's morn,
Tho' tyrant wars have made the earth a grave;
The good, the great, and true, are, if so, born,
And so with slaves, *chains do not make the slave!*
If high-souled birth be what the mother gave,—   50
If manly birth, and manly to the core,—
Whate'er the test, the man will he behave!
Crush him to earth and crush him o'er and o'er,
A man he'll rise at last and meet you as before.

XX

So with our young Atlassa, hero-born,—   55
Free as the air within his palmy shade,

The nobler traits that do the man adorn,
In him were native: Not the music made
In Tampa's forests or the everglade
Was fitter, than in this young Seminole   60
Was the proud spirit which did life pervade,
And glow and tremble in his ardent soul —
Which, lit his inmost-self, and spurned all mean control.

XXXIII

"Come now, my love, the moon is on the lake;
Upon the waters is my light canoe;   65
Come with me, love, and gladsome oars shall make
A music on the parting wave for you, —
Come o'er the waters deep and dark and blue;
Come where the lilies in the marge have sprung,
Come with me, love, for Oh, my love is true!"   70
This is the song that on the lake was sung,
The boatman sang it over when his heart was young.

XXXIV

The boatman's song is hushed; the night is still,
Still as the vault of heaven, — a plashy oar
Starts from the shadows by the darkling hill,   75
And softly dips towards the farther shore;
Now stops, now dips again — is heard no more.
But follow the nook by yonder tree, —
Where spouts a tiny stream with fretish roar,
His light canoe is riding noiselessly —   80
A Chieftain's light canoe, in which his maid you see.

XXXV

Ah! how her wild dark wealth of tresses spread
Below the arm that round her partly lies!
And as she leans her half reluctant head,
See how intense the glances that she tries!   85
Her very soul is mounting to her eyes
Lit with the fires of her proud ancestry;

And as her chieftain hears her faint replies,
How his high spirit doth adore to see
His princess-child, the bright star of his destiny!   90

XXXVI

"A maid from islands in a far, far sea,
Came to our shores, upon a day, a day;
A beauty fair, a beauty fair was she,
And took our young Chief's heart away, away;
Tho' all the world could not we heard him say.   95
And oh! we love our chieftain and his maid,
And so will we, and so will we for aye!"
This was the night-song on the lake delayed,—
The boatman sang it over in the willows' shade.

. . . .

CANTO II

. . . .

IV

Is manhood less because man's face is black?   100
Let thunders of the loosened seals reply!
Who shall the rider's restive steed turn back,
Or who withstand the arrows he lets fly,
Between the mountains of eternity?
Genius ride forth! thou gift and torch of heav'n!   105
The mastery is kindled in thine eye;
To conquest ride! thy bow of strength is giv'n—
The trampled hordes of caste before thee shall be driv'n!

V

Who is't would beg? What man permission crave
To give his thoughts their scope and rightful reign?   110
Let him be cursed! a self-manacled slave!
He's a polution to the mind's domain—
A moral garbage scattered on the plain—

An execration of the world!—God's arm
Defend not him! Oh! if there is disdain 115
To freeze the bosom's every impulse warm,
I crave it for all who to Favor's alm's house swarm.

VI

Shall thunders ask of man what time to beat
The march of clouds? Or oceans beg his leave
To rock their under-worlds? In his dread seat, 120
Doth Blanc consider him? When did he weave
A mantle for the hurricane, or give
The Rockies leave to hold the dying Sun!—
Sooner all these—sooner an earthquake heave,
And sink earth back where broods oblivion, 125
Than God-giv'n mind submit for gyves to be put on.

VII

'Tis hard to judge if hatred of one's race,
By those who deem themselves superior-born,
Be worse than that quiesence in disgrace,
Which only merits—and *should* only—scorn! 130
Oh! let me see the negro, night and morn,
Pressing and fighting in, for place and power!
If he a proud escutcheon would adorn,
All earth is place—all time th' auspicious hour,
While heaven leans forth to see, oh! can he quail or cower? 135

VIII

Ah! I abhor his protest and complaint!
His pious looks and patience I despise!
He can't evade the test, disguised as saint,
The manly voice of freedom bids him rise,
And shake himself before Philistine eyes! 140
And, like a lion roused, no sooner than
A foe dare come, play all his energies,
And court the fray with fury if he can;
For hell itself respects a fearless manly man!

XI

I never was a slave—a robber took   145
My substance—what of that? The *law* my rights—
And that? I still was free and had my book—
All nature. And I learned from during hights
How silence is majestic, and invites
In admiration far beholding eyes!   150
And heaven taught me, with her starry nights,
How deepest speech unuttered often lies,
And that Jehovah's lessons mostly he implies.

XII

My birth-place where the scrub-wood thicket grows,
My mother bound, and daily toil my dower;   155
I envy not the halo title throws
Around the birth of any; place and power
May be but empty phantoms of an hour,—
For me, I find a more enduring bliss:
Rejoicing fields, green woods—the stream—the flower, 160
To me have speech, and born of God, are his
Interpreters, proclaiming what true greatness is.

XIII

Where'er I roam, in all the earth abroad,
I find *this* written in the human chart:
A love of Nature is the love of God,   165
And love of man 's the religion of the heart.
Man's right to think, in his majestic part
In his Creator's works—to others bless—
This is the point whence god-like actions start,
And open, conscientious manliness   170
Is the divinest image mortals can possess.

XIV

Almighty fairness smiling heaven portends,
In sympathy the elements have tears;

The meekest flow'rs are their Creator's friends,
The hungry raven He in patience hears;   175
And e'en the sparrow's wishes reach His ears!
But when He treads the tyrant in His wrath,
And to crush wrong the horn of battle rears,
The pestilence goes forth on him who hath
Transgressed, and empires fall imploring in His path.   180

XV

A god-like man is fair to fellow-men,
And gentleness is native in his soul!
He sees no fault in man till forced, and then
He wonders 't were not greater. He is whole
In valor, mercy, love, and self-control.   185
Virtue is his religion — Liberty
His shrine — honest contentment is his goal
And sum of bliss, and his life aims to be
In nothing excellent, save that which leaves man free.

XVI

I envy not the man whose want of brains   190
Supplies a roost for race-hate's filthy brood!
The little eminence his soul attains
Is more the pity when 'tis understood,
That he, perhaps, has done the best he could!
Tread not upon him just to see him squirm!   195
Pity, forsooth! to crawl is his best good,
And 'tis his nat'ral way, I do affirm;
So, let him crawl his fill, he is a harmless worm!

LXVII

Dark rose the walls, a church and prison joined,
Their kindred glooms to blend and intermix.   200
Dungeon'd in one, the unknown victim pined,
And in the other mid quaint candlesticks,
Sombre and weird arose a crucifix:
How fitly these portrayed the men who built

A house of God o'ershadowed by old Nick's—   205
Vain man, to thus offend thy Maker! wilt
Thou look on images to take away thy guilt!

LXVIII

How slight the transit superstition makes
From common crime to acts of righteousness!
E'en human life in willful hate she takes,   210
Makes earth a waste and desert of distress,
Where lust and rapine rival in excess;
Then from the smoke of some mysterious rite,
She shadows forth in all as if to bless!
And whose disputes must perish in her sight,   215
An heretic, an enemy of God and right!

LXIX

Man will hold some religion, most believe,
Mainly to hush the soul's rebuke of wrong;
They would their very conscious selves deceive,
By hearing God's will in an unknown tongue,   220
And recitals not understood and long.
Hence, from the conscience, they with ease appeal
To crime's high court, the mysteries among.
What then are human hearts?—earth's woe or weal
When man wrongs man, inspired divinely *not* to *feel*.   225

LXXI

Thus, San Augustine's church and prison joined,
Fitly portrayed crime's eminent success;
When hounds and murderous troops were loosed to find
The unsuspecting exile, and to press
The wretched Seminole from his recess   230
In hommock far, or by the dark bayou;
To burn his corn-fields in the wilderness,
And drag the helpless child and mother, thro'
Infested swamps to die in chains as felons do.

LXXII

Start not! the church and prison are our text.   235
The Seminole and exile far removed
From busier scenes, led harmless lives, unvexed
And unmolested mid the groves they loved;
Till proud Columbia for all time proved
How much her high religion could perform,   240
When her slave-holding sons were truly moved!—
How soon her pious bosom could grow warm,
When heathen tribes submitted to her cruel arm.

. . . .

CANTO IV

. . . .

XL

Hail! home of exiles and of Seminoles!
Hail! Mexico, thou weak but goodly land!   245
The Day of Freedom onward grandly rolls,
And thou shalt yet receive the greeting hand
Of her, who once did like a vulture stand,
To gorge upon thy sons by slave power slain!
The world's respect, ere long thou shalt command;   250
And when the hosts of Freedom come amain;
Thy sons shall join their shouts ascending from the plain!

XLI

Those who once came upon thee with the sword,
Are coming now with pruning hooks and plows;
And plains, once trampled by the spoiler's horde,   255
Are green with fields, and sweet with fruitful boughs.
Awake thou ebon maid! awake! arouse!!
Throw wide thy gates! unlock thy treasures now!
The proud cause of humanity espouse;
And from thy miser-clutching hills shall flow   260
The wealth that yet must glitter in thy sunny brow!

XLIV

We leave thee with thy guests, thou sunny maid!
The daughter of Twasinta dwells with thee;
The chief of Tampa and the everglade
Is with her, and will strive to keep thee free.   265
Rise thou into a nation's dignity,
And freedom's acclamations spread around!
As Rio Grande rolls down to the sea,
Let the omnific waters catch the sound,
"A queen of beauty in the West is Mexic crowned!"   270

LI

Thus ends my lay: Reluctantly I leave
Atlassa and his sweet-eyed Southern maid;
Palmecho, too, with whom I much did grieve,
I turn from sadly! Could they but have stayed
Beneath their "vines and fig trees," not afraid!   275
Yet by their Santa Rosa let them dwell,
Rejoicing in their freedom, long delayed!
And while my heart's untrained emotions swell,
Once more I turn to gaze and sigh: farewell! farewell!

Notes

The poem is in 251 Spenserian stanzas, a form invented by the English poet
Edmund Spenser; Whitman probably learned the stanza from Byron's *Childe
Harold* (1812–18). *Rape of Florida* reviews events of two Seminole Wars—waged
sporadically from 1816 to 1842 by the U.S. Army against the Seminole Indians,
their black slaves, and free black allies, the Maroons—which culminated in
eviction of the defeated Indians from Florida. In the poem, the army attacks Chief
Palmecho's Seminoles. Atlassa, a noble, handsome Indian warrior, loves Palmecho's
daughter Ewald, a beauty of Spanish, Indian, and black heritage, and heroically
helps rout the attackers. Under a flag of truce the Seminoles come to parley in
San Augustine, Texas (where "church and prison" join), but the perfidious whites
take them captive and ship them to exile in Santa Rosa, Mexico. The narrative
is often interrupted by Whitman's musings on honor, freedom, race pride, love,
death, and nostalgia for an Edenic pastoral world. The treacherous rape of Florida
is a parable of the American experience: a land once paradisical is corrupted by
greed, hatred, and hypocrisy, and its native peoples, red and black, are doomed
by race prejudice.

13, 17. *bard of Cedarmere* ... *Bryant:* William Cullen Bryant (1794–1878), a popular American nature poet, editor, and abolitionist. 112. pollution. 121. *Blanc:* Mont Blanc, highest peak in the Alps. 126. *gyves:* shackles. 133. *escutcheon:* shield bearing a coat of arms. 148. heights. 253–54. *sword* ... *plows:* "They shall beat their swords into plowshares, and their spears into pruning-hooks; nations shall not lift up sword against nation, neither shall they learn war anymore" (Isa. 2:4).

from "The Octoroon"

18

These creatures of the languid Orient, —
    Rare pearls of caste, in their voluptuous swoon
And gilded ease, by Eunuchs watched and pent,
    And doomed to hear the lute's perpetual tune,
Were passion's toys — to lust an ornament;   5
    But not such was our thrush-voiced Octoroon, —
The Southland beauty who was wont to hear
Faith's tender secrets whispered in her ear.

19

"An honest man's the noblest work of" — No!
    That threadbare old mistake I'll not repeat.   10
A lovely woman — do you not think so? —
    Is God's best work. That she is man's helpmeet,
The Bible says, and I will let it go;
    And yet she crowns and makes his life complete.
Who would not shrive himself in her dear face,   15
And find his sinless Heaven in her embrace!

20

Young Maury loved his slave — she was his own;
    A gift, for all he questioned, from the skies.
No other fortune had he ever known,
    Like that which sparkled in her wild blue eyes.   20
Her seal-brown locks and cheeks like roses blown,
    Were wealth to him that e'en the gods might prize.
And when her slender waist to him he drew,
The sum of every earthly bliss he knew.

21

They had grown up together, — he and she —   25
    A world unto themselves. All else was bare, —

A desert to them and an unknown sea.
    Their lives were like the birds' lives—free and fair,
And flowed together like a melody.
    They could not live apart, Ah! silly pair!   30
But since she was his slave, what need to say,
A swarm of troubles soon beset their way?

22

Just in the dawn of blushing womanhood;
    Her swan-neck glimpsed through shocks of wavy hair;
A hint of olives in her gentle blood,   35
    Suggesting passion in a rosy lair;
This shapely Venus of the cabins stood,
    In all but birth a princess, tall and fair;
And is it any wonder that this brave
And proud young master came to love his slave?   40

28

If it be shame to love a pretty woman,
    Then shameful loving is a pretty thing.
And of all things the most divinely human
    Is this:—Love purifies life's Fountain Spring;
And he who has not quaffed that fount is no man—   45
    I'd rather be a lover than a king.
And then, preach as we will or may, we'll find
That Cupid, dear young god, is sometimes blind.

55

Before the world, I hold that none of these:
    The Shushan slave, the Oreb shepherdess,   50
Nor Moab's gleaner, ever had the ease
    Of carriage, grace of speech, the stateliness
Of step and pose, nor had the art to please
    And charm with symphonies of form and dress,
Nor had such wond'rous eyes, such lovely mouth,   55
As had this blue-eyed daughter [Lena] of the South!

56

Had priest or prophet ever heard her singing,
    Or seen her, where the clover was in bloom,
Wading knee-deep, while larks were upward springing,
    And winds could scarcely breathe for want of room—   60
Thus seen her from the dappled hillsides bringing
    The cows home, in the sunset's golden gloom,
Our good old Bible would have had much more
Of love and romance mixed with sacred lore.

57

What man is there who would not dare defend   65
    A life like this? Is doing so a sin?
Or who should blush to be known as her friend?
    White wonder of creation, fashioned in
The moulds of loveliness; kings might contend
    On martial fields a prize like her to win,   70
And yet, the cabin's hate and mansion's scorn,—
She suffered both, betwixt them being born.

59

When genial Spring first hears the mating thrush,
    Where waters gossip and the wild flowers throng,
Love rears her altar in the leafy bush,   75
    And Nature chants the sweetest bridal-song.
When love is free, with madness in its rush,
    Its very strength defends the heart from wrong.
Love, when untutored, walks a harmless way,
With feet, though bare, that never go astray.   80

153

Mind knows no death. Life is the "first and last."
    The falling leaf leaves its source living still;
The flower which withers in the autumn blast
    Dies not, but thus escapes the winter's chill,
And will return, through changes strange and vast,   85

When summoned forth to range o'er vale and hill.
Shall mind which thus perceives Life's changes die?
Hath only matter immortality?

156

But, "if a man die, shall he live again?"
    This baffling question comes from long ago.   90
Shall ashes only of Life's torch remain?
    The mind cries out, and Nature answers, "No!"
Ye who have heard the prophesying rain,
    And seen the flowery Resurrection glow:
Ye know of better things than eye hath seen;   95
Ye know sere Earth is Mother of the green.

157

The wild moose shivers in the north land's breath,
    Where Huron's wave upbraids the fretful shore;
The marsh fowl far to southward wandereth
    And calls her tribes to milder climes explore;   100
All Nature seems to sigh: "Remember death,
    For all the living soon shall be no more."
But mark how Faith sweeps on with tireless wing,
To find for e'en the fowl an endless spring.

159

Let scoffers mock, let unbelief deny—   105
    Agnosticism stolidly ignore;
Let worldly wisdom proudly ask us, "Why?"
    And still the soul cries out for something more—
For something better than philosophy—
    Still longs for higher joys and looks before;   110
And cannot rest—will ne'er contented be,
Till triumph over matter leaves mind free.

160

Then hail we all the spirits of the just,
    With Lena we shall join them all. The mind

Now risen looks down on Life's unmeaning dust, 115
   And soars to higher spheres—all unconfined;
To spheres of love and duty, hope and trust;
   And leaves the sordid and corrupt behind.
The Virgin is the sign of vanquished night,
Her child is born—born of the soul—the Light. 120

161

Farewell! In grandeur sinks the closing day,
   And on our vision slowly fades the light;
And bygone scenes, like shadows fall away,
   To settle in the blank of coming night.
The Octoroon has passed, but not for aye; 125
   To those who have the gift of inner sight,
The spirit of all nature prophesies
A home for love and beauty in the skies.

An Idyll of the South (1901)

Notes

The poem of 161 stanzas (in ottava rima) is a lyrical tribute to love, women, and the mind's immortality. A handsome patrician youth, Sheldon Maury, falls deeply in love with his octoroon slave Lena, but their interracial love is doomed. Maury's father sells Lena into slavery; Maury rides to her rescue, only to find Lena, escaped untainted from a brutish owner, dying in a woodsman's cottage. Stanza 18. *Orient:* the Far East, also meaning the luster of pearls; *pearls of caste:* female slaves in a harem, guarded by *Eunuchs*, castrated men. Lena, the *Southland beauty,* is loved; therefore, she surpasses the slaves who merely serve their master's lust. 9. *"An honest man's the noblest work of [God]":* Alexander Pope, *An Essay on Man*, IV: 247. 37. *Venus:* Roman goddess of love and beauty. 48. *Cupid:* Roman god of love; son of Venus. 50–51. *Sushan slave, the Oreb shepherdess. . . . Moab's gleaner:* respectively, Esther was crowned queen of Persia in Shusan (Esth. 1–2); Zipporah, wife of Moses, was a shepherdess and daughter of a Midianite priest; Oreb was in Midian; Ruth was a faithful woman who redeems her kinswoman's land (Ruth 1–4).

HENRIETTA CORDELIA RAY

Henrietta Cordelia Ray (1850/1852?–1916) was the daughter of Charlotte Augusta (Burrough) and Charles Bennett Ray, the pioneer abolitionist, editor of the *Colored American,* Congregational minister, and
distinguished civic leader. Born in New York City, Ray earned a master
of pedagogy degree from the University of the City of New York in
1891. For some thirty years she taught in the New York City public
school system. After retiring, Ray tutored pupils in music, mathematics,
and languages and taught English literature to classes of teachers. She
lived on Long Island with her elder sister Florence; neither married,
and together they wrote a biography of their father. Ray was a prolific
and well-known poet: her ode, *Lincoln,* was read at the unveiling of
the Freedmen's Monument in Washington, D.C. in 1876, and she
published many poems in periodicals and 146 poems in her collections.

   Ray's favorite subjects are a benignly beautiful earth and heaven,
Christian idealism and morality, love, and literature. She does not versify
current racial issues, but past struggles for freedom and equality inspire
several tributes to race heroes. Ray's technical skills are unusually rich:
she successfully employs varied stanzaic forms; her rhythms are diver-
sified and appropriately irregular at times; end rhymes are perfect and
occasionally fall into original schemes. However, possibly as a result
of her fine education and genteel respectability, Ray's language, thought,
and sentiments seem stilted and generic. She is fond of archaic diction
and syntax, personifications, mythological allusions, and copious ad-
jectives. Ray's artificial landscapes, abstract musings, and cultured tributes, bereft of the vitalizing heat of personal emotions and concrete
realities, remain superior examples of the polite, poetical-picturesque
orthodoxies beloved by readers of her time.

   Sonnets (New York: J. J. Little, 1893); *Poems* (New York: Grafton
Press, 1910).

God's Ways, Not Our Ways

Men choose a crystal goblet filled with wine,
    That thirst and sense of beauty in all haste
May be indulged; but soon the wine is spilled
    Or proves unpleasant to the sated taste;
The crystal chasteness of the goblet slow   5
    Grows dimmer, and thus beauty is a loss;
And man full weary, to the wayside flings
    That wealth of pleasure which has turned to dross,
Close hugs a wooden bowl—no substitute
    For grace and radiance—and with pleading eyes,   10
Begs his Creator humbly to send down
    One drop of water from the plenteous skies;
God grants the boon, man drinks and is content.

Most men refuse to tread on this or that,
    In their attempts to climb where angels are;   15
Some fain would walk on roses, some on down,
    Some reach on waves of light the nearest star;
But from the devious modes that they devise,
    One has adjusted been to ev'ry need;
The fiat born of Wisdom goeth forth,   20
    And man must reck not that his feet will bleed;
Nor dare to say in lofty arrogance,
    "Walk thou in that path, I will walk in this!"
For he who would attain where angels bathe
    Their willing souls in affluence of bliss,   25
Must climb on *Patience'* ladder up to God.

Verses to My Heart's-Sister

We've traveled long together,
    O sister of my heart,
Since first as little children
    All buoyant, we did start
Upon Life's checkered pathway,   5
    Nor dreamed of aught save joy;
But ah! To-day can tell us
    Naught is without alloy.

Rememb'rest thou the gambols
    Of those sweet, early days,   10
When siren Fancy showed us
    Our dreams through golden haze?
Ah, well thou dost remember
    The mirth we then did share,
The sports, the tasks, the music,   15
    The all-embracing prayer.

Somehow my own sweet sister,
    Our heart-strings early twined;
Some rare bond of affection
    Of tastes and aims combined;   20
Made us, e'en in our Springtime,
    Soul-sisters fond and leal;
And how that love has strengthened
    The years can well reveal.

We've seen our loved ones vanish   25
    Far from our yearning gaze,
Into the peace of Heaven.
    O those sad, saddest days,
When we two clung together,
    So lonely and forlorn,   30
With our crushed hearts all quiv'ring,
    All bruised, and scarred and torn.

So nearer clung we, sister,
  And loved each other more;
The tendrils of our natures   35
  Twined closer than before.
We could speak to no other
  Of those sweet, holy things,
So tender yet so nameless,
  Which sorrow often brings.   40

The troubles that have thickened
  Around our daily path,
We've borne together, sister,
  And oft when courage hath
Grown feeble, and the future   45
  Was dark with naught of cheer,
Could one have faced the conflict
  Without the other near?

And sister, dear Heart's-Sister,
  When all the mystery   50
Of this strange life is ended
  In Immortality,
We'll love each other dearly
  As now we do, and more;
For sacred things in Heaven   55
  Grow richer than before.

And shall not those sweet loved ones
  Missed here so long! so long!
Join with us in the music
  Of an all-perfect song?   60
We feel a gladder cadence
  Will thrill their rapt'rous strain,
When we are with them, sister,
  All, ne'er to part again!

So now as here we linger,   65
  May ours be happy days!

O generous-hearted sister,
 In all Life's winding ways
May we have joy together!
 And this I fondly pray,—   70
God bless thee, dear Heart's-Sister!
 Forever and for aye!

Sea Cadences

Many are thy tones, O Ocean,
Filling us with strange emotion
As we hear the murmurs wild;
 In their weird and solemn power,
 Thou dost send them ev'ry hour   5
To thy yearning, list'ning child.

Like a voice subdued and tragic,
Many of thy songs bring magic,
Others to us hoarsely call;
 Some are sweet and fraught with gladness, 10
 Some have strains akin to sadness,
Yet we prize and love them all.

In the heart nigh crushed with sorrow,
Dreading the unknown to-morrow,
Wishing past the drear to-day,   15
 In the soul its burden bearing
 While the lip a smile is wearing,
They have waked an answering lay.

Thou hast psalms of glad thanksgiving,
Choral anthems for the living,   20
Dirges for the silent throng;
 For the beautiful who, lying
 Where the mermaids low are sighing,
Nevermore shall join thy song.

There is freedom in thy dashing   25
As thy waves the rocks are lashing,
Singing loud their mad refrain;
 Of unrest the chords are telling,
 And from many a soul's depth welling,
Comes an echo to the strain.   30

Like some lone heart's plaintive throbbing,
Leap the billows, wildly sobbing,
Flinging to the pulseless air, —
 Now, a cadence hushed and calming,
 Now, a peal fierce and alarming,   35
Now a wail of deep despair.

As the sad mysterious surges
Chant their melancholy dirges,
In a whisper ne'er repressed,
 So within the realm of feeling,   40
 Hopes and longings softly stealing,
Moan forever unexpressed.

When thy sweetly chiming chorus
Throws its fascination o'er us,
We would fain translate it all;   45
 But in vain is e'en our trying,
 For thy notes are never-dying,
And they baffle as they fall.

Soft thy hymns of awed devotion
Float on waves of ceaseless motion,   50
To the throne of God above.
 Many are thy tones, O Ocean,
 Filling us with strange emotion,
Tuning souls to praise and love.

To My Father

A leaf from Freedom's golden chaplet fair,
We bring to thee, dear father! Near her shrine
None came with holier purpose, nor was thine
Alone the soul's mute sanction; every prayer
Thy captive brother uttered found a share   5
In thy wide sympathy; to every sign
That told the bondman's need thou didst incline.
No thought of guerdon hadst thou but to bear
A loving part in Freedom's strife. To see
Sad lives illumined, fetters rent in twain,   10
Tears dried in eyes that wept for length of days—
Ah! was not that a recompense for thee?
And now where all life's mystery is plain,
Divine approval is thy sweetest praise.

Note

8. *guerdon:* reward.

Antigone and Œdipus

Slow wand'ring came the sightless sire and she,
Great-souled Antigone, the Grecian maid,
Leading with pace majestic his sad steps,
On whose bowed head grim Destiny had laid
A hand relentless; oft the summer breeze   5
Raised the gold tresses from her veinèd cheek,
As with a dainty touch, so much she seemed
A being marvelous, regal yet meek.

Thus spake sad Œdipus: "Ah! whither now,
O daughter of an aged sire blind,   10
Afar from Thebes' pure, crested colonnades,
Shall we, sad exiles, rest and welcome find?
Who will look on us with a pitying eye?
But unto me sweet resignation's balm
Suff'ring and courage bring; yet moments come   15
When naught restores my spirit's wonted calm.

"O rare dim vales and glitt'ring sunlit crags!
O vine-clad hills soft with the flush of dawn!
O silver cataract dancing to the sea,
And shad'wy pines and silent dewy lawn!   20
I ne'er can see you more. Alas! alas!
But whither go we? Speak! O daughter fair;
Thou must indeed be sight unto thy sire.
Does here a temple consecrate the air?"

"My father! grieve not for our distant land."   25
Thus made Antigone reply: "I see
Amid the forest's music-echoing aisles,
A spot of peace and blest repose for thee.
In solemn loftiness the towers rear
Their stately pinnacles; my eyes behold   30
The holy laurel decked in festive robes,
The olive pale, waving in sunset-gold.

"In the green leafage, tender nightingales
Are chanting dulcet harmonies meanwhile,
In the clear river's liquid radiance   35
The early stars, of sheen resplendent, smile.
It is a sacred spot; here we may shun
Dangers that threaten, and in sweet content
Ere we need wander more, a few short days
May in these hallowed shades be calmly spent.   40

"My father! sorrow not because of Fate!
Perchance the gods may kindly deign to look
With glance benignant on our mournful doom.
Together thou and I, can we not brook
Th' assaults of stern-browed Destiny? May not   45
The fatal mesh contain some golden thread,
Ere it be spun complete with all of woe?
Father! my father! raise thy drooping head!"

"Immortal asphodels ne'er crowned a brow
More queenlike than is thine, my peerless child,   50
Calm-browed Antigone! ah woe! sad fate!"
Then spake Antigone with aspect mild:
"My father! cease thy sadness! wherefore grieve?
Oh! let us dream that from the azure sky,
The gods gaze on us with a pitying glance.   55
Oh! let us hope a little ere we die!"

Notes

In Greek legend, Antigone is a daughter of Oedipus and his mother Jocasta.
For his unwitting sins of killing his father and marrying his mother, Oedipus blinds
himself and is driven out of his kingdom, Thebes. Antigone alone shares his
wanderings. Sophocles' trilogy of plays (ca. 442–406 B.C.) dramatizes this legend,
and Ray's poem draws on one play, *Oedipus at Colonus.* 49. *asphodels:* lilylike
flowers.

In Memoriam

(*Frederick Douglass*)

One whose majestic presence ever here,
Was as an inspiration held so dear,
Will greet us nevermore upon the earth.
The funeral bells have rung; there was no dearth
Of sorrow as the solemn cortege passed;   5
But ours is a grief that will outlast
The civic splendor. Say, among all men,
Who was this hero that they buried then,
With saddest plaint and sorrow-stricken face?
Ay! 'twas a princely leader of his race!   10

. . . .

Panting for freedom early, he did dare
To throw aside his shackles, for the air
Of slavery is poison unto men
Moulded as Douglass was; they suffer, then
Manhood asserts itself; they are too brave,   15
Such souls as his, to die content a slave.
So being free, one path alone he trod,
To bring to liberty — sweet boon from God —
His deeply injured race; his tireless zeal
Was consecrated to the bondman's weal.   20

. . . .

He saw the slave uplifted from the dust,
A freeman! Loyal to the sacred trust
He gave himself in youth, with voice and pen,
He had been to the end. And now again
The grandest efforts of that brain and heart   25
In ev'ry human sorrow bore a part.
His regnant intellect, his dignity,
Did make him honored among all to be;
And public trusts his country gladly gave
Unto this princely leader, born a slave!   30

He thought of children sobbing round the knees
Of hopeless mothers, where the summer breeze
Blew o'er the dank savannas. What of woe
In their sad story that he did not know!
He was a valiant leader in a cause   35
Than none less noble, though the nation's laws
Did seem to spurn it; and his matchless speech
To Britain's sea-girt island shores did reach.
Our Cicero, and yet our warrior knight,
Striving to show mankind might is not right!   40

Shall the race falter in its courage now
That the great chief is fallen? Shall it bow
Tamely to aught of injury? Ah, nay!
For daring souls are needed e'en to-day.
Let his example be a shining light,   45
Leading through duty's paths to some far height
Of undreamed victory. All honored be
The silv'ry head of him we no more see!
Children unborn will venerate his name,
And History keep spotless his fair fame.   50

. . . .

Yes! our great chief has fallen as might fall
Some veteran warrior, answering the call
Of duty. With the old serenity,
His heart still strung with tender sympathy,
He passed beyond our ken; he'll come no more   55
To give us stately greeting as of yore.
We cannot fail to miss him. When we stand
In sudden helplessness, as through the land
Rings echo of some wrong he could not brook,
Then vainly for our leader will we look.   60

But courage! no great influence can die.
While he is doing grander work on high,
Shall not his deeds an inspiration be
To us left in life's struggle? May not we

Do aught to emulate him whom we mourn?   65
We are a people now, no more forlorn
And hopeless. We must gather courage then,
Rememb'ring that he stood man among men.
So let us give, now he has journeyed hence,
To our great chieftain's memory, reverence!   70

Notes

Douglass (1817–95), a slave in Maryland, escaped to Massachusetts in 1838, earned acclaim as a lecturer, writer (*Narrative of the Life of Frederick Douglass,* 1845), founder of the antislavery newspaper *North Star* (1847–64), statesman, and minister after the Civil War. Compare Cotter's "Frederick Douglass" and Dunbar's "Douglass." 39. *Cicero:* see Reason's "The Spirit Voice" (31).

Longfellow

The "Psalm of Life" for thee is o'er,
O bard serenest! on the shore
Of shad'wy Time, we see complete
Thy life so rounded, fair and sweet.

Thy tender thoughts, thy soothing rhyme,   5
Like sweet bells ringing, e'er will chime
With much of hope and joy and need,
For thou couldst soothe and cheer indeed.

Like pictures in some stately hall,
Hung where the loving gaze of all   10
May seek contentment, thy true verse
May to each one some truth rehearse.

Who now can climb the Alpine height,
Nor see clear in the gleaming light,
The word that mystic banner bore,   15
That potent word,—"Excelsior?"

When dainty moonlight veils the stars,
We see framed in its "golden bars,"
"Endymion and Dian" fair,
While Love floats radiant through the air.   20

Shall we not oft at midnight hour
When silence reigns with mystic pow'r,
Hear loud "the old clock on the stairs,"
Its requiem mingling with our prayers?

When fierce the tempest roars o'erhead   25
And e'en the mariner knows dread,
Behold the little maiden fair,
The seaweed clinging to her hair!

Evangeline and Gabriel!
When woman's constancy we tell,   30
Her name in brightest hues shall shine,
Who made devotion so divine.

And Minnehaha! we can see
A scene of grace and witchery
When her we call; and then the grief   35
And pathos of her warrior chief.

When round the hearth some vacant chair
Is all the answer to our prayer,
We hear thee say, "Death is transition"
But leading to the "life elysian."   40

When "day is done" and misty shades
Are deep'ning all the solemn glades,
And sadness comes, who well as thou,
Can rest and cheer and calm us now?

We fain—the "architects of Fate"—   45
Would wisely build; though naught of great
May be the end of all our care,
We still will hope and nobly dare.

So runs our life with thine, sweet friend,
And now when all thy soul-songs blend   50
With Heaven's music, shall not we
Still sweeter rev'rence give to thee?

Note

Henry Wadsworth Longfellow (1807–82) of Maine, was an eminent Harvard professor, prose writer, and the most beloved poet of his age. Ray's tribute consists of titles, phrases, and references from Longfellow's poems: "A Psalm of Life," "Excelsior," "Endymion," "The Old Clock on the Stairs," "The Wreck of the Hesperus," *Evangeline, The Song of Hiawatha*, "Resignation," and "The Day Is Done." Ray's fondness for the "genteel" Longfellow is fitting: he, too, showed superior technical skills, but often his proper, mild verse lacked fire.

Robert G. Shaw

When War's red banners trailed along the sky,
And many a manly heart grew all aflame
With patriotic love and purest aim,
There rose a noble soul who dared to die,
If only Right could win. He heard the cry   5
Of struggling bondmen and he quickly came,
Leaving the haunts where Learning tenders fame
Unto her honored sons; for it was ay
A loftier cause that lured him on to death.
Brave men who saw their brothers held in chains,   10
Beneath his standard battled ardently.
O friend! O hero! thou who yielded breath
That others might share Freedom's priceless gains,
In rev'rent love we guard thy memory.

Note

Robert G.[ould] Shaw was the white commander of the Massachusetts 54th
Infantry, the first black regiment raised in the North in the Civil War. Colonel
Shaw and many of his soldiers were killed in the battle of Fort Wagner, South
Carolina in 1863 and were buried together on the battlefield. Some forty poems
(four by black poets) and several monuments and paintings honor Shaw.

My Spirit's Complement

Thy life hath touched the edges of my life,
All glistening and moist with sunlit dew.
They touched, they paused,—then drifted wide apart,
Each gleaming with a rare prismatic hue.

'Twas but a touch! the edges of a life   5
Alone encolored with the rose, yet lo!
Each fibre started into strange unrest,
And then was stilled, lulled to a rhythmic flow.

Perchance our spirits clasp on some fair isle,
Bright with the sheen of reveries divine;   10
Or list'ning to such strains as chant the stars,
In purest harmony their tendrils twine.

God grant our souls may meet in Paradise,
After the mystery of life's sweet pain;
And find the strange prismatic hues of earth   15
Transmuted to the spotless light again.

JOHN WILLIS MENARD

John Willis Menard (1838–93) is distinguished as the first African American elected to Congress (from Louisiana, 1868). Although the House decided he was not entitled to the seat, Menard became the first back man to make a speech to the House of Representatives. Born in Kaskaskia, Illinois, Menard worked on a farm for his first eighteen years. He attended schools in Illinois and Ohio, and during the Civil War went to Washington, D.C. There, through his appointment in the Bureau of Emigration, Menard became the first federal clerk of his race in 1862. He wrote and spoke in support of black separatism and investigated British Honduras, for the government, as a site for colonization. From 1865 to 1871, Menard lived in New Orleans, worked for the city, and published a newspaper. During the next seventeen years, he published and edited three newspapers in Key West and Jacksonville while holding down several governmental posts, including a term in the Florida legislature. For the five years before he died of pulmonary emphysema, Menard clerked in Washington, D.C.

Almost half of the sixty-three verses in Menard's only published volume are love poems, addressed to many different women. Their language is banal, the imagery stale, execution clumsy, and sentiments repetitive and spiritless. More effective are Menard's tributes to famous people in which his race pride is stong.

Lays in Summer Lands (Washington, D.C.: Enterprise Publishing, 1879).

The Negro's Lament

How long, O God! how long must I remain
   Worse than an alien in my native land?
For long years past I've toiled for other's gain
   Beneath Oppression's ruthless iron hand.

Columbia! why art thou so great and fair,   5
   And so false and cruel to thine own?
Goodness and Beauty, a proverbial pair,
   They in thy heritage, themselves disown.

So fair and yet so false! thou art a lie
   Against both natural and human laws,—   10
A deformed dwarf, dropp'd from an angry sky
   To serve a selfish, and unholy cause!

Ye sun-kiss'd lakes and hills of Liberty!
   And silvery flowing streams and fields!
Your teeming gold and grain are not for me,   15
   My birthright only ostracism yields!

My life is burdensome; year suceeds year
   With feeble hope: I try to emulate
All that conspire to ennoble manhood's sphere;
   And yet I seem to war with angry Fate!   20

O Liberty! I taste but half thy sweets
   In this thy boasted land of Equal Rights!
Although I've fought on land and in thy fleets
   Thy foes, by day and by dim camp-fire lights!

What more wouldst have me do? Is not my life—   25
   My blood, an all-sufficient sacrifice?
Wouldst thou have me transformed in the vain strife
   To change the fiat of the great Allwise?

Of what avail is life—why sigh and fret,
   When manly hopes are only born to fade?   30
Although declared a man, a vassal yet
   By social caste—a crime by heaven made!

Far better for me not to have been born,
   Than live and feel the frownings of mankind;
Endure its social hatred and its scorn,   35
   With all my blighting, forlorn hopes combined.

O, cruel fate!—O, struggle which unmans,
   And burdens every hope and every sigh!
Thou art a boundless gulf over which spans
   Only the arching, storm-foreboding sky!   40

Ah, woe is me! I feel my yearnings crush'd
   Ere they are born within my sighing heart;
All hopes, all manly aspirations hush'd
   As with the power of Death's fatal dart!

The rice birds sing as if in mocking glee,   45
   Scorn my long felt sorrows and my burning tears,
Why mock me, birds? I only crave to be
   Like you, free to roam the boundless spheres!

But still sing on! your cheerful music gives
   My fading hope a gleam of brighter days;   50
Why should I grieve? the eternal God still lives!—
   The sun still shines though clouds obscure his rays!

The darkest hour is just before the break
   Of dawning victory of light and life,
When Freedom's hosts with armor bright awake,   55
   To quell Oppression in the deadly strife!

New hope is mine! for now I see the gleam
   Of beacon lights of coming liberty!
A continent is shock'd—a crimson stream
   Of blood has paid the debt, and I am free!   60

To My Wife

[At Kingston, Jamaica, West Indies.]

Thou art gone to thine island home,
  On the Caribbean shore —
Gone to thy dear old native scenes,
  Among thy friends of yore.

May health, and joy, and hope be thine,   5
  Dear comfort of my life;
May Heaven's protecting care attend
  My darlings and my wife!

Two little darlings, sweet and bright,
  With tiny hands and feet —   10
With raven hair and jetty eyes,
  And voices dear and sweet.

They are my jewels and my wealth —
  My joy, my life, my all;
And heavenly music 'tis to me   15
  Whene'er I hear them call!

But they are gone, and I, alone,
  Am lonesome and bereft;
My life has been a joyless blank
  E'er since my darlings left.   20

But, ah! this sadd'ning loneliness
  Will last but for a time:
They'll soon return, and, in my heart,
  I'll hear their voices chime!

My darling wife and little ones,   25
  Far o'er the foaming main,
Weeks will be months, and months long years,
  Until you come again!

———

Come back to me, come back to me,
From o'er the foaming, raging sea: 30
Come back—your home is in my heart,
And from its fold no more depart.

Come back, for days and nights are drear,
And home seems desolate and queer;
The sunny joys of home have fled,   35
And chaos reigns o'er floor and bed.

Come back, your chickens go half-fed;
The weeds have worn—your flow'rs are dead!
Disorder rules supreme o'er all,
And webs are thick on every wall.   40

Come back with sunny joys and smiles,
Come back with laughing hearts and eyes;
Come back to soothe, come back to cheer,
And all this sad confusion clear.

Good-bye! Off for Kansas

Good-bye ye bloody scenes of long ago!—
  Good-bye to cotton fields and hounds!
From you, vile sources of my earthly woe,
  My freed and leaping spirit bounds!

Though free, my work to me no profit yields,   5
  And for my politics, am mobb'd;
No more thank God! upon these bloody fields
  Shall I be of my labor robb'd!

Good-bye Aunt Polly! good-bye Uncle Ned!
  I am off, and shall not come back;   10
This land is cursed; we are in rags, half fed,
  Bull-dozed and killed by Yellow Jack!

Good-bye! I've sold my little cane and corn!
  And am off for the river's banks;
And when I step on board to-morrow morn,   15
  I'll sing and give the good Lord thanks!

Notes

Reference is to emigration of Southern blacks to Kansas in response to the
Kansas-Nebraska Act (1854); see Rogers's *The Repeal of the Missouri Compromise
Considered* and note. 12. *Yellow Jack:* yellow fever, a viral disease transmitted
by a mosquito, prevalent in the South.

ROBERT CHARLES O'HARA BENJAMIN

Robert Charles O'Hara Benjamin (1855–1900), by his own account, was born on St. Kitts in the British West Indies and went to school on the island and at Oxford's Trinity College. As a young man, he traveled in the East and West Indies and South America, settling in New York City about 1869. He lived in New York for eight years, became a United States citizen, got involved in Republican politics, and worked on newspapers and briefly as a letter carrier. Subsequently, Benjamin was a teacher and principal in four Southern states while he read law; he was admitted to the bar in Tennessee in 1880. Benjamin traveled extensively thereafter: he practiced law in twelve states, edited many newspapers, lectured, and wrote and published ten volumes of prose. According to a newspaper account, Southern Democrats murdered Benjamin for registering black voters in Kentucky.

The radical politics and strong race pride that strengthen Benjamin's prose are generally absent from his standard verses on nature, love, and other domestic topics. His freshest poems are the mocking folksy soliloquy and "political" summons printed here.

Poetic Gems (Charlottesville, Va.: Peck & Allan, 1883).

The Farmer's Soliloquy

"Oh! for a thousand tongues to sing
   My great Redeemer's praise:
The glories of my Lord and King,
   The triumphs of His grace."

Oh! for a thousand cedar posts   5
   To fence my garden 'round.
To hinder the neighbors' pigs and goats
   From rooting up my potato ground.

Oh! for a thousand hickory rails,
   To make my fence secure;   10
A thousand patent locks and keys,
   To lock my stable door.

Oh! for a thousand bricks and stones,
   To build my chimney higher,
To keep the neighbors' boys and girls   15
   From putting out my fire.

Oh! for a thousand old shot guns,
   That I might be a match,
For all the tramps that I can find
   In my watermelon patch.   20

Oh! for a thousand pumpkin seeds,
   To plant for my son John;
He says that pumpkin pies are good
   When the winter time comes on.

Oh! for a thousand cribs of corn,   25
   Filled chuck up to the beam;
And a thousand pails that's good and strong,
   To keep the milk and cream.

Oh! for a thousand turnip bads,
  Placed all into a row;   30
Lord! please send a little rain,
  To make the 'tatoes grow.

Oh! for a thousand tongues to ask
  My maker, who's on high,
To keep my smoke-house filled with meal,   35
  Fat bacon, rock and rye.

Now, Lord, I close my humble prayer,
  Which (to some) may seem a vision;
Numbers ask for all I've named,
  Whilst few ask for RELIGION.   40

Note

29. beds.

Colored Heroes, Hark the Bugle

Political

Colored heroes seek your standard,
  Know you not the foeman's near,
Know you not how they'll enslave you,
  You and yours, who are so dear.
Gather then, combine for freedom,   5
  Fight for that and bravely die,
Only cowards turn their faces,
  Cowards they, who turn and fly.

Colored heroes, hark, your masters
  Have combined and are as one,   10
They have sworn they will enslave you,
  Will you now the battle shun?
Gather then, combine for freedom,
  Wealth would claim you 'till you die,
Only cowards turn their faces,   15
  Cowards they, who turn and fly.

Colored heroes, get your armor,
  Each be worthy of the name.
Better far than be a coward,
  You be numbered with the slain.   20
Gather then, combine for freedom,
  They would crush you till you die.
Only cowards turn their faces,
  Cowards they, who turn and fly.

Colored heroes, hark the bugle,   25
  O'er the land sounds the alarm,
Bravely charge the foemen's trenches,
  On each breast there is a charm.
Gather then, combine for freedom,
  Predjudice will have to die,   30

'Tis but cowards turn their faces,
Cowards they, who turn and fly.

Note

Author's footnote: "This poem was written for the Pittsburg [*sic*], Pa. 'Citizen' and published during the political campaign of 1882; the author being an active member of the Independent Party at that time."

TIMOTHY THOMAS FORTUNE

Timothy Thomas Fortune (1856–1928) wrote the fifty poems of *Dreams of Life* from 1875 to 1900, when he reigned as the "Dean of Negro Editors" and the "Prince of Negro Journalists" in the United States. He was born in Marianna, Florida, to slaves of mixed racial heritage, Sarah Jane (Bush) and Emanuel Fortune. As he grew to manhood, living primarily in Jacksonville, Fortune had fewer than three years of formal schooling; he worked as a page in the Florida senate, printer's devil and typesetter, mail route agent, customs inspector, and school teacher. He studied law at Howard University and in 1877 married Caroline Charlotte Smiley; they had five children. In 1879, in New York City, Fortune embarked on a fifty-year career in journalism as a publisher, editor, printer, and the author of thousands of trenchant articles, editorials, monographs, and books. In all his writings and in his newspapers, the New York *Globe, Freeman,* and *Age,* he agitated for African-American independence and power in all areas of life. To this end Fortune also organized several radical black organizations that flourished nationwide. In the early 1900s, beset by economic woes, political and personal attacks, marital problems, and heavy drinking, Fortune lost control of the *Age* and suffered a breakdown that left him sick and destitute (1907). He returned to journalism, however, and in the last fourteen years of his life worked as editor and correspondent for many major newspapers. Fortune died of heart disease in Philadelphia.

Fortune's poetry offers glimpses of his ideals, aspirations, self-image, and sentimental nature that his fine prose writings never reveal. His recurring poetic themes are: all is vanity, and the paths of glory lead but to the grave; "love is life and life is love," but true love is defeated; liberty must be fought for and cherished; and the Promethean-Byronic hero is the most admirable of men. Fortune's lyrics are often weakened by banal language, forced end rhymes, choppy meters, moralistic digressions, and repetitions. Some lyrics, however, effectively blend natural diction, formal pattern, and deep feeling. Among his long narrative poems, "The Bride of Ellerslee," faithful in form and tone to Byron's *Tales,* is a compelling saga of love's triumph over race prejudice. Although Fortune's poetic art seldom measures up to his powerful prose, his strengths are a sensitive romantic vision and courageous race pride.

Dreams of Life: Miscellaneous Poems (New York: Fortune and Peterson, 1905).

Bartow Black

'Twas when the Proclamation came,—
  Far in the sixties back,—
He left his lord, and changed his name
  To "Mister Bartow Black."

He learned to think himself a man,   5
  And privileged, you know,
To adopt a new and different plan,—
  To lay aside the hoe.

He took the lead in politics,
  And handled all the "notes,"—   10
For he was up to all the tricks
  That gather in the votes;

For when the war came to a close
  And negroes "took a stand,"
Young Bartow with the current rose,   15
  The foremost in command.

His voice upon the "stump" was heard;
  He "Yankeedom" did prate;
The "carpet-bagger" he revered;
  The Southerner did hate.   20

He now was greater than the lord
  Who used to call him slave,
For he was on the "County Board,"
  With every right to rave.

But this amazing run of luck   25
  Was far too good to stand;
And soon the chivalrous "Ku-Klux"
  Rose in the Southern land.

Then Bartow got a little note, —
    'Twas very queerly signed, —   30
It simply told him not to vote,
    Or be to death resigned.

Young Bartow thought this little game
    Was very fine and nice
To bring his courage rare to shame   35
    And knowledge of justice.

"What right have they to think I fear?"
    He to himself did say.
"Dare they presume that I do care
    How loudly they do bray?   40

"This is my home, and here I die,
    Contending for my right!
Then let them come! My colors fly!
    I'm ready now to fight!

"Let those who think that Bartow Black, —   45
    An office-holder, too! —
Will to the cowards show his back,
    Their vain presumption rue!"

Bartow pursued his office game,
    And made the money, too,   50
But home at nights he wisely came
    And played the husband true.

When they had got their subject tame,
    And well-matured their plan,
They at the hour of midnight came,   55
    And armed was every man!

They numbered fifty Southern sons,
    And masked was every face;
And Winfield rifles were their guns, —
    You could that plainly trace.   60

One Southern brave did have a key,
  An entrance quick to make;
They entered all; but meek, you see,
  Their victim not to wake!

They reached his room! He was in bed,—   65
  His wife was by his side!
They struck a match above his head,—
  His eyes he opened wide!

Poor Bartow could not reach his gun,
  Though quick his arm did stretch,   70
For twenty bullets through him spun,
  That stiffly laid the wretch.

And then they rolled his carcass o'er,
  And filled both sides with lead;
And then they turned it on the floor,   75
  And shot away his head!

Ere Black his bloody end did meet
  His wife had swooned away;
The Southern braves did now retreat,—
  There was no need to stay!   80
A.M.E. *Church Review* 3 (Oct. 1886): 158–59

Notes

Author's footnote: "The facts upon which this poem is based are substantially correct. Black was well known to me, by his proper name, Calvin Rogers. He was far above the average of his race in intelligence and courage. He was killed, as here described, in Jackson County, Florida (where I was born), in the early part of 1870, a reference to which can be found in volume 13, page 192, of the 'Ku-Klux Conspiracy,' reported to Congress in 1872 by the Joint Select Committee." 1. *Proclamation*: Emancipation Proclamation, January 1, freeing some slaves. 19. *"carpetbagger"*: a Northerner who went South after the Civil War to hold political office or otherwise exploit the social and political unrest of Reconstruction. 27. *"Ku-Klux"*: During Reconstruction, the Ku Klux Klan, a secret society of white supremacists, spread terror with violent and murderous acts against Southern blacks and carpetbaggers, especially those who rose to political power. An official organization, Knights of the Ku Klux Klan, was founded in 1915 and remains active.

Dreams of Life

I

O, Life of Dreams! O, Dreams of Life!
    Ye mysteries are that breathe and thrill—
In times of peace, in times of strife—
    Through all the pulses of our will.

In hours of joy, in hours of pain,   5
    In all of Love, in all of Hate,
We strive t' evade thee, but in vain,
    For ye are messengers of Fate!

How vain is man! How passing vain!
    The son of Macedon see stride   10
His day upon the battle plain,
    And sate with blood his vaulting pride!

Conquered he all of earth then known,
    And for more worlds to conquer sighed!
Then, drunk with crime, Death claimed his own—   15
    The cruel monster drank and died!

II

Then Caesar took the world's command,
    And savage millions cut he down!
E'en mighty Pompey, great and grand,
    Fell like the fresh green grass, new mown!   20

And Rome, Imperial Rome! the Fates
    Resigned to his corrupt embrace!
And all of Rome's dependent states
    Implored the boon of Caesar's grace!

He who had conquered from the Nile   25
    To where the Rhone and Thamès stray,

Who basked in beauty's fickle smile
    And thought supreme to end his day —

The master of the world was slain
    In the swift movement of the eye;   30
In torture that subdued e'en pain
    He went to judgment in the sky!

His grasp of power the world in thrall
    As adamantine chains did hold;
No arm was raised to stay his fall —   35
    And treason triumphed, treason bold!

The mind grows faint the blood to view
    That selfish man has spilt — for what?
To dull his hate, or chain renew
    That binds the helot to his lot!   40

That mad ambition may o'erleap
    The bounds of Reason and of Right,
Or in cursèd chains doomed millions keep
    On plea of Wisdom and of Might.

.   .   .   .

V

Upon the future life we build,   45
    As built the toilers of the Nile,
Whose rude and ruthless tyrants willed
    That God's eternal sun should smile

On monuments of dust and stone
    Which should defy the flight of Time,   50
Beneath dumb hieroglyphics groan,
    The wonder of each age and clime!

And still they stand, in Winter's storms
    And vernal Summer's rays benign,

Lifting on high grand, gloomy forms 55
   Round which eternity may twine!

VI

The Pyramids! When did they rear
   Their sombre bulk to Time's stern gaze?
Canst estimate the thought—the care—
   The lives condemned—the flight of days— 60

That went to consecrate the pile
   Where Egypt's tyrants now repose,
The sentient serpents of the Nile,
   At whose commands the phantoms rose?

Each stone cemented with the gore, 65
   The tears and sweat of some poor slave!
For each dead king the millions bore
   Into the gloomy vaults, his grave,

A thousand men, perchance, had bled,
   Had sacrificed their all in death, 70
To guard the tyrant in his bed
   And watch for his returning breath!

VII

Yes; on the Future Life we build,
   Rear crumbling monuments to fame,
When Death's remorseless clasp has stilled 75
   The currents of the mortal frame!

Man's labors here are all in vain,
   Are scattered on the cyclone blast—
Scattered afar like tiny seed,
   Upon a barren desert cast, 80

If Duty and Justice be not
   The objects of his care and zeal;

Or in the granary will rot,
  As time eats up the blade of steel!

The universal law ordains,   85
  Nor can we change the just decree,
That man to man, as man, remains,
  By kindred ties, each as each free!

VIII

There were no kings of men till men
  Made kings of men, and of the earth;   90
There were no privileged classes when
  First Nature, man and beasts, had birth.

Man was sole monarch of his sphere,
  And each with equal power was made;
Each from the earth partook his share;   95
  Each shared with each earth's sun and shade.

No fetters on the limbs were bound;
  The intellect was free as light;
Man's every wish abundance found;
  He gloried in his earth-wide right.   100

God made the earth and sky—the breath
  Of mountain and of smiling vale—
And filled them all with life, not death,
  As bracing as the ocean gale!

IX

The giant warrior clothed in steel,   105
  The high-walled city, ravaged plain,
The angry millions as they reel
  To battle, death, or woe and pain—

The world in thrall to him whose might
  And cunning triumph o'er his kind—   110

Did God make Might the test of Right,
Or man—blind leader of the blind!

No; Vanity has reared on high
  The grandeur of its fragile power,
But it will fall, will prostrate lie,   115
  The broken idol of an hour.

X

O, Life of Dreams! O, Dreams of Life!
  Ye mysteries are that breathe and thrill—
In times of peace, in times of strife—
  Through all the pulses of our will.   120

Notes

10. *son of Macedon:* see Horton's "Gen. Grant" (35). 17. *Caesar:* Gaius Julius
(ca. 100–44 B.C.), Roman general and emperor-dictator of the Roman Empire,
who with great bloodshed conquered vast areas of Britain, Europe, Asia, and
Africa. 19. *Pompey:* (106–48 B.C.), Roman general and statesman; like Caesar,
Pompey was stabbed to death. 25–26. *Nile . . . Rhone and Thames:* rivers flowing
through Northeast Africa, France, and England, respectively. 34. *adamantine:* hard
as steel. 40. *helot:* slave. 51. *hieroglyphics:* picture and symbol alphabet used by
ancient Egyptians. 57. *Pyramids:* huge triangular stone structures, the royal tombs
of Egypt.

Byron's Oak at Newstead Abbey

Through thy battlements, Newstead, the hollow winds whistle;
 Thou, the hall of my fathers, art gone to decay;
In the once smiling garden, the hemlock and thistle
 Have choked up the rose that once bloomed in the way.
                                        Lord Byron (1803)

> The little twig that Byron planted here,
> In manhood's hope and early prime,
> The twig he gave his constant love and care
> In Britain's far-famed classic clime,
> Has grown to be a towering, stalwart tree; —   5
> But Byron, master mind, O where is he!
>
> And Newstead Abbey, where he lived and dreamed,
> Still marks the sacred precincts well;
> But long ago the stranger's banners streamed
> O'er towers where Byron's heart did swell!   10
> His lofty oak, with arms outstretched to God,
> Speaks for the Bard—as Missolonghi's sod.
>
> Old Newstead and its giant oak may stand
> The fury of the storm and age,
> But they must both decay, ere Byron's wand   15
> Shall lose its power of love and rage!
> Ere from the human heart shall fade away
> The magic spell he breathed in life's short day!
>
> I love him well, this wayward child of song,
> Whose life in all was passing strange;   20
> With mind so bitter sweet, so weak, so strong—
> With power to soothe, to charm, estrange; —
> Within his grasp the harp was made to flow
> The sweetest, saddest notes the heart can know!
>
> And he will live when Newstead and its tree   25
> Have crumbled back to mother dust;

His name is linked with song and liberty,
And time such fame can never rust!
E'en Albion's glorious name must pale and wane,
While Byron's fame through endless time will reign!   30

Notes

George Gordon, Lord *Byron* (1788–1824), a greatly admired English Romantic poet, was famed for his extravagant life-style and gloomy, passionate super-heroes. Newstead was his ancestral estate. Byron died in *Missolonghi* (12), Greece, while helping the Greeks fight for independence from Turkey. Fortune's note to the poem says: "The oak tree planted by Lord Byron at Newstead Abbey is large and flourishing." 29. *Albion's:* an archaic term for Britain.

Edgar Allan Poe

I know not why, but it is true — it may,
In some way, be because he was a child
Of the fierce sun where I first wept and smiled —
I love the dark-browed Poe. His feverish day
Was spent in dreams inspired, that him beguiled,   5
When not along his path shone forth one ray
Of light, of hope, to guide him on the way,
That to earth's cares he might be reconciled.
Not one of all Columbia's tuneful choir
Has pitched his notes to such a matchless key   10
As Poe — the wizard of the Orphic lyre!
Not one has dreamed, has sung, such songs as he,
    Who, like an echo came, an echo went,
    Singing, back to his mother element.

Note

Poe (1809–49) was born in Boston but raised in Virginia; Fortune's "where I first wept," refers to the South. Poe suffered a troubled and painful life and wrote fiction, essays, and poetry that was characteristically melancholy, musical, and dreamlike.

JAMES EDWIN CAMPBELL

James Edwin Campbell (1867–96) published dynamic folk poetry in periodicals several years before his friend Paul Laurence Dunbar popularized dialect verse. The son of Lethia (Stark) and James Campbell was born in Pomeroy, Ohio, and graduated from Pomeroy High School in 1884. He taught school in Ohio and participated in Republican politics there. In West Virginia, where he lived from 1890 to 1894, Campbell served as principal of Langston School in Point Pleasant and the newly opened Collegiate Institute in Charleston, an agricultural and mechanical arts school for black youths. He married Mary Champ, a teacher, in 1891. Moving to Chicago, Campbell joined the staff of the *Times-Herald* and contributed articles and poems to several periodicals. His promising career as a poet, educator, and journalist was tragically cut short when, on a visit to Pomeroy, he died of pneumonia.

Campbell's *Echoes* contains the finest group of dialect poems of the century, praised by leading critics for their originality, hard realism, authentic dialect and spirit, and aptness of phrasing, rhymes, and rhythms. In more than a dozen spirited lyrics, Campbell captures the folk ways and values of "the Negro of the old regime" (to whom he dedicated these poems) without lapsing into minstrelsy or surrendering race pride. He varies verse forms, alters moods and speech patterns to suit individual subjects, and he leavens the pungent satire with sympathetic appreciation for the joy and pathos of cabin life. In standard English, Campbell toasts wine, women, song, and the beauties of nature in verse that is serious, correct, and esthetically superior to most of his contemporaries' efforts, but his authentic dialect poems remain his most notable work.

Driftings and Gleanings (Charleston, W.Va., 1887 [these poems are all in standard English and are reprinted in *Echoes*]); *Echoes from the Cabin and Elsewhere* (Chicago: Donohue & Henneberry, 1895).

The Pariah

Owned her father all the fact'ries
   Which their black'ning smoke sent up,
Miles and miles all 'round the country,
   From the town by hills pent up.
Traced he back his proud ancestry   5
   To the Rock on Plymouth's shore,
Traced I mine to Dutch ship landing
   At Jamestown, one year before.
Thus was she of haughty lineage,
   I of mongrel race had sprung;   10
O'er my fathers in the workfield
   Whips of scorpions had been swung.
Years of freedom were her race's,
   Years of cruel slavery mine;
Years of culture were her race's,   15
   Years of darkest ign'rance mine.
She a lily sought by all men,
   I a thistle shunned by all;
She the Brahmin, I the Pariah
   Who must e'er before her crawl.   20
Fair was I as her complexion,
   Honest came my fairness, too,
For my father and my mother
   Were in wedlock banded true.
Yes, this mixing of the races   25
   Had been years, long years ago,
That you could not trace the streamlet
   To the fountain whence the flow.

* * * * * * * * * * * *

Like an eagle long imprisoned
   Soared I into realms of light,   30
Scorning all the narrow valley,
   Where my wings had plumed for flight.

In the SUN of modern science
  I had soaring bathed my wings,
And rose higher, *higher,* HIGHER,   35
  'Bove a world of narrow things.
Then on proudly soaring pinions
  I forgot my lowly birth,
When Caste's arrow, venom laden,
  Struck me, shot me down to Earth.   40

*   *   *   *   *   *   *   *   *   *   *   *   *

Kind and friendly had she ever
  Seemed and acted unto me,
Till of late a cold restrainment
  Seemed to bar her manners free.
Then my sens'tive soul quick thinking   45
  That the Pride of Caste was born
In her mind, grew cold and distant,
  Though it pricked me like a thorn,
And my thoughts grew dark and bitter,
  Bitter as the wild aloe.   50
I became a sneering cynic,
  Deeming every man a foe,
Scorning books while scorning people.
  In their pages naught I saw
But I libelled, but I censured,   55
  Every sentence found a flaw;
Till one night the mad mob gathered,
  Called in voices wild and loud
I should quickly come before them,
  And address the raging crowd.   60
They were strikers, who were workmen
  For her father stern and proud,
And they threatened to destroy him
  And his works in curses loud.
At the call I stepped before them,   65
  And they greeted wild and strong,
And my heart grew hot with hatred
  Of Oppression, Caste and Wrong,

While the words poured out like lava
   From the crater of my brain—   70
Burning, seething, hissing, raging
   With the years of pent-up pain.
They had gathered by the great works,
   With their blazing furnace doors,
And the lofty, flaming chimneys,   75
   Up whose throats the hot blast roars;
And the furnace threw its hot light
   'Pon their toilworn, swarthy faces,
While the flames from out the chimnies
   Painted heaven with their blazes.   80
In their hands they held their weapons—
   Tools for toil, and not for war;
On the great mill rolled and thundered,
   Shaking heaven with its jar.
And their brows were dark with hatred,   85
   And their cheeks were hot with rage,
And their voices low were growling,
   Like wild beasts penned in a cage.
And the tiger rose within me
   With a growl that was a curse,   90
And I breathed his breath of passion,
   And I felt his awful thirst.
But her image came before me,
   With her sad, reproachful eyes,
And her locks of sunset splendor   95
   When the summer daylight dies.
Then banished was hot Passion,
   While Mercy pleaded low,
And I cooled their angry fury,
   As hot iron is cooled in snow.   100

* * * * * * * * * * * * *

And she comes and stands before me
   As I gaze into the stream,
And I see her, I behold her
   As some vision in a dream,

And the waves of love come surging   105
  And they sweep my will away,
For I love her, O I love her—
  Aye, forever and a day!
And I called her: "Edie! Edie!"
  As I'd called her oft before,   110
When as little guileless children
  We plucked lilies from this shore.
Oh my voice sobbed like a harp string
  When the rough hand breaks a chord,
And it wailed and moaned as sadly   115
  As some broken-hearted bard.
And she came up to me quickly
  When I thus wailed out her name,
All her soul rose in her blue eyes
  There was ne'er a look of shame,   120
And she threw her arms up to me
  And I caught her to my heart,
While the whole earth reeled beneath me
  And the heavens fell apart!

  * * * * * * * * * * * *

Faint and trembling then I asked her   125
  What the cruel world would say,
While she blushed but spoke out bravely:
  "We'll forget the World to-day.
This I only know, I love you,
  I have loved you all the while;   130
What care I then for your lineage
  Or the harsh world's frown or smile.
Men are noble from *their* actions,
  From *their* deeds and theirs alone,
Father's deeds are *not* their children's—   135
  Reap not that by others sown.
They are naught but dwarfish pigmies
  Who would scorn you for your birth;
Who would scorn you for your lineage,
  Raise they not their eyes from Earth.   140

What is blood? The human body?
  Trace it back, it leads to dust,
Trace it forward, same conclusion,
  Naught but vile dust find you must.
But the *soul* is sent from heaven   145
  And the Sculptor-Hand is God's
Part and parcel of his being,
  While our bodies are but clods!"
                    (1889; revised 1895)

Notes

6–8. *Rock on Plymouth's . . . Jamestown:* see Whitfield's, "A Poem Written . . ."
(5–54). 10, 21–28. *mongrel race:* mixed black and white lineage. The "tragic
mulatto" had long been a popular literary theme. Usually the lover of mixed race
was the fated woman, as in the first African-American novel, William Wells Brown's
Clotel, or The President's Daughter (1853) and in the highly successful play by
Dion Boucicault, *The Octoroon* (1859). Albery Whitman continued the tradition
in his epic poem "The Octoroon" (1901). Here Campbell reverses the sexes, with
the speaker of mixed blood a man who is rejected by a white woman. An
autobiographical element may be present in "The Pariah"; Campbell himself was
very light-complexioned, with Caucasian features. 19. *Brahmin . . . Pariah:* members of the highest and lowest castes among Hindus of India; a pariah is an outcast.
79. chimneys. 137. pygmies.

Ol' Doc' Hyar

Ur ol' Hyar lib in ur house on de hill,
He hunner yurs ol' an' nebber wuz ill;
He yurs dee so long an' he eyes so beeg,
An' he laigs so spry dat he dawnce ur jeeg;
He lib so long dat he know ebbry tings   5
'Bout de beas'ses dat walks an' de bu'ds dat sings—
    Dis Ol' Doc' Hyar,
    Whar lib up dar
Een ur mighty fine house on ur mighty high hill.

He doctah fur all de beas'ses an' bu'ds—   10
He put on he specs an' he use beeg wu'ds,
He feel dee pu's' den he look mighty wise,
He pull out he watch an' he shet bofe eyes;
He grab up he hat an' grab up he cane,
Den—"blam!" go de do'—he gone lak de train,   15
    Dis Ol' Doc' Hyar,
    Whar lib up dar
Een ur mighty fine house on ur mighty high hill.

Mistah Ba'r fall sick—dee sont fur Doc' Hyar,
"O, Doctah, come queeck, an' see Mr. B'ar;   20
He mighty nigh daid des sho' ez you b'on!"
"Too much ur young peeg, too much ur green co'n,"
Ez he put on he hat, said Ol' Doc' Hyar;
"I'll tek 'long meh lawnce, an' lawnce Mistah B'ar,"
    Said Ol' Doc' Hyar,   25
    Whar lib up dar
Een ur mighty fine house on ur mighty high hill.

Mistah B'ar he groaned, Mistah B'ar he growled,
W'ile de ol' Mis' B'ar an' de chillen howled;
Doctah Hyar tuk out he sha'p li'l lawnce,   30
An' pyu'ced Mistah B'ar twel he med him prawnce

Den grab up he hat an' grab up he cane
"Blam!" go de do' an' he gone lak de train,
                    Dis Ol' Doc' Hyar,
                    Whar lib up dar   35
Een ur mighty fine house on ur mighty high hill.

But de vay naix day Mistah B'ar he daid;
Wen dee tell Doc' Hyar, he des scratch he haid:
"Ef pashons git well ur pashons git wu's,
Money got ter come een de Ol' Hyar's pu's;   40
Not wut folkses does, but fur wut dee know
Does de folkses git paid" — an' Hyar larfed low,
                    Dis sma't Ol' Hyar,
                    Whar lib up dar
Een de mighty fine house on de mighty high hill!   45

Note

Campbell writes in Gullah, the dialect spoken by blacks of the Sea Islands and coastal regions of South Carolina and Georgia. This satire of the money-getting ethic of a rising black middle class cleverly employs the animal fable of folk tradition.

'Sciplinin' Sister Brown

Shet up dat noise, you chillen! Dar's some one at de do'.
Dribe out dem dogs; you 'Rastus, tek Linkum off de flo'!

Des ma'ch yo'se'f right in sah! (Jane, tek dem ashes out!
Dis house look lak ur hog-pen; you M'randy, jump erbout!)

W'y bress my soul, hit's Ef'um—w'y, Ef'um, how you do?   5
An' Tempie an' de chillen? I hopes dey's all well too.

Hyuh, M'randy, bresh dat stool off; now, Ef'um, des set down.
Wut's de news f'um off de Ridge an' wut's de news in town?

Now doan' you t'ink dem niggahs hed Susan 'fo de chu'ch
'Bout dawncin' at de pa'ty—dey call dat sinnin' much.   10

Dey up an' call ur meetin' ter 'scipline Sistah Brown,
But de night dey hol' de meetin' she tuk herse'f to town.

Dey sont de Bo'd ob Deacons, de pahstah at de head,
Ter wait urpon de sistah an' pray wid her, dey said,

But Susan mighty stubbo'n, an' wen dey lif' ur pra'r   15
She up an' tell de deacons she des wawn' gwine ter cyar.

An' wen de Reb'ren' Pa'son prayed 'bout ur "sheep wuz los',"
An' 'bout de "po bac'slidah," she gin her head ur toss!

I seed de debbil raisin' in de white ob Susan's eyes—
Fyeah she blow dat deacon-bo'd ter "mansions in de skies,"   20

I des tuk down my bawnjer an' den I 'gins an' plays;
"Come dy fount ob ebbry blessin', chune my ha't ter sing dy praise."

De pa'son an' de deacons dey jined me pooty soon;
Lawd! Dat bawnjer shuk itse'f ur-playin' ob de chune!

An' wen dey mos' wuz shoutin', I tightened up er string,   25
Drapped right inter "Money Musk" an' gin de chune full swing.

De "Debbil's Dream" come arter—de debbil wuz ter pay,
Dem niggahs fell ter pattin'—I larf mos' ebbry day!

Deacon Jones got on his feet, de pa'son pulled him down;
I played ur little fastah, an' sho's my name am Brown,   30

De pa'son an' de deacons jined han's right on dis flo',
Su'cled right and su'cled lef'—it sutny wuz ur show.

Dey 'naded up an' down de flo' an' w'en hit come ter swing,
De pa'son gin hisse'f a flirt an' cut de pidgin-wing!

An' we'n urfo' de meetin' dat 'mittee med its 'po't   35
'Bout Sistah Susan's dawncin', dey cut it mighty sho't.

De chyuhsman, Mr. Pa'son, said in tones so mil' an' sweet:
"Sistah Brown wa'n't guilty, caze—SHE NEBBER CROSSED HER FEET!"

De Cunjah Man

O chillen run, de Cunjah man,
Him mouf ez beeg ez fryin' pan,
Him yurs am small, him eyes am raid,
Him hab no toof een him ol' haid,
Him hab him roots, him wu'k him trick, 5
Him roll him eye, him mek you sick—
 De Cunjah man, de Cunjah man,
 O chillen run, de Cunjah man!

Him hab ur ball ob raid, raid ha'r,
Him hide it un' de kitchen sta'r, 10
Mam Jude huh pars urlong dat way,
An' now huh hab ur snaik, dey say.
Him wrop ur roun' huh buddy tight,
Huh eyes pop out, ur orful sight—
 De Cunjah man, de Cunjah man, 15
 O chillen run, de Cunjah man!

Miss Jane, huh dribe him f'um huh do',
An' now huh hens woan' lay no mo';
De Jussey cow huh done fall sick,
Hit all done by de cunjah trick. 20
Him put ur root un' 'Lijah's baid,
An' now de man he sho' am daid—
 De Cunjah man, de Cunjah man,
 O chillen run, de Cunjah man!

Me see him stan' de yudder night 25
Right een de road een white moon-light;
Him toss him arms, him whirl him 'roun',
Him stomp him foot urpon de groun';
De snaiks come crawlin', one by one,

Me hyuh um hiss, me break an' run—   30
De Cunjah man, de Cunjah man,
O chillen run, de Cunjah man!

Note

The subject is the conjurer or witch doctor who practices magical healing or casts harmful spells.

Mobile-Buck

O, come erlong, come erlong,
    Wut's de use er hol'in back;
O, hit it strong, er hit it strong,
    Mek de ol' flo' ben' an' crack.
O, hoop tee doo, uh, hoop tee doo!　　　　　5
Dat's de way ter knock it froo.
        Right erlong, right erlong,
        Slide de lef' foot right erlong.
        Hoop tee doo, O, hoop tee doo,
        See, my lub, I dawnce ter you.　　　10
        Ho, boy! Ho, boy!
        Well done, meh lady!

O, slide erlong, slide erlong—
    Fas'ah wid dat pattin', Sam!
Dar's music in dis lef' heel's song,　　　　15
    Mis'ah right foot, doan' you sham!
O, hoop tee doo, oh, hoop tee doo!
Straight erlong I dawnce ter you.
        Slide erlong, slide erlong,
        Mek dat right foot hit it strong.　　　20
        Hoop tee do, O, hoop tee doo,
        See, my lub, I dawnce ter you.
        Ho, boy! Ho, boy!
        Well done, meh lady!

Note

Author's footnote: "The above is an attempt to catch the shuffling, jerky rhythm of the famous negro dance, the Mobile-Buck. The author has watched by the hour the negro roustabouts of Ohio and Mississippi river steamboats 'buck' against each other, to use their own expression. One roustabout called on by the crew steps out and begins the shuffle. Suddenly he makes a tremendous slide forward on one foot, like the swift stroke of a skater, while with the other foot he beats a perfect tattoo. Each dancer in succession tries to outdo his predecessor, while all are cheered on by the comments and laughter of their rude but picturesque audience."

Song of the Corn

O, hits time fur de plantin' ur de co'n;
   De groun' am wa'm, de furrers made—
    ("Caw! caw!" de black crow larf,)
   Put ur han'le in yo' ol' hoe blade—
    ("Caw! caw!" de black crow larf)   5
O, hits time fur de plantin' ur de co'n.

O, hits time fur de plantin' ur de co'n,
   De chipmunk sot on top ur clod—
    ("Cheat! cheat!" de rahskil say)
   He flirt his tail an' wink an' nod—   10
    ("Cheat! cheat!" de rahskil say,)
O, hits time fur de plantin' ur de co'n.

O, hits time fur de hoein' ur de co'n,
   De co'n am up an' full ur grass—
    (Hot, hot, de sun hit shine,)   15
   Hit beat de wu'l' how weeds grow fas'—
    (Hot, hot, de sun hit shine,)
O, hits time fur de hoein' ur de co'n.

O, hits time fur de hoein' ur de co'n,
   Hit stan'in' knee-high in de row—   20
    (Hot, hot, de sun hit shine,)
   One mo' time an' we'll let hit go—
    (Hot, hot, de sun hit shine,)
O, hits time fur de hoein' ur de co'n.

O, hits time fur de cuttin' ur de co'n,   25
   De blades am dry, de milk am ha'd—.
    (Hack, hack, de co'n knives say,)
   De hawgs am killed an' ren'nered la'd—.
    (Hack, hack, de co'n knives say,)
O, hits time fur de cuttin' ur de co'n.   30

O, hits time fur de cuttin' ur de co'n,
    Dars w'ite fros' in de still night a'r—
    (Hack, hack, de co'n knives say,)
    Come urlong, Sam, le's grin' ur pa'r—
    (Hack, hack, de co'n knives say,)   35
O, hits time fur de cuttin' ur de co'n.

O, hits time fur de huskin' ur de co'n,
    De boys an' gyurls am all come out—
    (Rip, rip, de brown pegs go,)
    You hyuh 'em sing an' larf an' shout—   40
    (Rip, rip, de brown pegs go,)
O, hits time fur de huskin' ur de co'n.

O, hits time fur de huskin' ur de co'n,
    Dar's Reuben's side am a'mos' froo—
    (Rip, rip, de brown pegs go,)   45
    Hurry up, Sam, deys leabin' you—
    (Rip, rip, de brown pegs go,)
O, hits time fur de huskin' ur de co'n.

O, hits time fur de grin'in' ur de co'n,
    Run 'long, honey, an' git yo' sack—   50
    ("Clack, clack," de mill wheel say,)
    An' put hit on ol' Betsy's back—
    ("Clack, clack," de mill wheel say,)
O, hits time fur de grin'in' ur de co'n.

O, hits time fur de grin'in' ur de co'n,   55
    Des ride five mile ur roun' de hill—
    ("Clack, clack," de mill wheel say,)
    Den dump yo' load at Thompson's mill—
    ("Clack, clack," de mill wheel say,)
O, hits time fur de grin'in' ur de co'n.   60

O, hits time fur de eatin' ur de co'n,
    Mammy, bake us ur co'n pone brown—
    ("Good, good," de chillen cry,)

Draw up yo' chyuh an des sot down—
    ("Good, good," de chillen cry,)   65
O, hits time fur de eatin' ur de co'n.

O, hits time fur de eatin' ur de co'n,
    Wid ham an' aigs an' coffee strong—
    ("Good, good," de chillen cry,)
    Dat big co'n pone hit woan' las' long—   70
    ("Good, good," de chillen cry,)
O, hits time fur de eatin' ur de co'n.

When Ol' Sis' Judy Pray

When ol' Sis' Judy pray,
De teahs come stealin' down my cheek,
De voice ur God widin me speak';
I see myse'f so po' an' weak,
Down on my knees de cross I seek,   5
When ol' Sis' Judy pray.

When ol' Sis' Judy pray,
De thun'ers ur Mount Sin-a-i
Comes rushin' down f'um up on high—
De Debbil tu'n his back an' fly   10
While sinnahs loud fur pa'don cry,
When ol' Sis' Judy pray.

When ol' Sis' Judy pray,
Ha'd sinnahs trimble in dey seat
Ter hyuh huh voice in sorrow 'peat: 15
(While all de chu'ch des sob an' weep)
"O Shepa'd, dese, dy po' los' sheep!"
When ol' Sis' Judy pray.

When ol' Sis' Judy pray,
De whole house hit des rock an' moan   20
Ter see huh teahs an' hyuh huh groan;
Dar's somepin' in Sis' Judy's tones
Dat melt all ha'ts dough med ur stones,
When ol' Sis' Judy pray.

When ol' Sis' Judy pray,   25
Salvation's light comes pourin' down—
Hit fill de chu'ch an' all de town—
Why, angels' robes go rustlin' 'roun',
An' hebben on de Yurf am foun',
When ol' Sis' Judy pray.   30

When ol' Sis' Judy pray,
My soul go sweepin' up on wings,
An' loud de chu'ch wid "Glory!" rings,
An' wide de gates ur Jahsper swings
Twel you hyuh ha'ps wid golding strings,   35
When ol' Sis' Judy pray.

When ol' Sis Judy die —
Froo triberlations justerfied,
I know de gates will des fly wide
An' wid King Jesus by huh side,   40
Straight froo dem gold-paved streets she'll ride,
When ol' Sis' Judy die!

Mors et Vita

Into the soil a seed is sown,
Out of the soul a song is wrung,
Out of the shell a pearl is gone,
Out of the cage a bird is flown,
      Out of the body, a soul!   5

Unto a tree the seed is grown,
Wide in the world the song is sung,
The pearl in a necklace gleams more fair,
The bird is flown to a sweeter air,
And Death is half and Life is half,   10
      And the two make up the whole!

Note
The Latin title means death and life.

JOSEPH SEAMON COTTER, SR.

Joseph Seamon Cotter, Sr. (1861–1949) began his formal schooling at age twenty-two, but he achieved prominence as an educator; an advocate of race progress, working with social, educational, and literary organizations; a writer of verse and prose for periodicals; and as author of nine books of poetry, plays, and fiction (1895–1947). Born in Bardstown, Kentucky, to Martha Vaughn and Michael J. Cotter, Joseph worked as a laborer from the age of eight until he enrolled in a Louisville night school in 1883. Soon he began to teach and continued his part-time evening education until 1892, when he earned certificates for grammar school teacher and principal. For more than fifty years, Cotter was an educator in several Louisville schools, an active member of organizations, and a prolific writer. He married Maria F. Cox in 1891; their eldest son, Joseph Jr., was a promising poet (*The Band of Gideon*, 1918) who died at twenty-three. Cotter died in his Louisville home and was buried in Greenwood Cemetery.

In both dialect and standard English verse, Cotter urges social and moral reform, sectional reconciliation, and brotherhood. He satirizes the foibles and frailties of blacks but also praises their strengths and achievements; he philosophically examines God's ways and the mysteries of human nature; he comments on historical events and pays tribute to notables from Frederick Douglass to W. E. B. DuBois as well as to many literary idols. In five decades of writing poetry, Cotter's interests range from industrial education to the atom bomb, and his verse forms and techniques are as various as his subjects. His major concern is advancement of the race, to be gained by a mixture of pride, hard work, education, and optimism. The quality of his poetry is uneven, ranging from trite, dully didactic, or sentimental verses to others that are delightfully clever, musical, ingenious in language and thought, and freshened by a personal point of view.

A Rhyming (Louisville, Ky.: New South Publishing, 1895); *Links of Friendship* (Louisville, Ky.: Bradley & Gilbert, 1898); *A White Song and a Black One* (Louisville, Ky.: Bradley & Gilbert, 1909).

Frederick Douglass

O eloquent and caustic sage
Thy long and rugged pilgrimage
   To glory's shrine has ended;
And thou hast passed the inner door,
And proved thy fitness o'er and o'er,   5
   And to the dome ascended.

In speaking of thy noble life
One needs must think upon the strife
   That long and sternly faced it;
But since those times have flitted by,   10
Just let the useless relic die
   With passions that embraced it.

There is no evil known to man
But what, if wise enough, he can
   Grow stronger in the bearing;   15
And so the ills we often scorn
May be of heavenly wisdom born
   To aid our onward faring.

Howe'er this be, just fame has set
Her jewels in thy coronet   20
   So firmly that the ages
To come will ever honor thee
And place thy name in company
   With patriots and sages.

Now thou art gone; the little men   25
Of fluent tongue and trashy pen
   Will strive to imitate thee;

And when they find they haven't sense
Enough to make a fair pretense,
   They'll turn and underrate thee.   30
(1898)

Note

See Ray's "In Memoriam (*Frederick Douglass*)" and Dunbar's "Douglass."

Answer to Dunbar's "After a Visit"

[The following is an answer to a poem written
by Paul L. Dunbar after his visit to Kentucky.]

So, you be'n to ole Kentucky,
  An' you want to go ag'in?
Well, Kentucky'll doff her kerchief
  An' politely ask you in.
An' she'll loosen from her girdle   5
  What perhaps you didn't see —
Keys that fit the other cupboards
  Of her hospitality.

Not that she's inclined to hold back
  With the good, and give the worst;   10
But, you know, in all fair dealin',
  What is first must be the first.
So, when she takes key the second
  An' gives it a twist er two
(Maybe I ought not to say it)   15
  It'll most nigh startle you.

An' then keys the third and fourth, sir,
  (Not to speak of all the rest)
Wouldn't stop at crackin' buttons,
  They'd jest smash that Sunday vest.   20
And your happiness would find, sir,
  A momentum then and there
That would carry it a-sweepin'
  Through the stronghold of despair.

Now, the grippin' o' the hand, sir,   25
  An' the welcome that you say
Was so firm an' true an' all that
  Has a kind o' curious way.
At the first it's sorter slow like,
  Till it forms a league with you,   30

Then it makes a kind o' circuit
   That jest thrills you thro' an' thro'.

But it may be I had better
   Not discuss this aftermath
Fur it might stir up your feelings   35
   To the righteous point of wrath
As you brood o'er what you lost, sir,
   By not stayin' with us longer.
Ah, well, come to see us often,
   Ole Kentucky'll make you stronger.   40

So, you be'n to ole Kentucky,
   An' you want to go ag'in?
Well, Kentucky's standin' waitin'
   Jest to take you wholly in,
An' she'll loosen her vast girdle   45
   So that you can fully see
All the roots, fruits, leaves, an' branches
   Of her hospitality.

                            (1898)

On Hearing James W. Riley Read

[From a Kentucky standpoint.]

To tell the truth, each piece he read
Set up a jingle in my head
That bumped and thumped and roared about,
Then on a sudden just crept out,
Gently and slowly at the start,   5
Then made a bee-line for my heart.

And more than once I thought maybe
His charming Hoosier poetry
Would be a guide to lead me over
To the Elysian fields of clover.   10

To find fault with his worst or best
Would be like finding fault with rest
After a fellow has been in
The dirt and dust up to his chin,
And bathed and stretched beneath the trees   15
Whose branches fairly hug the breeze.

In these hackneyed and sordid days,
When censure thorns the bud of praise
And many think they ought not to
Give genius half its honest due,   20
And never fail to bombard it
With silly quips and shallow wit,
I like to just go hunt it up
And sup and sip and sip and sup;
And then I like to speak my praise   25
In honest thought and simple phrase,

And let the giver know that I
Delight in him and tell him why,

And not go wavering to and fro
But just come out and tell him so.   30
(1898)

Notes

James Whitcomb Riley (1849–1916) wrote popular sentimental poetry of rustic life in his native Indiana (*Hoosier,* 8) dialect (see Dunbar's "Deacon Jones' Grievance"). 10. *Elysian fields:* Elysium, in classical mythology, the blissful abode of the blessed after death.

William Lloyd Garrison

His country seared its conscience through its gain,
   And had not wisdom to behold the loss.
It held God partner in the hellish stain,
   And saw Christ dying on a racial cross.

What unto it the shackled fellowman,   5
   Whose plea was mockery, and whose groans were mirth?
Its boasted creed was: "He should rule who can
   Make prey of highest heaven and dupe of earth."

From out this mass of century-tutored wrong
   A man stood God-like and his voice rang true.   10
His soul was sentry to the dallying throng,
   His thought was watchword to the gallant few.

He saw not as his fellow beings saw;
   He would not misname greed expediency.
He found no color in the nation's law,   15
   And scorned to meet it in its liberty.

He saw his duty in his neighbor's cause,
   And died that he might rise up strong and free—
A creature subject to the highest laws
   And master of a God-like destiny.   20

The thunder of a million armed feet,
   Reverberating 'till the land was stirred,
Was but the tension of his great heart-beat,
   The distant echo of his spoken word.

He speaks again: "Such as would miss the rod   25
   That ever chastens insufficiency,

Must purge their lives and make them fit for God,
Must train their liberty and make it free."

(1909)

Note

A radical abolitionist from Massachusetts (1805–79), Garrison founded *The Liberator* and the New England Antislavery Society, both in 1831, and the American Anti-Slavery Society in 1833.

Dr. Booker T. Washington to the National Negro Business League

'Tis strange indeed to hear us plead
  For selling and for buying
When yesterday we said: "Away
  With all good things but dying."

The world's ago, and we're agog   5
  To have our first brief inning;
So let's away through surge and fog
  However slight the winning.

What deeds have sprung from plow and pick!
  What bank-rolls from tomatoes!   10
No dainty crop of rhetoric
  Can match one of potatoes.

Ye orators of point and pith,
  Who force the world to heed you,
What skeletons you'll journey with   15
  Ere it is forced to feed you.

A little gold won't mar our grace,
  A little ease our glory.
This world's a better biding place
  When money clinks its story.   20
                (1909)

Note

Washington (1856?–1915), born a slave in Virginia, became an internationally prominent and influential African-American leader. He founded (and headed) Tuskegee Institute in Alabama in 1883 and the National Negro Business League in 1900, and in his lectures and writings championed industrial education, self-help, and the acquisition of money for race progress (see Fordham's "Atlanta Exposition Ode").

The Don't-Care Negro

Neber min' what's in your cran'um
   So your collar's high an' true.
Neber min' what's in your pocket
   So de blackin's on your shoe.

Neber min' who keeps you comp'ny   5
   So he halfs up what he's tuk.
Neber min' what way you's gwine
   So you's gwine away frum wuk.

Neber min' de race's troubles
   So you profits by dem all.   10
Neber min' your leaders' stumblin'
   So you he'ps to mak' dem fall.

Neber min' what's true tomorrow
   So you libes a dream today.
Neber min' what tax is levied   15
   So it's not on craps or play.

Neber min' how hard you labors
   So you does it to de en'
Dat de judge is boun' to sen' you
   An' your record to de "pen."   20

Neber min' your manhood's risin'
   So you habe a way to stay it.
Neber min' folks' good opinion
   So you habe a way to slay it.

Neber min' man's why an' wharfo'   25
   So de world is big an' roun'.
Neber min' whar next you's gwine to
   So you's six foot under groun'.

                (1909)

Ned's Psalm of Life for the Negro

Dis is Ned dat am er-speakin',
    Wid no wuds dat's cute an' fine.
Dis is Ned dat am er-seekin'
    Light fur dis heah race o' mine.

I don' know as I'se er prophit—   5
    Ef I is, I prophersy—
Smart folks, don' you dar ter scoff it:
    Dis race feelin's gwine ter die.

'Tain't er thing dat has er color—
    I'se gwine lib ter see it ain't.   10
Hit goes 'long wid black an' yeller,
    Kase you's not er wukin' saint.

When you wuks so dat de folks is
    Boun' ter lib by whut you does,
All dey feelin's an' dey jokes is   15
    Fur de man dat once you wuz.

Folks will 'cept you when you takes 'em
    By supplyin' all dey needs;
Dey will paint you when you makes 'em
    Jes' de color o' yo' deeds.   20

Atter while dey will be treatin'
    You de bery bes' dey can,
An' you'll nebber 'gret de meetin'
    Wid yo' brudder feller man.

Yes, dey's feelin' 'twixt de races,   25
    An' hit's gwine ter las' until
We jes' wuks ourselves ter places
    Udder folks has got ter fill.

Dis is Ned dat am er-speakin' —
   Smart folks, don' you dar ter scorn —   30
I'se er-prayin' an' er-seekin'
   Ways ter let dis race be born.

I'se got faith 'nuff in de Marster
   Fur ter know He'll do His part;
Ef we stomps out dire disarster   35
   Wid er wukin' brain an' heart.
                   (1909)

Algernon Charles Swinburne

All earth is a poet,
All nature doth know it,
Each firefly doth show it,
    Each frost work doth rhyme.
Poor man who the fool is,   5
And prone as the pool is,
May yet learn God's rule is:
    All prose is part crime.

The dust that we tread in,
The swirls we are sped in,   10
The throes we are wed in,
    Were dust, dust and dust.
If out of God's treasure
There came not a measure
Of rhythmical pleasure   15
    In sibilant trust.

Thy gift was a yearning
That paradised learning,
And ended in turning
    All seasons to Junes   20
Through death that caresses,
Through hatred that blesses,
And love that distresses,
    And words that are tunes.

A Milton may ghoul us,   25
A Shakespeare may rule us,
A Wordsworth may school us,
    A Tennyson cheer;
But thine is the glory,

Star-sprung from the hoary,   30
Flame-dependent story
    Of the munificent ear.
        (1909)

Note

An English lyric poet (1837–1909), Swinburne's work is marked by repetitive sounds and rhythms and sensual language often imprecise in meaning. Cotter's verse parodies and compliments Swinburne's style in contrast to the more intellectual or didactic measures of the English poets (15–28): John *Milton*, William *Shakespeare*, William *Wordsworth*, and Alfred, Lord *Tennyson*.

The Book's Creed

Reader, listen ere we go,
    I will furnish line and page;
You must bring a soul aglow
    And an eye that scans the age.

I am but a shadow sent,   5
    Telling of a shape that's gone;
I am just an instrument
    All mankind may play upon.

If you would behold the shape,
    You must carve it all alone.   10
I, as shadow, will be crepe
    On your door till you are grown.

All my myriad silent keys
    Are responsive to the touch
That has lived the mysteries   15
    Former masters knew as such.

I am but a skeleton.
    Flesh and blood and soul and speech
Were the property of one—
    Now the property of each.   20

If you see a Godlike eye,
    Give it not an ancient name.
Would you stamp a wanton lie
    On the helmet of your fame?

If you hear a charming tongue,   25
    Do not think it from the dead.
This old world proclaims it young
    Through your heart and through your head.

If I am a ghastly find,
 You are poor beyond compare—   30
You of empty heart and mind,
 Dweller in a world of air.

You are dead to all the Then,
 You are dead to all the Now,
If you hold that former men   35
 Wore the garland for your brow.

Time and tide were theirs to brave,
 Time and tide are yours to stem.
Bow not o'er their open grave
 Till you drop your diadem.   40

Honor all who strove and wrought,
 Even to their tears and groans;
But slay not your honest thought
 Through your reverence for their bones.

Reader, listen ere we part,   45
 Search to know and know to read;
And, by owning brain and heart,
 You will live this simple creed.
       (1909)

GEORGE CLINTON ROWE

George Clinton Rowe (1853–1903), a minister, editor, and author, was born in Litchfield, Connecticut, to Adeline S. (Johnson) and Solomon D. Rowe. He attended school, served an apprenticeship on a newspaper, and studied theology privately in Litchfield until 1876. For four years in Hampton, Virginia, Rowe worked on three black periodicals and began his missionary activities. He was ordained by the Georgia [Congregational] Association in 1881; thereafter, Rowe pastored, ran church schools, and worked for race advancement as an officer of religious and educational organizations in Georgia and South Carolina until his death. During these years, he edited and published the *Charleston Enquirer* (1893–96) and won honors for his poetry. Rowe married Miranda Jackson in 1874 and had nine children. He died of heart disease in Charleston.

All but a handful of Rowe's seventy-one "thoughts in verse" are versified sermons that preach virtuous living, labor, and love of God as the road to racial progress. The other selections in his first volume praise women of his family, eulogize the dead, or recall his earlier life. Rowe's prosaic, repetitive verses lack fervor and esthetic merit. The fifteen tributes to black heroes and leaders in Rowe's second volume are technically smoother and more varied, but they remain humdrum verses; the tributes, however, do fulfill Rowe's stated goal of elevating the race by creating race pride in the "noble deeds, inspiring sayings, and . . . true manhood and womanhood" of African Americans.

Thoughts in Verse (Charleston, S.C.: Kahrs, Stolze & Welch, 1887); *Our Heroes: Patriotic Poems on Men, Women and Sayings of the Negro Race* (Charleston, S.C.: Walker, Evans & Cogswell, 1890).

God Speed

Go forth my little volume,
  And do thy work of love;
Cheer up the tired and lonesome,
  And raise their thoughts above.
Thy lessons of humility,   5
  With faith and patience teach;
Where shadows fall the darkest,
  May thy rays of brightness reach.

Go forth to teach salvation,
  A saviour's dying grace;   10
Go forth to all the nation
  And cheer our struggling race.
May blessings rest upon thee,
  And all thy course be bright.
Go forth in faith and purity,   15
  And carry truth and light.

(1887)

The Reason Why

It is the eve of battle;
  The soldiers are in line;
The roll of drum and bugle's blast
  Marshal that army fine.

The hour is fraught with mystery—   5
  A hush pervades that throng,
And each one thinks of home and friends,
  And says at heart, "How long?"

The colonel rides before his men,
  His thoughtful brow is bare;   10
He calls the color-sergeant,
  And tenders to his care

The nation's pride, the dear old flag—
  The loved *red, white and blue,*
And says, with earnest tones and grave: 15
  "I intrust *this* now to you.

"Yes, color-bearer, take in charge
  Your country's flag to-day,
And to the conflict bear it—
  The thickest of the fray.   20

"Bear it with lofty courage,
  And to it faithful be;
This flag has inspired thousands,
  And led to victory.

"Take it and never leave it,   25
  'Tis a solemn charge to thee;
Bring back to *me* this banner,
  This ensign of the free!"

"Colonel," the color-sergeant said,
    Holding the flag on high;   30
"I'll bring it back or else report
    To *God* the reason why!"

Away to the front he bears it,
    Cheered on by comrades brave,
Anxious to liberate his race,   35
    Bring freedom to the slave.

They charge upon Port Hudson,
    Where, sheltered by a wall,
The foemen cut them down like grass.
    They bravely charge—but fall.   40

Yes, on that field, where thousands
    Unheeding the tumult lie,
He left the flag, reporting
    To *God* the reason why.

Another bears that flag along,   45
    Holding it proud and high;
But the sergeant has reported
    To *God* the reason why.

Oh, Christian soldier, going forth
    To battle for the Lord,   50
Be filled with manly courage,
    And proudly bear God's word.

It is the standard of your King,
    Who rules the earth and sky;
You must win, through it, the vict'ry   55
    Or tell *Christ* the reason why.

The war will soon be ended:
    In the dust you soon will lie;

Go forth and conquer, or report
To *God* the reason why.   60
(March 1885; 1887)

Note

Author's headnote: "In the December, 1884, number of the AMERICAN MIS-
SIONARY, an article published contained the following incident: 'The First Louisiana Regiment of colored soldiers, recruited in New Orleans, was about to take
its departure for the front. The Colonel, who for some reason could not accompany
his men, presented the regimental flags to the color-sergeant. After a brief speech,
full of patriotic feeling, he concluded with these words: 'Color-guard, protect,
defend, die for, but do not surrender these flags.' The sergeant, upon receiving
them, made this simple but noble response: 'Colonel, I will bring back these
colors to you in honor or report to God the reason why.' And when, a few days
afterward, during an assault on Port Hudson [Louisiana, 27 May 1863], he fell
defending the flag, and his dying blood crimsoned its fold, another took his place
and saved it from falling into the hands of the enemy. The brave standard-bearer
kept his word, and in failing to return the colors to the hands that had committed
them to his care, he 'reported to God the reason why.' "

We Are Rising

Among the sayings of our race,
　Suggestive and surprising,
That fills a most exalted place,
　Is, *"Tell them we are rising."*

The question came from Doctor Roy —　　　5
　What to the North your greeting?
The answer from a negro boy —
　"Tell them that we are rising!"

Within Atlanta's classic halls,
　This youth, self-sacrificing,　　　10
Wrote high his name upon her walls,
　His motto: "We are rising!"

Out in the world he makes his mark,
　Danger and fear despising,
E'er soaring upward like the lark,　　　15
　My Brethren: "We are rising!"

He meets the foe with voice and pen,
　With eloquence surprising!
Give us a chance, for we are men!
　Most surely we are rising!　　　20

Rising to take our place beside
　The noble, the aspiring;
With energy and conscious pride,
　To the best things, we're rising!

Within the class-room is his place,　　　25
　Greek, Latin, criticising,
To raise the youthful of his race,
　And show the world we're rising!

Go forth, my friend, upon your way,
   Each obstacle despising,   30
Prove by your efforts every day,
   To all that we are rising!

In farming, trade and literature,
   A people enterprising!
Our churches, schools, and home life pure,   35
   Tell to the world WE'RE RISING!
                          (1890)

Note

Author's footnote: "About a score of years since, Dr. Jos. Roy, of the American Missionary Association, on visiting one of their schools in Georgia, asked the children: 'What message shall I take from you to the people of the North?' An intelligent boy answered promptly: 'Tell them that we are rising!' That boy was Richard Wright, of Augusta, Ga., who has since graduated from Atlanta University, ably filled the editorial chair, and is now Principal of the High School of Augusta, Ga. Indeed, he is 'rising!' "

Mrs. Frances Ellen Harper

Faithful Frances Ellen Harper!
   Truly noble are thy deeds!
Using pen and voice with vigor,
   Thou hast scattered precious seeds!

Seeds of truth, of holy living,   5
   Seeds of wisdom, temperance;
Waking virtuous aspirations;
   Building up a sure defence,

Round our homes, our wives and mothers;
   Teaching lessons of great worth;   10
Leading on our sons and daughters,
   In the path of virtue—truth!

Lecturing in many a city,
   With a tongue of living fire!
Pungent, eloquent and witty,   15
   Thou dost reason and inspire!

With thy pen, in happy measure,
   Thou hast sung the poet's song;
Thou hast given us many a treasure—
   Rich and beautiful and strong!   20

We admire thy noble record,
   From thy spirit impulse take!
Earnestly contending upward,
   Every day real progress make.

Long live Frances Ellen Harper!   25
   Voice and pen instruction give!
Live thy earnest spirit ever!
   May thy work forever live!

When complete thy earthly missions
   And from toil thou art at rest: 30
Still, may coming generations
   Testify, and call thee blest!

                (1890)

from *Toussaint L'Overture*

HIS ANCESTRY

A tribe surnamed the Arradas,
Sojourned for years, on Africa's
      Southwestern coast.
Men of physique and strength of mind,
Excelling others of their kind   5
      Among a host.

Gaou-Gwinou, the chieftain's heir,
Hunting the wild beast in his lair,
      With ruthless hand,
Was seized, and hurried to the hold   10
Of a black ship, thence to be sold
      By slaver band.

For Hayti's Isle, the ship was bound,
Which years before the Spaniards found—
      Luxuriant, fair.   15
The land was rich in fruit and flower,
Mountains and valleys—Nature's dower!
      Oh! beauty rare!

. . . .

Gaou-Gwinou was purchased here
By a French prince, and many a year   20
      He spent—a slave—
Upon the Breda property;
And there he reared a family
      And made his grave.

HIS BOYHOOD

His eldest son, Arradas' heir,   25
Toussaint L'Overture, who there
      Was given birth,

In seventeen hundred forty-three,
Was destined by the gods to be
    A man of worth.   30

A slender boy, he grew apace;
A Prince-apparent of his race!
    Most eagerly
He sat him down at Learning's feast,
His teacher, pious Pierre Baptiste   35
    Exultingly

Taught him to read and write and pray,
Some Latin, French, Geometry;
    To meditate,
Upon the precious word of God,   40
His name to magnify, and laud
    His high estate.

. . . .

HIS MANHOOD

Thus, up to manhood he arose,
A man of wisdom, strength, repose,
    Integrity;   45
Beloved by all both far and near,
Respected for his character
    And industry.

Then he was married to Suzan,
A help-meet true for such a man;   50
    For many years
The loved companion of his life,
Sharing his honors, toils and strife,
    His hopes and fears.

. . . .

He saw with pain the cruel lot   55
Of Brethren dear, and ne'er forgot
    To humbly pray,

That He, who calms the ocean's wave,
Would bring deliverance to the slave,
    And haste the day.   60

In reading, 'neath his gaze there fell
Prophetic words, which long and well,
    And thoughtfully,
He pondered, for in them appear
Visions of a deliverer   65
    From slavery.

"Where is the man whom Nature owes
To her vexed children — the negroes?
    He will appear!
With standard raised for liberty,   70
Impetuous as a stormy sea,
    And conquer here."

. . . .

HIS PRIME

The years pass on, and overhead,
Portentious clouds of fear and dread,
    Obscure the sky!   75
No ray of hope for bondmen sad,
"Whom gods destroy they first make mad!"
    Then seize their prey.

In seventeen hundred ninety-one,
Mid-August at the set of sun,   80
    There suddenly
Appeared upon the evening sky
A ruddy glow; we hear the cry —
    For liberty!

The horror of those days, no pen   85
Can tell, of children, women, men,
    Hurried to death!
The masters tortured, shot and burned;

The slaves their hideous crimes returned;
The very breath   90

Of realms infernal filled the air!
Nor cry, nor groan, nor pleading prayer,
Could stay the hand
Of violence, 'twas deaths mælstrom!
It seemed indeed the day of doom   95
Throughout the land!

From peaceful toil to take his place,
As the deliverer of his race
Toussaint came forth.
This is the man of prophecy,   100
Who, for a noble destiny
Was given birth!

A leader-born, in manhood's prime,
Called to command in God's own time,
When there was need;   105
Large-hearted, pure, magnanimous,
His policy was glorious,
With noble deed!

. . . .

Yes, 'twas Toussaint L'Overture,
Who boldly *opened* freedom's door   110
To Afric's son,
Who met the men of Britain, Spain,
In war-array, on hill and plain,
And nobly won!

. . . .

New laws are made, and order reigns;   115
No more the clank of servile chains;
But far and near,
With one accord—"Our Governor,

Shall be Toussaint L'Overture!"
    From all we hear. 120

This man is chosen for his life,
To govern Hayti, freed from strife,
    And takes his place,
Among the rulers of the earth.
Destined to rule e'en from his birth! 125
    Again we trace!

. . . .

In eighteen one, great Bonaparte,
Proud conqueror with a treacherous heart,
    Sent forth the word;
"That slavery in the Colonies, 130
And in the French Dependencies,
    Shall be restored!"

Now consternation everywhere,
And maledictions fill the air.
    "For *liberty!* 135
We'll fight until the latest breath!
We'll fight for freedom unto death
    Or victory!"

. . . .

'Twas all in vain! The Frenchmen found
On St. Domingo's battle-ground, 140
    And Hayti's field,
A foe they could not overcome;
They fought for freedom and for home!
    They would not yield!

Le Clerc in disappointment sore; 145
His troops discouraged, more and more,
    Issues decree:
"Each one who will refuse to fight,

Shall have all privilege and right!
      He shall be free!"   150

Deceived; his [Toussaint's] brother Paul withdraws;
Bellair, and gallant Maurepas
      Submit to France!
But brave Toussaint his *aid-de-camps*
Valiant Christoph and Dessalaines   155
      With sword advance!

A solemn message is received:
The wise Toussaint is not deceived,
      But fear awakes!
To pacify his followers,   160
With chief of Frenchmen he confers,
      And treaty makes.

"Submit, and truly, I declare,
Shall rights and freedom everywhere
      Respected be!   165
In rule my colleague thou shalt be;
Full rank, and general amnesty,
      And lenity."

"I might in mountains still remain,
And harass thee on hill and plain   170
      With brigand's shield;
But constant bloodshed I disdain!
I fought our freedom to maintain!
      To terms I yield!"

. . . .

A letter couched in language fair,   175
Invites our hero to repair
      To Brunet's home:
"Your welfare and the colony,
My highest pleasure e'er shall be;
      Believe me, come!"   180

Without a thought of treachery;
Trusting in his sincerity,
    Nor doubt, nor fear;
For love of country he goes forth,
To treachery's hand, this man of worth,   185
    From freedom dear!

Received with honour and respect,
Naught but good-will could he detect—
    A noble part!
His host examined heartily   190
The interests of the colony,
    With map and chart.

'Tis evening's hour, when suddenly
Armed men appear, and forcibly,
    Before he wist,   195
They seize the veteran with the word:
"Surrender! Death at point of sword
    If you resist!"

He rose to meet them in his might!
'Tis useless—an unequal fight!   200
    No help is near.
Such are Injustice's cruel laws!
"Heaven will avenge my righteous cause!
    My God will hear!"

'Tis midnight. With his wife and child,   205
Breast raging with a tempest wild,
    A storm of grief;
Chained—manacled—the guards beside—
Toussaint is hurried o'er the tide,
    Beyond relief!   210

. . . .

Without a charge or just complaint,
To Castle Joux they bear Toussaint
    A captive lone,

Upon the verge of Switzerland,
On Jura's height the castles stand   215
On summit stone!

. . . .

Reduced by peril, hunger, cold,
By longings that can ne'er be told;
With failing breath;
He bowed beneath the heavy rod,   220
With perfect trust and faith in God,
And slept in death!

A warrior true of great renown,
A *hero, martyr,* him we crown!
He led the van!   225
His heaven-born soul to God has flown!
This world of ours has never known
A nobler man!

(1890)

Notes

In seventy stanzas Rowe surveys the Haitian leader's life and death. Toussaint's revolution won freedom for the slaves, but in 1801 Napoleon's armies invaded Haiti to restore slavery; Toussaint was captured and died in a Swiss prison. However, Haitian patriots (and yellow fever) finally defeated the French armies. 145. *LeClerc:* Victor Emanuel LeClerc, Napoleon's brother-in-law, led the French forces. 152. *Bellair. . . . Maurepas:* aides to Toussaint. 155. *Christophe and Dessalaines:* aides to Toussaint. Jean-Jaques Dessalaines led the troops that defeated Napoleon at Le Cap (1803); he then ruled Haiti as Emperor Jacques I (1804–6) until he was assassinated. Subsequently, Henri Cristophe ruled as Henri I. 177. *Brunet:* French general, aide to LeClerc. Author's note: "L'Overture means—The Opening." Author's footnote: "Toussaint died of starvation and exposure to cold in a cell, in Castle Joux, near the border of Switzerland, in 1803, at the age of 60 years. He was confined there eight months, and France refused to give him a trial or to answer his communications. Madame Toussaint sank under the weight of her great afflictions. Her health became very feeble, and at times her mind wandered.

When the power of Bonaparte was overthrown, and a new Government was introduced into France, a pension was granted for her support, and her two sons were released from prison. She died in their arms in 1816, thirteen years after the death of our hero."

See Reason's "Freedom" (58) and Vashon's "Vincent Ogé."

JOSEPHINE DELPHINE HENDERSON HEARD

Josephine Delphine Henderson Heard (1861–1921) was born in Salisbury, North Carolina, of slave parents, Annie M. (Henderson) and Lafayette Heard. Educated in Charlotte, at Scotia Seminary in Concord, N.C., and Bethany Institute in New York, she taught school in South Carolina and Tennessee until her marriage to the Reverend William Henry Heard in 1882. With Heard, a prominent A.M.E. bishop, she lived and traveled throughout the United States, Europe, and Liberia, where Heard served as minister from 1909 to 1917.

Heard's favorite poetic subjects are love, lost and found, and God, here and in eternity. She also writes compliments to literary figures and to African-American clergy and leaders; the latter group, with two other poems, are Heard's only acknowledgment of her race. With rare exceptions, her seventy-eight verses do not rise above the ordinary in topic and execution; emotions are limited to sentimentality and religious piety, and the language is insipid.

Morning Glories (Philadelphia: Author, 1890, 2d ed. 1901).

To Whittier

In childhood's sunny day my heart was taught to love
Thy name, all other poet's names above,
And when to womanhood at last I came,
Behold the spark was fanned into a flame,
Nor did I dare presume that I should live,   5
And to the honored, white-haired poet give
My sentiment in rude constructed rhyme;
O, wondrous change wrought by the hand of time!

When he who came the slaves among to dwell,
From frigid Idaho (we loved him well,)   10
Athirst for knowledge I stood at his side,
With quickening thought and eyes astonished, wide.
He nightly read, and held me on his knee,
From Whittier's "Snowbound" filling me with glee.
The seed sown by his hand in infant heart,   15
Has lived and grown, and cannot now depart.

Now to the sunset thou hast set thy face,
And silvery crown thy head doth grace;
The mind of fertile thought doth not decline
Preserved yet from the ravages of time   20
Since I can never hope my first desire,
To shake thy hand, which would my soul inspire,
Now e're yet "the cord is loosed or pitcher broken,"
Grant me with thine own hand this little token:
Ere yet that hand by feebleness grows lame,   25
With condescension write for me thy name.

Note

See Holly's "A Wreath of Holly" (38). Whittier's response to Heard's request
for his "name" or autograph appears in her book's Appendix of congratulatory
letters. Whittier's finest poem, *Snow-bound: A Winter Idyl* (1866), recalls family
life in New England.

"They Are Coming?"

They are coming, coming slowly —
They are coming, surely, surely —
In each avenue you hear the steady tread.
From the depths of foul oppression,
Comes a swarthy-hued procession,   5
And victory perches on their banners' head.

They are coming, coming slowly —
They are coming; yes, the lowly,
No longer writhing in their servile bands.
From the rice fields and plantation   10
Comes a factor of the nation,
And threatening, like Banquo's ghost, it stands.

They are coming, coming proudly —
They are crying, crying loudly:
O, for justice from the rulers of the land!   15
And that justice will be given,
For the mighty God of heaven
Holds the balances of power in his hand.

Prayers have risen, risen, risen,
From the cotton fields and prison;   20
Though the overseer stood with lash in hand,
Groaned the overburdened heart;
Not a tear-drop dared to start —
But the Slaves' petition reach'd the glory-land.

They are coming, they are coming,   25
From away in tangled swamp,
Where the slimy reptile hid its poisonous head;
Through the long night and the day,
They have heard the bloodhounds' bey,
While the morass furnished them an humble bed.   30

They are coming, rising, rising,
And their progress is surprising,
By their brawny muscles earning daily bread;
Though their wages be a pittance,
Still each week a small remittance,   35
Builds a shelter for the weary toiling head.

They are coming, they are coming —
Listen! You will hear the humming
Of the thousands that are falling into line:
There are Doctors, Lawyers, Preachers;   40
There are Sculptors, Poets, Teachers —
Men and women, who with honor yet shall shine.

They are coming, coming boldly,
Though the Nation greets them coldly;
They are coming from the hillside and the plain.   45
With their scars they tell the story
Of the canebrakes wet and gory,
Where their brothers' bones lie bleaching with the slain.

They are coming, coming singing,
Their Thanksgiving hymn is ringing.   50
For the clouds are slowly breaking now away,
And there comes a brighter dawning —
It is liberty's fair morning,
They are coming surely, coming, clear the way.

Yes, they come, their stepping's steady,   55
And their power is felt already —
God has heard the lowly cry of the oppressed:
And beneath his mighty frown,
Every wrong shall crumble down,
When the *right* shall triumph and the world be blest! 60

Note

12. *Banquo's ghost:* In Shakespeare's *Macbeth,* the spirit of the murdered thane
Banquo terrorizes his murderer Macbeth. 29. bay.

An Epitaph

When I am gone,
Above me raise no lofty stone
Perfect in human handicraft,
No upward pointing gleaming shaft.
Say this of me, and I be content,   5
That in the Master's work my life was spent;
Say not that I was either great or good,
But Mary-like, "She hath done what she could."

Note

8. *Mary-like:* Mary of Bethany sat quietly, listening to and worshipping Jesus, while her sister Martha busily occupied herself with material things. Jesus defended the prayerful one, saying: "Mary hath chosen that good part which shall not be taken away from her" (Luke 10:38–42).

DANIEL WEBSTER DAVIS

Daniel Webster Davis (1862–1913) was honored by having three schools in Virginia named for him. For thirty-three years, he was an educator, Baptist minister, popular orator, historian and poet, and a leader of Richmond's African-American community. His parents, Charlotte Ann (Christian) and John Davis, were slaves in Caroline County, Virginia, where Davis was born. He moved to Richmond after the Civil War, graduated from Richmond High and Normal School in 1878, and two years later began a long teaching career in Virginia, West Virginia, and the Carolinas. Davis married Elizabeth Eloise Smith in 1893—they had three children—while attending Lynchburg Baptist Seminary. After ordination in 1896, he served as pastor of the Second Baptist Church in South Richmond until his death. Davis's erudite lectures and flamboyant platform style gained him wide popularity as a lecturer to church, college, and civic groups throughout the United States and Canada. In Richmond, Davis worked for racial betterment with many economic, social, and literary organizations. At his funeral, the *Richmond Planet* reported that prominent citizens of both races, teachers and students, ministers from many cities, and nine civic organizations mourned the loss to Richmond of "one of the most prominent and influential colored men the South had ever produced."

Like his prose and lectures, Davis's poetry aims to instruct and entertain; he amplifies the race's achievements, teaches Gospel idealism and self-help, and offers a humorous, nostalgic view of antebellum plantation life. His poems in standard English, about one-third of his output, are generally sentimental or moralistic in tone, and the language is commonplace or stiffly classical; he versifies a wide range of subjects in a variety of metrical forms. Davis's dialect poems portray church-going, holiday celebrations, good eating, superstitions, and recreations of the old days "way down South." He wrote many of these plantation portraits as exempla of evil habits bequeathed to the race by slavery and often inserted them into his lectures demanding racial justice and equal opportunities. Davis's best dialect verses happily blend lilting melodies, mocking humor, and colorful details.

Idle Moments (Baltimore, Md.: Educator of Morgan College, 1895); *'Weh Down Souf* (Cleveland, Ohio: Helman-Taylor Co., 1897).

De Nigger's Got to Go

Dear Liza, I is bin down town,
To Massa Charley's sto',
An' all de talk dis nigger hear
Is — "niggers got to go;"
I 'fess it bodders my ole head,   5
An' I would like to kno',
What all we cullud folks is done,
Dat now we's got to go?

I hear dem say dat long ago,
To ole Virginny's sho',   10
Dar kum a ship wid cullud folks,
Some twenty odd or mo',
Dey tells me dat dey hoed de corn,
An' wuz good wuckers sho';
Dey made Virginny like de rose,   15
But now dey's got to go.

Dat, when ole Ginnel Washington
Did whip dem red coats so,
A nigger wuz de fus to fall,
A-fightin' ub de foe;   20
Dat in de late "unpleasan'ness"
Dey watched at massa's do'
Proteckin' ub his lubin' ones,
But now we's got to go.

I 'fess I lubs dis dear ole place,   25
'Twuz here we buried Jo',
An' little Liza married off
So menny years ago,
An' now wez feeble, an' our lims
Is a-gittin mighty slo',   30
I'd hate to lebe dis dear ole place
But den wez got to go.

I don' kno' much 'bout politicks,
An' all dem things fur sho',
But de las leckshun I jes vote   35
Like de white folks tole me to;
Dey tole me vote for Dimikrats
An' 'twould be better sho',
But now dey don de leckshun win
But dey sez we's got to go.   40

Dey sez de white folks mad long us,
Kas wez-a-kummin up you kno',
An' sum un us is gittin' rich,
Wid do' bells on de do':
Dat wez get lawyers, doctors too,   45
An all dem things fur sho':
But den, it kan be jes for dis
Dat we all got to go.

De Lord he made dis lubly lan'
For white an' black folks too,   50
An' gin each man his roe to ten,
Den what we gwine to do?
We habes ourselbes, an' 'specks de laws,
But dey's peckin' mo' an' mo'
We aint don nuffin tall to dem,   55
Den huc-kum we mus' go.

Fur ebry nashun on de glob'
Dis seems to be a hom',
Dey welkums dem wid open arms,
No matter whar dey from   60
But we who here wuz bred an born,
Don' seem to hab no sho';
We hoped to make it what it is,
But den wez got to go.

It 'pears to me, my Liza dear,   65
Wez got a right to stay,

An' not a man on dis brod uf
Gwine dribe dis nigger way;
But why kan white folks lef us lone,
An weed dar side de roe,   70
An what dey all time talkin' 'bout
"De nigger's got to go?"

"But Rastus," Liza sed, "Trus' in God,
He'll brung things right fur sho',
He don' hate us bekase wez black,   75
He made us all you kno';
He lubs us if wez cullud folks,
Our hearts is white an puh
An' less de Lord sez, forward march!
Wez not a gwine to go."   80

                              (1895)

Note

19-20. *A nigger wuz de fus to fall:* Crispus Attucks, a mulatto sailor, was killed before the Revolutionary War (1770) when British soldiers fired into a hostile crowd in Boston. See Subject Index: African-American Race: Colonization.

De Linin' ub De Hymns

Dare a mighty *row* in Zion an' de *debbil's gittin' high*,
An' de *saints* done beat de *sinners, a-cussin' on de sly;*
What for it am? you reckon, well, I'll tell how it 'gin
Twuz 'bout a *mighty leetle thing, de linin' ub de hyms.*

De *young folks* say *taint stylish* to *lin' out* no mo',   5
Dat *dey's* got *edikashun,* an' dey wants us all to know
Dat *dey* likes to hab dar *singin' books* a-holin' fore dar eyes,
An *sing de hymns right straight along* to mansion in de skies.

Dat it am *awful fogy* to gin um out *by lin'*,
An' ef de ole folks will kumplain 'cause dey is ole an' blin   10
An' slabry's chain don kep dem back from larnin how to read,
Dat *dey* mus' take a *corner seat,* and let de *young folks* lead.

We *bin* peatin' *hine* de pastor when he sez dat lubly pray'r
Cause some un us *don kno'* it an' kin not say it squar,
But dey sez we *mus' peat wid* him, an' ef we kan keep time,   15
De gospel train will drap us off from follin' long behin'.

Well p'haps dez's right, I kin not say, my lims is growin' ole,
But I likes to sing dem dear ole hymns 'tis *music to my soul,*
An' 'pears to me twon't do *much* harm to gin um out *by lin'*,
So we *ole folk* dat *kin not read* kin *foller long behin'.*   20

But few ub us am lef here now dat bore de slabry's chain,
We don edekate our boys an' gals we'd do de sam' agin
An *Zion's* all dat's lef us now to cheer us wid its song,
Dey *mought* 'low us to *sing wid dem,* it kin not be fur long.

De *sarmons* high-falutin' an' de *chuch* am mighty fin',   25
We trus' dat *God still understans* ez he did in olden times;
When we do ign'ant po an' mean still worshiped wid de soul
Do oft akross our peac'ful breas' de wabes ub trouble rolled.

De ole time *groans* an' *shouts* an' *moans* am passin' out ub
  sight,
Edikashun changed all dat, and we believe *it right:*   30
We *should* serb God *wid 'telligence* but fur dis thing I plead,
Jes lebe a leetle place in chuch fur dem as kin not read.

                        (1895)

My Childhood's Happy Days

To My Parents

Many poets great and gifted whom the muse's touch had
   blessed,
Have sung in rhythmic measure, at the spirit's high behest,
Of the days of childish glory, free from sorrow and from pain,
When all was joy and pleasure, and wished them back again,
But, somehow, when my mind turns back to sing in joyous   5
   lays,
I remember great discomforts, in my childhood's happy days.

Why, my earliest recollections are of pains and colics sore,
And the meanest kinds of medicines the grown folks down
   would pour,
Ipecac and paregoric, and though I hard would kick
They still would dose and physic "Cause the baby must be   10
   sick!"
When I think of this how can I sing a song in joyous lays,
And speak in tones of rapture of my childhood's happy days.

Off to school I then was started and the simple rule of three
Was as hard as now quadratics or geometry's to me:
And then the awful thrashings, with a paddle at the school,   15
And again at home with switches if I broke the simplest rule,
Oh, my life was one vast torment, so, of course I'm bound
   to praise
The time that poet's nickname "our childhood's happy
   days."

On a cold and snowy morning, when lying snug in bed,
"You Webster" was the sound I heard, and wished that I   20
   was dead;
For I knew I had to make the fires, bring water, and cut
   wood,
And then, perhaps, I might have chance to get a bit of food,
When off to school I trotted: these were the pleasant ways,

In which I spent that festive time, my childhood's happy
     days.

Father's breeches, cut to fit me, was, of course, the proper   25
     thing,
And no where would they touch me, my one "gallus" was a
     string,
I couldn't tell the front from back-part, and my coat of navy
     blue,
So variously was mended, it would match the rainbow's hue;
'Twill do all right for rich white boys to sing those merry
     lays,
But the average little "Jap" fared tough, in childhood's   30
     happy days.

I had a tender place where I couldn't bear the comb to
     touch,
I'd jump three feet when tested, at last I cried so much
Mother said that she would cut it, oh, fate! to see me
     then,
My head was picked by dull shears as if some turkey hen
Had gotten in his cruel work, and the boys, with jolly   35
     ways
Hallowed "buzzard" when they saw me in my childhood's
     happy days.

In the evening holding horses, selling papers—"Evening
     News,"
To earn an honest penny, for the folks at home to use,
Yet, of course I had my pleasures, stealing sugar, playing
     ball,
But I can not go in raptures o'er that season after all,   40
And, we repeat our childhood, and all life's sterner ways
Are mixed with rain and sunshine, as were childhood's
     happy days.

Still I find that life's one "hustle" from the cradle to the
     tomb,
With occasional rays of sunshine to lighten up the gloom.

And if we can help a brother, and mix our cares with joys,   45
We'll find old age as happy as the days when we were boys;
And above may sing in rapture heavenly songs of love and
    praise,
When at last our bark is anchored there to spend our
    happiest days.

                                        (1895)

I Can Trust

I can not see why trials come,
And sorrows follow thick and fast;
I can not fathom His designs,
Nor why my pleasures can not last,
Nor why my hopes so soon are dust,   5
But, I can trust.

When darkest clouds my sky o'er hang,
And sadness seems to fill the land,
I calmly trust His promise sweet,
And cling to his ne'er failing hand,   10
And, in life's darkest hour, I'll just
Look up and trust.

I know my life with Him is safe,
And all things still must work for good
To those who love and serve our God,   15
And lean on Him as children should,
Though hopes decay and turn to dust,
I still will trust.

                              (1895)

Miss Liza's Banjer

Hi! Miss Liza's got er banjer;
    Lemme see it, ef yo' please!
Now don' dat thing look pooty,
    A-layin' 'cross yer kneeze,
Wid all dem lubly ribbins,   5
    An' silber trimmin's roun'.
Now, mistis, please jes' tetch it,
    To lemme hear de soun'.

'Scuze me, mistis, but dar's sumfin'
    De matter wid dem strings;   10
I notis it don' zackly
    Gib de proper kinder ring;
An' den de way yo' hol' it
    Ain't lik' yo' orter do.
Now, mistis, won't yo' lemme   15
    Jes' try a chune fur yo'?

Now lis'n to de diffunce;
    I'se got the thing in chune,
An' de music's lik' de breezes
    Dat fills de air in June.   20
Fur a banjer's lik' a 'ooman—
    Ef she's chuned de proper pitch,
She'll gib yo' out de music
    Dat's sof', melojus, rich.

But when yo' fail to chune her,   25
    Or to strike de proper string,
Yo' kin no more git de music,
    Den mek' a kat-bird sing.
An' 'taint always de fixin's
    Dat makes a 'ooman bes',   30
But de kind ub wood she's made un
    Is de thing to stan' de tes'.

I s'pose yer plays yer music
　　Jes' lik' yo' hab it wrote,
Or—what is dat yo' call it—　　　　　　　35
　　A-playin' by de note?
Yo' kin fill yer head wid music
　　Ez full ez it kin hol',
But yo' nebber gwine ter play it
　　'Tell yo' gits it in yer soul.　　　　　　40

T'ain't de proper notes dat makes yo'
　　Feel lik' yo' wants to cry,
But de soul dat's in de music
　　Dat lif's yo' up on high;
An' 'taint always de larnin',　　　　　　　45
　　'Do' a splendid thing, I kno',
Dat lif's de low an' 'umble
　　To higher things belo'.

Keep larnin', den, Miss Liza,
　　An' when yo' wants ter know　　　　　50
Ef yo' kin play de banjer,
　　Jes' kum to Uncle Joe;
Jes' fill yer head wid music,
　　Ez full ez it kin hol'
But de music from de banjer　　　　　　　55
　　Must fust be in de soul.

　　　　　　　　(1897)

Aunt Chloe's Lullaby

Hesh! my baby; stop yer fuss,
I's 'fraid yuz gittin wuss an' wuss;
Doncher cry, an' I gwy mek'
Mammy's baby 'lasses cake.
Hesh! my lubly baby chil',   5
I gwy rock yo' all de whil';
Nuffin gwyne to ketch yo' now,
'Cause yer mammy's watchin' yo'.
Sleep! my little baby, sleep!
    Mammy's baby, Lou!   10

How dem dogs do bark to-night!
Better shet yer eyes up tight;
Dey kan't hab dis baby dear;
Mammy's watchin', doncher fear.
Hear dem owls a-hootin' so?   15
Dey shan't ketch dis baby, do'.
Jes' like mistis lub her chil',
Mammy lubs dis baby too.
Sleep! my little baby, sleep!
    Mammy's baby, Lou!   20

Mammy's baby, black an' sweet,
Jes' like candy dat you eat,
Mammy lay yo' in dis bed,
While she mek de whi' folk's bread.
Angels dey gwy look below,   25
Watch dis baby sleepin' so.
Go to sleep, my hunny, now,
Ain't yer mammy watchin' yo'?
Sleep! my little baby, sleep!
    Mammy's baby, Lou.   30

        (1897)

The Negro Meets to Pray

Written for the great Negro Congress held in Atlanta, Ga., 1902

In days of old, when our fond mother earth,
  Now seamed and wrinkled with her weight of years,
Was young and gay, rejoicing in her birth,
  Nor gave one thought of future cares and tears.

When prehistoric man roamed hill and dell,   5
  And gods and genii ruled the world below,
Came Odin, great, to drink of Mimir's well,
  That he all wisdom of the world might know.

"Who drinks of Mimir's well must leave behind,
  His gift most dear, that he doth highly prize."   10
The gift was made, and he, though wise, half blind,
  Has left in Mimir's grasp one of his eyes.

So gods of wisdom ask of men to-day, —
  Who would be wise, some sacrifice must make;
Some good give up, something of self away,   15
  Ere he the wisdom of this world can take.

So this black-child, our father's image fair,
  In eb'ny cut, as we, too, would be wise,
Our gift hath made, our pledges, too, are there,
  Of years of suffering, toil and sacrifice.   20

In life's hard school we've conned these lessons o'er,
  Mid sobs and tears of slavery's galling chain;
Mid darkening days, God grant may come no more;
  Mid opposition, prejudice and pain.

What lessons learned? That God and right must win,   25
  God is not dead, but guards the weak alway;
The stars still shine, though faith and hope grow dim.
  We still can trust — the Negro meets to pray.

We seek the truth, nor wish one fault to hide;
   The truth alone is that can make men free,   30
Expose the sores, the remedies applied
   Will soothe and heal, and give true liberty.

Not to complain of burdens hard to bear;
   To fret and whine, resolve and go away;
We meet to plan how we can do our share   35
   To lift the load—The Negro meets to pray.

We know full well of all the gloomy past;
   Of all the darkness in which now we grope;
Of all the night that seems will never pass;
   And still we meet with bosoms filled with hope.   40

No night so dark, but comes some cheering ray,
   No sky so drear, but some bright star is there;
The harbor bells still ring and seem to say,
   "Just look this way: the world is still so fair."

We needs must fear the foes that lie within,   45
   That spoil our youth. With hearts both brave and stout,
Must fight 'gainst our own ignorance and sin,
   More than the hate and prejudice without.

Let others hate, we'll teach our children love;
   Let others fight, we'll teach endure the wrong;   50
No cowards we, our teaching's from above,
   When met in right then only are we strong.

We've met each trust, when slave as well as free,
   Our record's made, go search it, ye who will.
Oh, Country fair, our fathers died for thee,   55
   From Boston field to blood-bought San Juan Hill.

Their children come; no special favors ask,
   In Dixie land, the fair place of our birth;
But equal chance in this God-given task,
   To make our home the fairest spot on earth.   60

Ye leaders here, no nobler work than thine
    Could men or angels ask. We vow to-day
To life our race, by lifting as we climb;
    For this great task the Negro meets to pray.

No flaming sword, no curses loud and deep,   65
    We bring to-day, though we have suffered long,
Oh, rouse, ye race, from calm indifferent sleep,
    And face life's work, — then only are we strong.

God hear us now, and guide our thoughts aright,
    Give inspiration from above to-day;   70
Plan for us well, and help us see the light;
    By thy command, thy children meet to pray.

And from our knees to rise to bear our load,
    To reach the unreached Negro youth and save;
To spend ourselves for Country, race and God,   75
    Each in his field with hearts both stout and brave.

So soon for aye the lights of earth are o'er,
    The gloom be past, the toil and conflict done;
And angels' voices sing on yonder shore,
    For war-scarred veterans, God's sweet welcome home.   80
      (1902; D. W. Davis and Giles B. Jackson,
      The Industrial History of the Negro Race, 1908)

Notes

7–12. *Odin . . . Mimir's well:* In Scandinavian mythology, one root of the great tree that binds the universe descends into the world of giants to the fountain or well of wisdom guarded by the giant Mimir. Odin, king of the gods, agreed to lose an eye in order to drink this water of prophecy, poetry, and knowledge. 56. *Boston field to . . . San Juan Hill:* the Revolutionary War to the Spanish-American War (1898) in which Theodore Roosevelt led his Rough Riders up San Juan Hill in Cuba.

EDWARD W. WILLIAMS

Edward W. Williams (1863–91). Nothing is known about the life of Williams. His slim volume consists of a series of monologues by John Brown (1800–1859). The verses, at once militant and pious, pay homage to the radical abolitionist who with twenty-one followers attacked the government arsenal at Harpers Ferry, Virginia, on October 16, 1859. Captured and tried for murder and treason, Brown was convicted and hanged in December. He was a hero for many writers such as Bell, Harper, and Herman Melville, who called him the "meteor" of the Civil War.

The Views and Meditations of John Brown (Washington, D.C., 1893).

At Harper's Ferry Just Before the Attack

1. The hour, the spot, are here at last
   Their purpose, cause and hope we know,
   Our duty is to hold on fast
   To all the vows we made before.

2. To such as yield to our demand   5
   For freedom here and everywhere,
   In homes of safety let them stand
   And all their household comforts spare.

3. Those who refuse us or resist,
   Be as it may by words or arms,   10
   Enroll their names on death's black list
   To meet their dooms at war's alarms.

4. The blood that must be shed to-night
   Can never stain the name we bear,
   We fight for God's own holy right   15
   Which is to all mankind so dear.

5. Virginia robbed it from a race
   For over two sad hundred years,
   Abused and kept it in disgrace
   Regardless of entreating tears.   20

6. Those ancient tears rejoice to see
   This retributive night's advance,
   While Negro blood to you, to me,
   Is crying aloud for vengeance.

7. Around us stand with cheering hand   25
   The ghost of every Negro dead,
   Each blesses the freedom we demand
   Each bids us press with zeal ahead.

8. Angels rejoice with gladness, too,
   While round the throne on high they stand,   30
   To see poor mortal men pursue
   The common foe of God and man.

9. Though we are few in numbers now
   We trust the promise Jesus made,
   That where a few for good shall bow   35
   His spirit will be there to aid.

10. The saints are singing music sweet
    All around the heavenly strand,
    To see us here as Christians meet
    To help and save our brother man.   40

11. Oh! Saviour, Angels, Saints, look on
    While we the fathers will obey,
    Befriend and comvort them that mourn
    And in the dust their burdens lay.

12. We open war at once to-night   45
    And liberty for all proclaim,
    We'll lead from darkness unto light
    The weak, the poor, the blind and lame.

13. Before to-morrow's sun displays
    Its golden colors in the East,   50
    We'll wake slaveholders in amaze
    To breakfast on a bloody feast.

14. My brothers what a holy war
    In which we all will soon engage,
    It will assert free equal law   55
    Against the tyrants of the age.

15. The broken heart, the tearful eyes
    The cheerless face none sought to please,
    Will ere the morning sun arise
    Have symptoms of a time of ease.   60

16. The runaways in forest wilds
    And children sold to foreign shore,
Will soon return with happy smiles
    To see their parents, friends, once more.

17. The screws, the lashes and the hounds   65
    Shall no more glut off Negro blood,
Our forward march, our bugle sounds,
    Will scatter them as by a flood.

18. Husband and wife, daughters and son,
    Forever more shall ne'er be sold,   70
Together they shall live as one
    Till choice or Heaven breaks the fold.

19. The fertile earth shall no more yield
    Her fruits for unrequited toil,
The riches of the harvest field   75
    Must be for him who tills the soil.

20. Ye children all of Africa
    "Possess your soul" and weep no more,
This night will force America
    To grant you all you asked of yore.   80

21. The laws of God your rights ordain
    We are the instruments they send—
To cut your way, to break your chain,
    And ages long of troubles end.

PAUL LAURENCE DUNBAR

Paul Laurence Dunbar (1872–1906) rose to fame as the most popular African-American writer of his day. Born in Dayton, Ohio, to Matilda (Murphy) and Joshua Dunbar, both former slaves, Dunbar attended that city's public schools and graduated from Central High School in 1891. He sent poems to newspapers, gave poetry readings, and privately printed a slim volume of verse in 1893; meanwhile, he worked as an elevator operator and messenger in Dayton; a clerical assistant to Frederick Douglass at the Haitian exhibit of the Chicago World's Fair; and a journalist. William Dean Howells's review of Dunbar's second volume of poems (1895) and his glowing Introduction to a third collection that combined the first two (1896) launched the young poet's career. In his short life, Dunbar gained international renown with four additional volumes of poems, four novels, four collections of short stories, and dozens of articles in magazines; he also wrote song lyrics, musical plays, sketches, and essays. Dunbar held an assistant's job at the Library of Congress from 1897 to 1898, took a poetry-reading tour of England in 1897, and later gave lectures and acclaimed performances of his poetry throughout the United States. He married Alice Ruth Moore in 1898 but separated from her in 1902. Dunbar's last six years of social prominence and literary lionization were marred by the pain of marital troubles, the pressures of overwork, severe illness, and alcoholism. He died of tuberculosis in Dayton.

For almost a century critics have evaluated the complexities of Dunbar's art with both praise and condemnation. In his own time, Dunbar's dialect verse was universally admired; more recently, it is disparaged, along with dialect verse by others, for perpetuating stereotypes of the plantation tradition popularized by white writers in the last quarter of the century. With humor and pathos, Dunbar does indeed romanticize antebellum slaves, frolicking joyously, spinning tales, fishing and hunting through harmonious Southern landscapes, while they devotedly serve generous, genial masters. Scarcely a glimpse of the pains of slavery appears in these verses or in dialect poems narrated by nostalgic postwar freedmen. However, Dunbar's genuine affection for the rural South and its folkways often inspires his idealizations; and he enriches many dialect poems with expert musicality, a strong dramatic sense, graphic realistic details, ironic laughter, and, as in the standard English poems, his unique religious skepticism and ambiguous race consciousness. Dunbar greatly preferred his poetry in standard literary English, two-thirds of his work, which the public, he felt, did not appreciate. Most are competent but unremarkable romantic verses on such topics as love, nature, the arts, children, death, dreams, aspiration, and loss. A few poems acknowledge the struggles of African Americans and heroism of black soldiers, but very few strongly protest racial injustice. Dunbar's most moving lyrics ring with the tragic cry of a poet convinced of his personal and artistic failures. Whatever his shortcomings, Dunbar's artistic talents were exceptional: he wrote more than four hundred poems, the best of them in dialect; he popularized African-American literature, raised racial consciousness, and proved to the world the race's creative excellence; and he significantly influenced writers of the Harlem Renaissance and afterward.

Oak and Ivy (Dayton, Ohio: Author, 1893); *Majors and Minors* (Toledo, 1895); *Lyrics of Lowly Life* (New York: Dodd, Mead, 1896); *Lyrics of the Hearthside* (New York: Dodd, Mead, 1899); *Lyrics of Love and Laughter* (New York: Dodd, Mead, 1903).

Sympathy

I know what the caged bird feels, alas!
  When the sun is bright on the upland
    slopes;
When the wind stirs soft through the springing
    grass,
And the river flows like a stream of glass;
  When the first bird sings and the first bud   5
    opes,
And the faint perfume from its chalice steals—
I know what the caged bird feels!

I know why the caged bird beats his wing
  Till its blood is red on the cruel bars;
For he must fly back to his perch and cling   10
When he fain would be on the bough a-swing;
  And a pain still throbs in the old, old scars
And they pulse again with a keener sting—
I know why he beats his wing!

I know why the caged bird sings, ah me,   15
  When his wing is bruised and his bosom
    sore,—
When he beats his bars and he would be free;
It is not a carol of joy or glee,
  But a prayer that he sends from his heart's
    deep core,
But a plea, that upward to Heaven he flings—   20
I know why the caged bird sings!

                (1893)

When de Co'n Pone's Hot

Dey is times in life, when Nature
  Seems to slip a cog an' go,
Jes' a rattlin' down creation,
  Lak an ocean's overflow;
When de worl' jes' stahts a-spinnin'   5
  Lak a picaninny's top,
An' yo' cup o' joy is brimmin'
  'Twel it seems about to slop.
An' you feel jes' lak a racah,
  Dat is trainin' fu' to trot—   10
When yo' mammy ses de blessin'
  An' de co'n pone's hot.

When you set down at de table,
  Kin' o' weary lak an' sad,
An' you'se jes' a little tiahed   15
  An' purhaps a little mad;
How yo' gloom tu'ns into gladness,
  How yo' joy drives out de doubt
When de oven do' is opened,
  An' de smell comes po'in' out;   20
Why, de 'lectric light o' Heaven
  Seems to settle on de spot,
When yo' mammy ses de blessin'
  An' de co'n pone's hot.

When de cabbage pot is steamin'   25
  An' de bacon good an' fat,
When de chittlin's is a sputter'n'
  So's to show you whah dey's at;
Take away yo' sody biscuit,
  Take away yo' cake an' pie,   30
Fu' de glory time is comin',
  An' its 'proachin' very nigh,

An' you want to jump an' hollah,
　　Do you know you'd bettah not,
When yo' mammy ses de blessin'　　　　　　35
　　An' de co'n pone's hot.

I have heerd o' lots o' sermons,
　　An' I've heerd o' lots o' prayers;
An' I've listened to some singin'
　　Dat has tuck me up de stairs　　　　　　40
Of de Glory-Lan' an' set me
　　Jes' below de Mahster's th'one
An' have lef' my hawt a singin'
　　In a happy aftah tone.
But dem wu'ds so sweetly murmured　　　　45
　　Seem to tech de softes' spot,
When my mammy ses de blessin',
　　An' de co'n pone's hot.

　　　　　　　　　　　(1895)

The Colored Soldiers

If the muse were mine to tempt it
  And my feeble voice were strong,
If my tongue were trained to measures,
  I would sing a stirring song.
I would sing a song heroic   5
  Of those noble sons of Ham,
Of the gallant colored soldiers
  Who fought for Uncle Sam!

In the early days you scorned them,
  And with many a flip and flout,   10
Said "these battles are the white man's
  And the whites will fight them out."
Up the hills you fought and faltered,
  In the vales you strove and bled,
While your ears still heard the thunder   15
  Of the foes' increasing tread.

Then distress fell on the nation
  And the flag was drooping low;
Should the dust pollute your banner?
  No! the nation shouted, No!   20
So when war, in savage triumph,
  Spread abroad his funeral pall —
Then you called the colored soldiers,
  And they answered to your call.

And like hounds unleashed and eager   25
  For the life blood of the prey,
Sprung they forth and bore them bravely
  In the thickest of the fray.
And where'er the fight was hottest —
  Where the bullets fastest fell,   30
There they pressed unblanched and fearless
  At the very mouth of hell.

Ah, they rallied to the standard
   To uphold it by their might,
None were stronger in the labors,   35
   None were braver in the fight.
At Forts Donelson and Henry
   On the plains of Olustee,
They were foremost in the fight
   Of the battles of the free.   40

And at Pillow! God have mercy
   On the deeds committed there,
And the souls of those poor victims
   Sent to Thee without a prayer.
Let the fullness of thy pity   45
   O'er the hot wrought spirits sway,
Of the gallant colored soldier
   Who fell fighting on that day!

Yes, the Blacks enjoy their freedom
   And they won it dearly, too;   50
For the life blood of their thousands
   Did the southern fields bedew.
In the darkness of their bondage,
   In their depths of slavery's night;
Their muskets flashed the dawning   55
   And they fought their way to light.

They were comrades then and brothers,
   Are they more or less to-day?
They were good to stop a bullet
   And to front the fearful fray.   60
They were citizens and soldiers,
   When rebellion raised its head;
And the traits that made them worthy—
   Ah! those virtues are not dead.

They have shared your nightly vigils,   65
   They have shared your daily toil;

And their blood with yours commingling
   Has made rich the Southern soil.
They have slept and marched and suffered
   'Neath the same dark skies as you,   70
They have met as fierce a foeman
   And have been as brave and true.

And their deeds shall find a record,
   In the registry of Fame;
For their blood has cleansed completely   75
   Every blot of Slavery's shame.
So all honor and all glory
   To those noble Sons of Ham—
To the gallant colored soldiers,
   Who fought for Uncle Sam!   80
                    (1895)

Notes

6, 78. *sons of Ham:* Ham, a son of Noah and forefather of the Canaanites, was cursed by his father and condemned with all his descendants to be servants (Gen. 9:20–27); the black race, supposedly descended from Ham, was thus by biblical authority deemed inferior and legitimately enslaved. 37–41. *Forts Donelson . . . Henry . . . Olustee . . . Pillow!:* significant battles of the Civil War in which African-American regiments bravely fought for the Union. At Fort Pillow, Tennessee the Confederates massacred some three hundred captured black soldiers in 1864 (see Bell's *The Day and the War* [8]).

Deacon Jones' Grievance

I've been watchin' of 'em, parson,
    An' I'm sorry fur to say
'At my mind is not contented
    With the loose an' keerless way
'At the young folks treat the music;   5
    'Tain't the proper sort o' choir,
Then I don't believe in Christuns
    A-singin' hymns for hire.

But I never would 'a' murmured
    An' the matter might 'a' gone   10
Ef it wasn't fur the antics
    'At I've seen 'em kerry on;
So I thought it was my dooty
    Fur to come to you an' ask
Ef you wouldn't sort o' gently   15
    Take them singin' folks to task.

Fust, the music they've be'n singin'
    Will disgrace us very soon,
It's a cross between a opry
    An' a ol' cotillion tune.   20
With its dashes an' its quavers
    An' its hifalutin style —
Why, it sets my head to swimmin'
    When I'm comin' down the aisle.

Now it might be almost decent   25
    Ef it wasn't fur the way
'At they git up there an' sing it,
    Hey dum diddle loud and gay.
Why, it shames the name o' sacred
    In its brazen worldliness,   30
An' they've even got "Ol' Hundred"
    In a bold, new-fangled dress.

You'll excuse me, Mr. Parson,
    Ef I seem a little sore;
But I've sung the songs of Isr'el   35
    For three-score years an' more,
An' it sort o' hurts my feelin's
    Fur to see 'em put away
Fur these harum-scarum ditties
    'At is capturin' the day.   40

There's anuther little happ'nin'
    'At I'll mention while I'm here,
Jes' to show 'at my objections
    All is offered sound and clear.
It was one day they was singin'   45
    An' was doin' well enough —
Singin' good as people could sing
    Sich an awful mess o' stuff —

When the choir give a holler,
    An' the organ give a groan,   50
An' they left one weak-voiced feller
    A-singin' there alone!
But he stuck right to the music,
    Tho' 'twas tryin' as could be;
An' when I tried to help him,   55
    Why, the hull church scowled at me.

You say that's so-low singin',
    Well I pray the Lord that I
Growed up when folks was willin'
    To sing their hymns so high.   60
Why, we never had sich doin's
    In the good ol' Bethel days,
When the folks was all contented
    With the simple songs of praise.

Now I may have spoke too open,   65
    But 'twas too hard to keep still,
An' I hope you'll tell the singers

'At I bear 'em no ill-will.
'At they all may git to glory
   Is my wish an' my desire,   70
But they'll need some extry trainin'
   'Fore they jine the heavenly choir.
                  (1895)

Note

One-fifth of Dunbar's dialect verse is in *white* rural vernacular, as here. Dunbar consciously emulates the midwestern dialect popularized by his friend James Whitcomb Riley (see Cotter's "On Hearing James W. Riley Read," p. 330).

The Corn-Stalk Fiddle

When the corn's all cut and the bright stalks shine
   Like the burnished spears of a field of gold;
When the field-mice rich on the nubbins dine,
   And the frost comes white and the wind blows cold;
Then its heigho fellows and hi-diddle-diddle,   5
For the time is ripe for the corn-stalk fiddle.

And you take a stalk that is straight and long,
   With an expert eye to its worthy points,
And you think of the bubbling strains of song
   That are bound between its pithy joints—   10
Then you cut out strings, with a bridge in the middle,
With a corn-stalk bow for a corn-stalk fiddle.

Then the strains that grow as you draw the bow
   O'er the yielding strings with a practiced hand!
And the music's flow never loud but low   15
   Is the concert note of a fairy band.
Oh, your dainty songs are a misty riddle
To the simple sweets of the corn-stalk fiddle.

When the eve comes on and our work is done
   And the sun drops down with a tender glance,   20
With their hearts all prime for the harmless fun,
   Come the neighbor girls for the evening's dance,
And they wait for the well-known twist and twiddle,
More time than tune—from the corn-stalk fiddle.

Then brother Jabez takes the bow,   25
   While Ned stands off with Susan Bland,
Then Henry stops by Milly Snow
   And John takes Nellie Jones's hand,
While I pair off with Mandy Biddle,
And scrape, scrape, scrape goes the corn-stalk fiddle.   30

"Salute your partners," comes the call,
   "All join hands and circle round,"
"Grand train back," and "Balance all,"
   Footsteps lightly spurn the ground.
"Take your lady and balance down the middle"   35
To the merry strains of the corn-stalk fiddle.

So the night goes on and the dance is o'er,
   And the merry girls are homeward gone,
But I see it all in my sleep once more,
   And I dream till the very break of dawn   40
Of an impish dance on a red-hot griddle
To the screech and scrape of a corn-stalk fiddle.

                   (1895)

An Ante-Bellum Sermon

We is gathahed hyeah, my brothah,
  In dis howlin' wildaness,
Fer to speak some words of comfo't
  To each othah in distress.
An' we chooses fer ouah subjic'   5
  Dis—we'll 'splain it by an' by;
"An' de Lawd said Moses, Moses,
  An' de man said, 'Hyeah am I.' "

Now ole Pher'oh, down in Egypt,
  Was de wuss man evah bo'n,   10
An' he had de Hebrew chillun,
  Down dah wukin' in his co'n;
'Twell de Lawd got tiahed o' his foolin;
  An' sez he: "I'll let him know—
Look hyeah, Moses, go tell Pher'oh   15
  Fu' to let dem chillen go.

An' ef he refuse to do it,
  I will make him rue de houah,
Fu' I'll empty down on Egypt
  All de vials of my powah."   20
Yes, he did—an' Pher'oh's ahmy
  Wasn't wuth a ha'f a dime;
Fu' de Lawd will he'p his chillun,
  You kin trust him ev'ry time.

An' yo' enemies may 'sail you   25
  In de back an' in de front;
But de Lawd is all aroun' you,
  Fu' to ba' de battle's brunt.
Dey kin fo'ge yo' chains an' shackles
  F'om de mountains to de sea;   30
But de Lawd will sen' some Moses
  Fu' to set his chillun free.

An' de lan' shall hyeah his thundah,
    Lak a blas' f'om Gab'el's ho'n,
Fu' de Lawd of hosts is mighty   35
    When he girds his ahmor on.
But fu' feah some one mistakes me,
    I will pause right hyeah to say,
Dat I'm still a-preachin' ancient,
    I ain't talkin' 'bout to-day.   40

But I tell you, fellah christuns,
    Things'll happen mighty strange;
Now, de Lawd done dis fu' Isrul,
    An' his ways don't nevah change,
An' de love he showed to Isrul   45
    Wasn't all on Isrul spent;
Now don't run an' tell yo' mastahs
    Dat I'se preachin' discontent.

'Cause I isn't; I'se a judgin'
    Bible people by deir ac's;   50
I'se a givin' you de Scriptuah,
    I'se a handin' you de fac's.
Cose ole Pher'oh believed in slav'ry,
    But de Lawd he let him see,
Dat de people he put bref in,—   55
    Evah mothah's son was free.

An' dahs othahs thinks lak Pher'oh,
    But dey calls de Scriptuah liar,
Fu' de Bible says "a servant
    Is a worthy of his hire."   60
An' you caint git roun' nor thoo dat,
    An' you cain't git ovah it,
Fu' whatevah place you git in,
    Dis hyeah Bible too 'll fit.

So you see de Lawd's intention   65
    Evah sence de worl' began,

Was dat His almighty freedom
  Should belong to evah man,
But I think it would be bettah,
  Ef I'd pause agin to say,   70
That I'm talkin' 'bout ouah freedom
  In a Bibleistic way.

But de Moses is a comin,
  An' he's comin, suah and fas'
We kin hyeah his feet a-trompin',   75
  We kin hyeah his trumpit blas.'
But I want to wa'n you people,
  Don't you git too brigity;
An' don't you git to braggin'
  'Bout dese things, you wait an' see.   80

But when Moses wif his powah,
  Comes an' sets us chillen free,
We will praise de gracious Mastah
  Dat has gin us liberty;
An' we'll shout ouah halleluyahs,   85
  On dat mighty reck'nin' day,
When we'se reco'nized ez citiz'—
  Huh uh! Chillen let us pray!
                (1895)

Note

See the poems on this subject (and their notes) in the Subject Index, Religion:
Moses.

We Wear the Mask

We wear the mask that grins and lies,
It hides our cheeks and shades our eyes—
This debt we pay to human guile;
With torn and bleeding hearts we smile
And mouth with myriad subtleties.   5

Why should the world be over-wise,
In counting all our tears and sighs?
Nay, let them only see us, while
   We wear the mask.

We smile, but oh great Christ, our cries   10
To Thee from tortured souls arise.
We sing, but oh the clay is vile
Beneath our feet, and long the mile;
But let the world dream otherwise,
   We wear the mask!   15

(1895)

A Negro Love Song

Seen my lady home las' night,
  Jump back honey, jump back.
Hel' huh han' an' sque'z it tight,
  Jump back honey, jump back.
Heahd huh sigh a little sigh,   5
Seen a light gleam f'um huh eye,
An' a smile go flitin' by —
  Jump back honey, jump back.

Heahd de win' blow thoo de pines,
  Jump back honey, jump back.   10
Mockin' bird was singin, fine,
  Jump back honey, jump back.
An' my hea't was beatin' so,
When I reached my lady's do',
Dat I couldn't ba' to go —   15
  Jump back, honey, jump back.

Put my ahm aroun' huh wais',
  Jump back, honey, jump back.
Raised huh lips an took a tase',
  Jump back, honey, jump back.   20
Love me honey, love me true?
Love me well ez I love you?
An' she ansawhd: " 'Cose I do" —
  Jump back, honey, jump back.

           (1895)

When Malindy Sings

G'way an' quit dat noise, Miss Lucy—
    Put dat music book away;
What's de use to keep on tryin'?
    Ef you practice twell you're gray,
You cain't sta't no notes a-flyin'   5
    Like de ones dat rants and rings
F'om de kitchen to de big woods
    When Malindy sings.

You ain't got de nachel o'gans
    Fu' to make de soun' come right,   10
You ain't got de tu'ns an' twistin's
    Fu' to make it sweet an' light.
Tell you one thing now, Miss Lucy,
    An' I'm tellin' you fu' true,
When hit comes to raal right singin',   15
    'Tain't no easy thing to do.

Easy 'nough fu' folks to hollah,
    Lookin' at de lines an' dots,
When dey ain't no one kin sence it,
    An' de chune comes in in spots;   20
But fu' real melojous music,
    Dat jes' strikes yo' hawt and clings,
Jes' you stan' an' listen wif me,
    When Malindy sings.

Ain't you nevah heerd Malindy?   25
    Blessed soul, take up de cross!
Look heah, ain't you jokin', honey?
    Well, you don't know what you los'.
Y'ought to heah dat gal a-wa'blin',
    Robins, la'ks an' all dem things,   30
Heish dey moufs an' hides dey faces
    When Malindy sings.

Fiddlin' man, jes' stop his fiddlin',
  Lay his fiddle on de she'f;
Mockin'-bird quit tryin' to whistle,   35
  'Cause he jes' so shamed hisse'f.
Folks a-playin' on de banjo,
  Draps dey fingahs on de strings—
Bless yo' soul—fu'gits to move 'em,
  When Malindy sings.   40

She jes' spreads huh mouf and hollahs,
  "Come to Jesus," twell you heah
Sinnahs' tremblin' steps and voices,
  Timid-like a-drawin' neah;
Den she tu'ns to "Rock of Ages,"   45
  Simply to de cross she clings,
An' you fin' yo' teahs a drappin',
  When Malindy sings.

Who dat says dat humble praises
  Wif de Master nevah counts?   50
Heish yo' mouf, I heah dat music,
  Ez hit rises up an' mounts—
Floatin' by de hills an' valleys,
  Way above dis buryin' sod,
Ez hit makes its way in glory   55
  To de very gates of God!

Oh, hits sweetah dan de music
  Of an edicated band;
And hits dearah dan de battle's
  Song o' triumph in de lan'.   60
It seems holier dan evenin'
  When de solemn chu'ch bell rings,
Ez I sit an' ca'mly listen
  While Malindy sings.

Towsah, stop dat ba'kin' heah me!   65
  Mandy, make dat chile keep still;
Don't you heah de echoes callin'

F'om de valley to de hill.
Let me listen, I can heah it,
  Th'oo de bresh of angel's wings,   70
Sof' an' sweet, "Swing Low, Sweet Chariot,"
  Ez Malindy sings.

                       (1895)

When All Is Done

When all is done, and my last word is said,
And ye who loved me murmur, "He is dead,"
Let no one weep, for fear that I should know,
And sorrow too that ye should sorrow so.

When all is done and in the oozing clay,   5
Ye lay this cast-off hull of mine away,
Pray not for me, for, after long despair,
The quiet of the grave will be a prayer.

For I have suffered loss and grievous pain,
The hurts of hatred and the world's disdain,   10
And wounds so deep that love, well-tried and pure,
Had not the pow'r to ease them or to cure.

When all is done, say not my day is o'er,
And that thro' night I seek a dimmer shore:
Say rather that my morn has just begun,—   15
I greet the dawn and not a setting sun,
   When all is done.

                (1899)

Harriet Beecher Stowe

She told the story, and the whole world wept
   At wrongs and cruelties it had not known
   But for this fearless woman's voice alone.
   She spoke to consciences that long had slept:
Her message, Freedom's clear reveille, swept   5
   From heedless hovel to complacent throne.
   Command and prophecy were in the tone
   And from its sheath the sword of justice leapt.
Around two peoples swelled a fiery wave,
   But both came forth transfigured from the flame.   10
Blest be the hand that dared be strong to save,
   And blest be she who in our weakness came—
   Prophet and priestess! At one stroke she gave
   A race to freedom and herself to fame.

                            (1899)

Note

See Harper's "Eliza Harris" and note, and Coffin's "Harriet Beecher Stowe's
Works. . . ."

The Paradox

I am the mother of sorrows,
  I am the ender of grief;
I am the bud and the blossom,
  I am the late-falling leaf.

I am thy priest and thy poet,   5
  I am thy serf and thy king;
I cure the tears of the heartstick,
  When I come near they shall sing.

White are my hands as the snowdrop;
  Swart are my fingers as clay;   10
Dark is my frown as the midnight,
  Fair is my brow as the day.

Battle and war are my minions,
  Doing my will as divine;
I am the calmer of passions,   15
  Peace is a nursling of mine.

Speak to me gently or curse me,
  Seek me or fly from my sight;
I am thy fool in the morning,
  Thou art my slave in the night.   20

Down to the grave will I take thee,
  Out from the noise of the strife;
Then shalt thou see me and know me—
  Death, then, no longer, but life.

Then shalt thou sing at my coming,   25
  Kiss me with passionate breath,
Clasp me and smile to have thought me
  Aught save the foeman of Death.

Come to me, brother, when weary,
  Come when thy lonely heart swells;   30
I'll guide thy footsteps and lead thee
  Down where the Dream Woman dwells.

                        (1899)

The Haunted Oak

Pray why are you so bare, so bare,
  Oh, bough of the old oak-tree;
And why, when I go through the shade you throw,
  Runs a shudder over me?

My leaves were green as the best, I trow,   5
  And sap ran free in my veins,
But I saw in the moonlight dim and weird
  A guiltless victim's pains.

I bent me down to hear his sigh;
  I shook with his gurgling moan,   10
And I trembled sore when they rode away,
  And left him here alone.

They'd charged him with the old, old crime,
  And set him fast in jail:
Oh, why does the dog howl all night long,   15
  And why does the night wind wail?

He prayed his prayer and he swore his oath,
  And he raised his hand to the sky;
But the beat of hoofs smote on his ear,
  And the steady tread drew nigh.   20

Who is it rides by night, by night,
  Over the moonlit road?
And what is the spur that keeps the pace,
  What is the galling goad?

And now they beat at the prison door,   25
  "Ho, keeper, do not stay!
We are friends of him whom you hold within,
  And we fain would take him away

"From those who ride fast on our heels
    With mind to do him wrong;   30
They have no care for his innocence,
    And the rope they bear is long."

They have fooled the jailer with lying words,
    They have fooled the man with lies;
The bolts unbar, the locks are drawn,   35
    And the great door open flies.

Now they have taken him from the jail,
    And hard and fast they ride,
And the leader laughs low down in his throat,
    As they halt my trunk beside.   40

Oh, the judge, he wore a mask of black,
    And the doctor one of white,
And the minister, with his oldest son,
    Was curiously bedight.

Oh, foolish man, why weep you now?   45
    'Tis but a little space,
And the time will come when these shall dread
    The mem'ry of your face.

I feel the rope against my bark,
    And the weight of him in my grain,   50
I feel in the throe of his final woe
    The touch of my own last pain.

And never more shall leaves come forth
    On a bough that bears the ban;
I am burned with dread, I am dried and dead,   55
    From the curse of a guiltless man.

And ever the judge rides by, rides by
    And goes to hunt the deer,
And ever another rides his soul
    In the guise of a mortal fear.   60

And ever the man he rides me hard,
   And never a night stays he;
For I feel his curse as a haunted bough,
   On the trunk of a haunted tree.

                      (1900)

Douglass

Ah, Douglass, we have fall'n on evil days,
   Such days as thou, not even thou didst know,
   When thee, the eyes of that harsh long ago
Saw, salient, at the cross of devious ways,
And all the country heard thee with amaze,   5
   Not ended then, the passionate ebb and flow,
   The awful tide that battled to and fro
We ride amid a tempest of dispraise.

Now, when the waves of swift dissension swarm,
   And Honor, the strong pilot, lieth stark,   10
Oh, for thy voice high-sounding o'er the storm,
   For thy strong arm to guide the shivering bark,
   The blast-defying power of thy form,
To give us comfort through the lonely dark.

                  (1903)

Note
Compare tributes to Douglass by Ray and Cotter.

The Poet

He sang of life, serenely sweet,
   With, now and then, a deeper note.
   From some high peak, nigh yet remote,
He voiced the world's absorbing beat.

He sang of love when earth was young,   5
   And Love, itself, was in his lays.
   But ah, the world, it turned to praise
A jingle in a broken tongue.

             (1903)

GEORGE MARION McCLELLAN

George Marion McClellan (1860–1934), a minister, teacher, fiction writer, and poet, was a man of rare intellectual gifts, deep faith, and personal courage. The son of Eliza (Leonard) and George Fielding McClellan, he was born in Belfast, Tennessee. McClellan earned a B.A. from Fisk University in 1885; studied at Hartford (Connecticut) Theological Seminary from 1885 to 1887; married Mariah Augusta Rabb in 1888; and served as a Congregational minister in Louisville, Kentucky, from 1887 to 1890. With additional degrees, an M.A. from Fisk in 1890 and Bachelor of Divinity from Hartford in 1891, McClellan spent a few years in the ministry and as financial agent for Fisk before pursuing a successful career as teacher and principal in Louisville from 1899 to 1919. In later years he taught school in Los Angeles and again in Kentucky. From about 1890, McClellan suffered greatly from poverty, marital problems, the death of his younger son, publication difficulties, and feelings of estrangement from both his race and white society.

McClellan's sixty-seven lyrics, written from the 1880s onward, treat such standard subjects as nature, love, and religion with restrained diction, sober thought, faultless rhyming, graceful, classical meters, and refined sensibilities. His verses are spiritual autobiographies communicating the poet's struggle to deal with his "double consciousness," defined by W. E. B. DuBois as the sense of "measuring one's soul by the tape of a world that looks on in amused contempt and pity" while longing to express the "soul-beauty" of the race. McClellan's felt conflict between two cultures emerges as a separation-estrangement-regeneration theme in the poems: the poet-speaker longs to recapture the innocence, peace, freedom, and ecstatic harmony with nature and God that he links to youth, the beloved Southland, and joyous "soul-beauty" of his race. In opposition he sets adulthood, lost love, the North, winter, and death to symbolize corrupting experiences in an alien white world. The poet's hope of healing rests in God's power. McClellan's pacific stoicism and devotion to Gospel idealism in his poems is belied by the bitter anger at racial discrimination in his fiction; such contradiction reinforces the complex duality suggested by the poems, whose decorous surface and cool, detached tone artfully conceal the nostalgic and painful emotions beneath.

Poems (Nashville, Tenn.: A.M.E. Church Sunday School Union, 1895, retitled *Songs of a Southerner,* Boston, 1896); *The Path of Dreams* (Louisville, Ky.: John P. Morton, 1916).

A September Night

The full September moon sheds floods of light,
And all the bayou's face is gemmed with stars
Save where are dropped fantastic shadows down
From sycamores and moss-hung cypress trees.
With slumberous sound the waters half asleep   5
Creep on and on their way, twixt rankish reeds,
Through marsh and lowlands stretching to the gulf.
Begirt with cotton fields Anguilla sits
Half bird-like dreaming on her summer nest
Amid her spreading figs, and roses still   10
In bloom with all their spring and summer hues.
Pomegranates hang with dapple cheeks full ripe,
And over all the town a dreamy haze
Drops down. The great plantations stretching far
Away are plains of cotton downy white.   15
O, glorious is this night of joyous sounds
Too full for sleep. Aromas wild and sweet,
From muscadine, late blooming jessamine,
And roses, all the heavy air suffuse.
Faint bellows from the alligators come   20
From swamps afar, where sluggish lagoons give
To them a peaceful home. The katydids
Make ceaseless cries. Ten thousand insects' wings
Stir in the moonlight haze and joyous shouts
Of Negro song and mirth awake hard by   25
The cabin dance. O, glorious is this night.
The summer sweetness fills my heart with songs
I cannot sing, with loves I cannot speak.
    Anguilla, Miss., September, 1892.

                                        (1895)

Notes

18. *muscadine . . . jessamine:* a variety of grapes and yellow jasmine, respectively. 22. *katydids:* shrill-sounding tree insects related to the grasshopper.

The Feet of Judas

Christ washed the feet of Judas!
The dark and evil passions of his soul,
His secret plot, and sordidness complete,
His hate, his purposing, Christ knew the whole,
And still in love he stooped and washed his feet.   5

Christ washed the feet of Judas!
Yet all his lurking sin was bare to him,
His bargain with the priest and more than this,
In Olivet beneath the moonlight dim,
Aforehand knew and felt his treacherous kiss.   10

Christ washed the feet of Judas!
And so ineffable his love 'twas meet,
That pity fill his great forgiving heart,
And tenderly to wash the traitor's feet,
Who in his Lord had basely sold his part.   15

Christ washed the feet of Judas!
And thus a girded servant, self-abased,
Taught that no wrong this side the gate of heaven
Was e'er too great to wholly be effaced,
And though unasked, in spirit be forgiven.   20

And so if we have ever felt the wrong
Of trampled rights, of caste, it matters not,
Whate'er the soul has felt or suffered long,
Oh heart! this one thing should not be forgot,
Christ washed the feet of Judas!   25

(1895)

Note

9. *Olivet:* the Mount of Olives where Jesus predicts his death and receives the kiss of betrayal from Judas.

The Sun Went Down in Beauty

The sun went down in beauty,
Beyond Mississippi's tide,
As I stood on the banks of the river,
And watched its waters glide;
Its swelling currents resembling   5
The longing restless soul,
Surging, swelling, and pursuing
Its ever-receding goal.

The sun went down in beauty,
But the restless tide flowed on,   10
And the phantoms of absent loved ones
Danced o'er the waves and were gone;
Nautical phantoms of loved ones,
Their faces jubilant with glee
In the spray, seemed to rise and beckon,   15
And then rush on to the sea.

The sun went down in beauty,
While I stood musing alone,
Stood watching the rushing river,
And heard its restless moan;   20
And longings, vague, intenable,
So far from speech apart,
Like the endless rush of the river,
Went surging through my heart.

The sun went down in beauty,   25
Peacefully sank to rest,
Leaving its golden reflection
On the great Mississippi's breast;
Gleaming on the turbulent river,
In the coming gray twilight,   30
Soothing its restless surging,
And kissing its waters good-night.

The sun went down in beauty,
The stars came one by one,
Speaking from the vault of heaven,   35
Of the mighty Father and Son;
Speaking to earthly mortals,
Whose souls like the river's tide,
Forever and ever are flowing,
But never are satisfied.   40

The sun went down in beauty,
But still in the calm starlight,
My feet were wont to linger
To the coming of gray midnight;
My heart was filled with musings,   45
Of past and coming years,
And the thoughts of friends departed,
Filled my eyes with tears.

The sun went down in beauty,
But still in visions fair,   50
My soul to the gate of heaven,
Was wafted through the air;
The gate of life eternal,
Where cease tumult and strife,
Where men borne down with sorrow,   55
Lay down the burden of life.

The sun went down in beauty,
Tinging the west with gold,
Gleaming as a symbol in heaven,
Of light in the Father's fold;   60
And, soul, why fret with emotions,
Of sorrow, joy or renown?
Soon life with all that is earthly,
Forever will be laid down.

The sun will go down in beauty,   65
'Mid summer and mid winter snow,
When we in the grave are sleeping,

Beyond its radiant glow;
Speak to our souls, my Father,
Their void with comfort fill,   70
And ease our anxious longings,
And bid them, "Peace, be still."

Tiptonville, Tenn., on the banks
of the Mississippi, August, 1892.
                                (1895)

Lines to Mount Glen

In this soft air perfumed with blooming May,
Stretched at thy feet on the green grass, Old Glen,
It is a joy unspeakable to me
To see again thy face and friendly crags.
My childhood friend, then height of heights to me,   5
I am come home to worship thee once more,
And feel that bliss in indolent repose
Of those long past delightful afternoons,
When first you smiled on me and gave to my
Imaginings such imagery, when I   10
Would lie down at thy base as I
Do now. My feet have wandered far since then,
And over heights with prouder heads than thine,
Such as would name thy majesty with hills.
But I, Old Glen, my early mountain friend,   15
Am come with loyalty and heart still true
As thy bald crags are to their kindred skies.
My own Olympus yet and pride thou art,
With thy Thessalian gates of clouds
Which hide the great Olympian Hall,   20
Where Hebe still sweet nectar pours
Out to the gods. And murmurs sweet and low
Of melting cadences Apollo from
His magic lyre sends gently wandering
In soft succeeding measures yet in air   25
Familiarly to me.

       And yet, Old Glen,
A stranger at thy base I lie to-day
To all but thee, save this soft yielding grass,
And blooming waste, thy pageantry of flowers.   30
All these with yond bald eagle circling in
The upper air with keen descrying for
Some timorous skulking hare, are but old friends

Who laughed and played with me in childhood hours
Full many a summer day and told me tales   35
Of fairy lore. With such immortal friends
To welcome me again, what care I then
For yon rude plowman's stare and taking me
For some trespassing rake. This broad domain
Of circling hills and intervening vales   40
Is thine by ancient rights to shelter me,
And take me in thy lap when I have come
With love to worship thee. Before Rome was,
Or Greece had sprung with poetry and art,
Thy majesty with impartiality   45
Was here. The first soft tread of moccasin
On Indian feet, in ages none can tell,
That bent this yielding grass was thine to hear.
And all the sons of men who since have brought
Their pulsing hearts to thee with loves, with aches,   50
With tragedies, with childhood innocence,
Have had thy welcoming. To thee no race
May come with arrogance and claim first right
To thy magnificence, and mighty heart,
And thy ennobling grace that touches every   55
Soul who may commune with thee.

                                     And so
It was Old Glen we came at first to love
In this soft scented air now long ago,
When first I brought my youthful heart to thee,   60
All pure with pulsing blood still hot
In its descent of years in tropic suns
And sands of Africa, to be caressed
By thee. And to your lofty heights you bore
Me up to see the boundless world beyond,   65
Which nothing then to my young innocence
Had aught of evil or deceptive paths.
With maddening haste I quit thy friendly side
To mix with men. And then as some young bison
Of the plain, which breathes the morning air   70

And restless snorts with mad excess of life,
And rushes heedless on in hot pursuit
Of what it does not know: So I, Old Glen,
As heedlessly went out from thee to meet
With buffeting, with hates and selfishness   75
And scorn. At first I stood abashed, disarmed
Of faith. Too soon I learned the ways of men,
Forgetting much I wish I had retained
Of once a better life. And in the fret
And fever of the endless strife for gain   80
I often sigh for thee, my native peaks,
And for that early life for me now past
Forevermore.

                    But for one day, my early friend,
I am come back to thee again, to feel   85
Thy gentle grace so indefinable,
So subtile is thy touch, yet to the heart
A never-failing gift to all who come
To thee. And so it is, Old Glen, that I am come,
But not with all-believing innocence   90
As in those unsuspecting days of yore.
And O Mount Glen! sin-stained my burning heart
With shame lifts up its face to thine, but with
A love as changeless as thy ancient crags
Does it still beat for thee. And I rejoice   95
To feel thy mighty heart here solace mine.
For when the day leads in the early dawn
With blushing rosy light and caroling
Of larks; and sleepy flowers half unclosed,
All wet with dew, unfold their buds and leaves,   100
There is enchantment in this lovely spot
Beyond, by far, all mortal utterances.
To come here then and lie down on thy side,
As I do now, and see the butterflies
Bobbing from flower to flower, and hear   105
The restless songs of birds as they in joy
Flit carelessly from bush and tree, is all
The bliss my heart could ask. Here I could lie

In such repose and let a lifetime pass.
And here, Old Glen, could I forget the fret   110
Of life and selfishness of men, and see
The face of him who is all beautiful.
And here in this perfume of May, and bloom
Luxuriant, and friendly rioting
Of green in all this blooming waste, is seen   115
A glimpse of that, which He, the Lord of all,
Intended there should be with things and men
In all this earth, a thing which yet will be,
A universal brotherhood.

                                        (1895)

Notes

18, 20. *Olympus . . . Olympian Hall:* the highest mountain in Greece, fabled to be the home of the gods. 19. *Thessalian gates:* Thessalia or Thessaly, a section of ancient Eastern Greece. 21. *Hebe:* cupbearer to the gods in Greek myth, the daughter of Zeus and Hera. 23. *Apollo:* see Holly's "The Patriot's Lament" (12).

Love Is a Flame

Love is a flame that burns with sacred fire,
And fills the being up with sweet desire;
Yet, once the altar feels love's fiery breath,
The heart must be a crucible till death.

Say love is life; and say it not amiss,   5
That love is but a synonym for bliss.
Say what you will of love—in what refrain,
But knows the heart, 'tis but a word for pain.

(1895)

A January Dandelion

All Nashville is a chill. And everywhere
Like desert sand, when the winds blow,
There is each moment sifted through the air,
A powdered blast of January snow.
O! thoughtless Dandelion, to be misled   5
By a few warm days to leave thy natural bed,
Was folly growth and blooming over soon.
And yet, thou blasted yellow-coated gem,
Full many a heart has but a common boon
With thee, now freezing on thy slender stem.   10
When the heart has bloomed by the touch of love's
    warm breath
Then left and chilling snow is sifted in,
It still may beat but there is blast and death
To all that blooming life that might have been.

(1895)

Hydromel and Rue

Lord, let me live to serve and make a loan
    Of life and soul in love to my heart's own.
And what if they should never care or know
    How dark sometimes and weary are the ways,
How piercing cold and pitiless the snow,   5
    How desolate and lonely are the days
Which life for me holds sometimes in reserve?
    And what if those I love esteem above
Me, others all untried and far less true,
    And lightly barter off my wealth of love   10
For careless, strange, and passing comrades new?
    Oh Lord, those, whom I love, I still would serve.

To be permitted, once in this short life,
    To hold a little child close to my heart
In fatherhood, as mine, is worth all strife   15
    Which circumstance and time to me impart.
To know the bliss of chaste and holy love,
    To have one friend to even half divine
My hungry heart, is heaven from above
    Come to this ever-longing soul of mine.   20

And so, dear Lord, I thank Thee for the cup
    Of hydromel Thou givest me to sup,
Though rue and hyssop pass my lips and fill
    My life with earthly sorrow, grief, and pain,
In faith my soul will rise to thank Thee still   25
    For garish day, for guerdon and its gain.
And though through time insentient clay, the
        sward,
    My erstwhile form may hold; for joy, for life,
For everlasting love, sunshine and rain,

My ardent heart above all earthly strife,   30
Unbound in space, soars up through joy and pain
Triumphantly, in thanks to Thee, dear Lord.

(1916)

Notes

Hydromel, a mixture of honey and water that becomes a potent brew, mead, when fermented; in Scandinavian mythology hydromel is a magical liquor bestowing powers of prophecy and poetry. *Rue,* a medicinal plant with bitter-tasting leaves. 23. *hyssop:* an aromatic plant of the mint family used in folk medicine and ancient religious ceremonies.

To Theodore

Such are the little memories of you;
They come and go, return and lie apart
From all main things of life; yet more than they,
With noiseless feet, they come and grip the heart.
Gay laughter leading quick and stormy tears,   5
Then smiles again and pulse of flying feet,
In breathless chase of fleeting gossamers,
Are memories so dear, so bitter-sweet.

No more are echoes of your flying feet.
Hard by, where Pike's Peak rears its head in state,   10
The erstwhile rushing feet, with halting steps,
For health's return in Denver watch and wait.
But love and memories of noiseless tread,
Where angels hovered once, all shining fair,
To tuck you in your little trundle bed,   15
Kneel nightly now in agony of prayer.

                                    Feb. 22, 1916.
                                        (1916)

Notes

McClellan's younger son suffered from tuberculosis. McClellan took him from Colorado to Los Angeles for treatment (July 1916), but Theodore was refused admission to a sanitarium because of his race. He died in Los Angeles on January 5, 1917, at the age of twenty-one. 10. *Pike's Peak:* mountain in central Colorado.

Daybreak

Awake! arise! Oh, men of my race,
　　I see our morning star,
And feel the dawn-breeze on my face
　　Creep inward, from afar.

I feel the dawn, with soft-like tread,　　　　　　5
　　Steal through our lingering night,
Aglow with flame our sky to spread
　　In floods of morning light.

Arise! my men, be wide awake
　　To hear the bugle call,　　　　　　　　　　10
For Negroes everywhere to brake
　　The bands that bind us all.

Great Lincoln, now with glory graced,
　　All God-like with the pen,
Our chattel fetters broke, and placed　　　　　15
　　Us in the ranks of men.

But even he could not awake
　　The dead, nor make alive,
Nor change stern nature's laws which make
　　The fittest to survive.　　　　　　　　　　20

Let every man his soul inure,
　　In noblest sacrifice,
And with a heart of oak endure,
　　Ignoble, arrant prejudice.

Endurance, love, will yet prevail　　　　　　25
　　Against all laws of hate;
Such armaments can never fail
　　Our race its best estate.

Let none make common cause with sin,
    Be that in honor bound,   30
For they who fight with God must win
    On every battle ground.

Though wrongs there are and wrongs have been
    And wrongs we still must face,
We have more friends than foes within   35
    The Anglo-Saxon race.

In spite of all the babel cries,
    Of those who rage and shout,
God's silent forces daily rise
    To bring His will about.   40

Our portion is, and yet will be,
    To drink a bitter cup
In many things, yet all must see
    The race is moving up.

Oh! men of my race, awake! arise!   45
    Our morning's in the air,
There's scarlet all along the skies,
    Our day breaks everywhere.
                                    (1916)

Note

11. break.

ELOISE ALBERTA VERONICA BIBB

Eloise Alberta Veronica Bibb (1878–1928) published her volume of verse when she was only seventeen. The daughter of Catherine Adele and Charles H. Bibb, she was born and raised in New Orleans. Bibb attended Oberlin Academy from 1899 to 1901, graduated from Teachers' College of Howard University in 1908, and became a social worker in Washington, D.C. She married Noah D. Thompson and moved to Los Angeles in 1911, where she was active in Catholic organizations and wrote special features for newspapers as well as articles and poems for magazines.

More than half of Bibb's poems are romantic narratives of star-crossed lovers and agonized heroes; their catastrophes differ, but the characters vary in little more than their names, and the narrative lines may be complicated and illogical, or, more often, single and smoothly developed with sustained suspense. Bibb's verses on biblical and historical subjects are frequently successful, with simple language and even and consistent metrics, tone, and story line.

Poems (Boston: Monthly Review Press, 1895).

Gerarda

The day is o'er and twilight's shade,
Is darkening forest, glen and glade;
It steals within the old church door,
And casts its shadows on the floor;
It throws its gloom upon the bride,   5
And on her partner by her side:
But ah! it has no power to screen
The loveliest form that e'er was seen.

Sweet tones as from the angels' lyre,
Came pealing from the ancient choir;   10
They rouse the brain with magic power,
And fill with light that twilight hour.
Some artist's soul one easily sees,
Inspires the hands that touch the keys;
A genius sits and wakes the soul,   15
With sounds that o'er the passions roll.

"Till death we part," repeats the bride,
She shuddered visibly and sighed;
And as she leaves the altar rail,
She's startled, and her features pale,   20
For in the ancient choir above,
The man who sits and plays of love,
Has held her heart for many a year.
Alas! her life is sad and drear.

He never dreamed he roused a thrill,   25
Within that heart that seemed so still;
He never knew the hours of pain,
That racked that tired and troubled brain.
He could not see that bleeding heart,
From which his face would not depart;   30
He never could have known her grief,
From which, alas! there's no relief.

At last she thought the fire had cooled,
And love's strong guardian she had ruled;
'Twas then she vowed to be the bride   35
Of him who stands at her side.
Ill-fated hour! she sees too late,
This man she cannot help but hate;
He, whom she promised to obey,
Until from earth she's called away.   40

This life is sometimes dark and drear,
No lights within the gloom appear.
Gerarda smiled and danced that night,
As though her life had been all bright;
And no one knew a battle waged,   45
Within that heart so closely caged.
The few who've never felt love's dart,
Know not the depth of woman's heart.

II

Gerarda sat one summer day,
With easel, brush, and forms of clay,   50
Within her much-loved studio,
Where all that makes the senses glow
Were placed with great artistic skill;
Content, perhaps, she seems, and still,
She'd give this luxury and more,   55
To ease that heart so bruised and sore.

Her paintings hang upon the wall,
The power of genius stamps them all;
On this material soil she breathes,
But in her spiritual world she leaves   60
Her mind, her thoughts, her soul, her brain,
And wakes from fancy's spell with pain.
And thus her pictures plainly show,
Not nature's self but ideal glow.

And now to-day o'er canvas bent,   65
She strives to place these visions sent

From that bright world she loves so well,
But fancy fails to cast her spell,
And sick at heart, Gerarda sighs,
And wonders why her muse denies   70
The inspiration given before,
When oft in heaven her soul would soar.

But now her ear has caught a sound,
That causes heart and brain to bound,
With rapture wild, intense, sincere,   75
For, list! those strains are coming near;
She grasps the brush, her muse awoke,
Within those notes her genius spoke;
An Angelo might e'en be proud,
Of forms that o'er her vision crowd.   80

What power is this that swells that touch,
And sends it throbbing with a rush,
That renders all its hearers dumb!
If he be man, whence did he come?
Lo! 'tis the same who played with power   85
The wedding march that twilight hour;
The strains seem caught from souls above,
It is the very food of love.

And yet, he's neither old nor bent,
A comeliness to youth is lent;   90
A radiant eye, a natural grace.
An eager, noble, passionate face, —
All these are his, with genius spark,
That guides him safely through the dark,
To hearts that throb and souls that feel,   95
At every grand and solemn peal.

Triumphant Wagner's soul he reads,
And then with Mozart gently pleads,
And begs the weary cease to mope,
But rise and live in dreams of hope.   100
The sounds have ceased, — how drear life seems!

He wakes from out his land of dreams,
And finds Gerarda rapt, amazed.
In speechless ecstacy she gazed.

"Neville! thou king of heroes great,   105
A tale of love thou dost relate,
In tones that rend my heart in twain.
With intense agony and pain,
Forgive whate'er I say to-day,
Thy touch has ta'en my sense away: 110
O man that dreams, thou can'st not see,
That I, alas! doth worship thee!

"Behold! thou Orpheus, I kneel
And beg thee, if thou e'er canst feel,
Or sympathize with my unrest,   115
To thrust this dagger in my breast.
Shrink not! I can no longer live
Content in agony to writhe;
And death with thy hand given to me,
Will be one blissful ecstacy."   120

He starts, and lifts her from her knees,
Her features pale, and soon he sees
That tired heart so sick and sore
Can bear its grief and woe no more.
She swoons—her pulse has ceased to beat,   125
A holy calm, divine and sweet,
Has settled on the saintly face,
Lit up with beauty, youth and grace.

Neville amazed, in rapture stands,
Admiring hair, and face, and hands.   130
Forgetful then of hour and place,
He stoops to kiss the beauteous face,
And at the touch the fire of love,
So pure as to come from above,
Consumes his heart and racks his brain,   135
With longing fear and infinite pain.

The kiss, as with a magic spell,
Has roused Gerarda,—it seems to tell,
'Tis time to bid her conscience wake,
And off her soul this burden shake.   140
"Neville, forgive" with downcast eyes,
Gerarda sorrowfully cries:
"I've told thee of my love and woe,—
The things I meant thou should'st not know."

"Gerarda thou hast woke the heart,   145
That ne'er before felt passion's smart;
Oh! is it true thou'rt lost to me,
My love, my heart knows none but thee!"
"Enough! Neville, we must forget,
That in this hour our souls have met.   150
Farewell! we ne'er must meet in life,
For I'm, alas! a wedded wife."

III

Why ring those bells? what was that cry:
The night winds bear it as they sigh;
What is this crushing, maddening scene?   155
What do those flames of fire mean?
They surge above Gerarda's home,
Through attic, cellar, halls, they roam,
Like some terrific ghost of night,
Who longs from earth to take his flight.   160

Gerarda stands amid the fire,
That leaps above with mad desire,
And rings her hands in silent grief,
She fears for her there's no relief.
But now she hears a joyous shout,   165
A breathless silence from without,
That tells her God has heard her prayer,
And sent a noble hero there.

And here he comes, this gallant knight,
Her heart rejoices at the sight,   170

For 'tis Neville, with aspect grave,
Who risked his life, his love to save.
And all have perished now but she,
Her husband and her family.
Mid tears and sobs she breathes a prayer,   175
For loved ones who are buried there.

Neville has brushed her tears away,
Together silently they pray
And bless the Lord with thankful prayer
For all his watchfulness and care.   180
"Gerarda, love," he whispers now,
Implanting kisses on her brow,
"This earth will be a heaven to me,
For all my life, I'll share with thee."

Notes

97. *Wagner's soul:* Richard Wagner (1813–83), German composer. 98. *Mozart:* Wolfgang Amadeus Mozart (1756–91), Austrian composer. 113. *Orpheus:* see Payne's "The Pleasures" (117).

MARY WESTON FORDHAM

Mary Weston Fordham (1862?–?) was the daughter of Louise (Bonneau) and the Reverend Samuel Weston. She lived in South and North Carolina. In her volume of verse, bearing an "Introductory" by Booker T. Washington, a group of "In Memoriam" poems identifies members of her family and suggests that Mrs. Fordham suffered the loss of six young children.

In subject and tone Fordham's sixty-six "leaves" are identical to the work of myriad white "female poets" of the century: sentimentality dominates verses on death and motherhood; nature typifies moral virtues; patriotism and devout Christianity are celebrated. Her attractive poetic skills include use of diverse stanzaic patterns and well-sustained rhythms and rhymings; her language, however, ranges from pedestrian to "high poetic" clichés. Except for a handful of brisk poems on unusual topics, Fordham's art conforms to prevailing formulas.

Magnolia Leaves (Charleston, S.C.: Walker, Evans & Cogswell, 1897).

The Saxon Legend of Language

The earth was young, the world was fair,
And balmy breezes filled the air,
Nature reposed in solitude,
When God pronounced it "very good."

The snow-capped mountain reared its head,   5
The deep, dark forests widely spread,
O'er pebbly shores the stream did play
On glad creation's natal day.

But silence reigned, nor beast nor bird
Had from its mate a whisper heard,   10
E'en man, God's image from above,
Could not, to Eve, tell of his love.

Where the four rivers met there strayed
The man and wife, no whit afraid,
For the arch-fiend expelled from heaven   15
Had not yet found his way to Eden.

But lo! a light from 'mid the trees,
But hark! a rustling 'mongst the leaves,
Then a fair Angel from above,
Descending, sang his song of love.   20

Forth sprang the fierce beasts from their lair,
Bright feathered songsters fill the air,
All nature stirred to centre rang
When the celestial song began.

The Lion, monarch of the plain,   25
First tried to imitate the strain,
And shaking high his mane he roared,
Till beast and bird around him cowered.

The little Linnet tuned her lay,
The Lark, in turn, did welcome day,   30
And cooing soft, the timid Dove
Did to his mate tell of his love.

Then Eve, the synonym of grace,
Drew nearer to the solemn place,
And heard the words to music set   35
In tones so sweet, she ne'er forgot.

The anthems from the earth so rare,
Higher and higher filled the air,
Till Seraphs caught the inspiring strain,
And morning stars together sang.   40

Then laggard Adam sauntered near,
What Eve had heard he too must hear,
But ah! for aye will woman's voice
Make man to sigh or him rejoice.

Only the fishes in the deep   45
Did not arouse them from their sleep,
So they alas! did never hear
Of the Angel's visit to this sphere.
Nor have they ever said one word
To mate or man, or beast or bird.   50

Atlanta Exposition Ode

"Cast down your bucket where you are,"
From burning sands or Polar star
From where the iceberg rears its head
Or where the kingly palms outspread;
'Mid blackened fields or golden sheaves,   5
Or foliage green, or autumn leaves,
Come sounds of warning from afar,
"Cast down your bucket where you are."

What doth it matter if thy years
Have slowly dragged 'mid sighs and tears?   10
What doth it matter, since thy day
Is brightened now by hope's bright ray.
The morning star will surely rise,
And Ethiop's sons with longing eyes
And outstretched hands, will bless the day,   15
When old things shall have passed away.

Come, comrades, from the East, the West!
Come, bridge the chasm. It is best.
Come, warm hearts of the sunny South,
And clasp hands with the mighty North.   20
Rise Afric's sons and chant with joy,
Good will to all without alloy;
The night of grief has passed away—
On Orient gleams a brighter day.

Say, ye that wore the blue, how sweet   25
That thus in sympathy we meet,
Our brothers who the gray did love
And martyrs to their cause did prove.
Say, once for all and once again,
That blood no more shall flow in vain;   30
Say Peace shall brood o'er this fair land
And hearts, for aye, be joined with hand.

Hail! Watchman, from thy lofty height;
Tell us, O tell us of the night?
Will Bethlehem's Star ere long arise   35
And point this nation to the skies?
Will pæans ring from land and sea
Fraught with untrammelled liberty
Till Time's appointed course be run,
And Earth's millenium be begun?   40

"Cast down your bucket," let it be
As water flows both full and free!
Let charity, that twice blest boon
Thy watchword be from night to morn.
Let kindness as the dew distil   45
To friend and foe, alike, good will;
Till sounds the wondrous battle-call,
For all one flag, one flag for all.

Note

Booker T. Washington in a conciliatory speech to the Cotton States and International Exposition (Atlanta, 1895) urged blacks to cultivate morality and pursue opportunities for economic advancement in the South, where both races, although socially segregated, could work together for the South's prosperity. The poem's first line comes from Washington's speech (see Cotter's "Dr. Booker T. Washington. . . ." and note).

In Memoriam
Alphonse Campbell Fordham

Aged 6 Years, 2 Months, 20 Days

Almost whose last words were
"We shall meet beyond the River."

Yes, my darling, when life's shadows
   Over me do darkly fall,
Meet me surely at the river
   As I haste to obey the call.
Gladly through the darksome valley,   5
   Through its portals, grim and cold,
Will I hasten 'till my nestling
   Meets me at the "Gates of Gold."

Sadly do I miss my wee one,
   None can fill thy vacant place,   10
Only in my dreams I fold thee,
   Only then behold thy face.
See thee in thy childish beauty,
   Clasp thy little hand in mine,
Ever will those moments chain me,   15
   Ever in my heart enshrined.

Little Heartsease, "bud of promise,"
   Broken off in early morn,
Now can sin no more pollute thee
   In the angels' bosom borne.   20
In that land no pain or anguish
   Ever can my child enfold,
Then my darling meet thy mother
   Surely at the "Gates of Gold."

FRANK BARBOUR COFFIN

Frank Barbour Coffin (1870/71–1951) was born in Holly Springs, Mississippi, to Josephine (Barton) and Samuel Coffin. He attended Rust and Fisk universities from 1886 to 1890 and earned a Ph.G. from Meharry Medical College in 1893. Coffin owned a pharmacy in Little Rock, Arkansas; he married Lottie E. Woodford in 1913, was active in the Wesley Methodist Episcopal Church, wrote for local newspapers, and published a second volume of poetry and prose in 1947.

Coffin's poems consider religion, love, nature, and literature, and his "Ajax" verses dwell on racial wrongs. Esthetically the work is weak, deficient in language, metrical and rhyming skills, and inventiveness.

Coffin's Poems with Ajax' Ordeals (Little Rock, Ark.: Colored Advocate, 1897).

Mother's Songs

The summer's sun was beaming hot,
  The boys had played all day;
And now beside a rippling stream,
  Upon the grass they lay.

Tired of games and idle jest,   5
  As swept the hours along,
They called on one who mused at times,
  "Come pard, give us a song."

"I fear I cannot please," he said,
  "The only songs I know   10
Are those my mother used to sing
  To me long years ago."

"Sing one of those," a rough voice said,
  "There's none but true men here;
To ev'ry mother's son of us   15
  A mother's song is dear."

Then sweetly rose the singer's voice,
  Amid unwonted calm:
"Am I a soldier of the cross
  A follower of the lamb."   20

"And shall I fear to own his cause"
  Every heart seemed stilled,
And hearts that never throbbed with fear,
  With tender thoughts were filled.

As the singer closed he said,   25
  "Boys, we must face the foes"
Then thanking them for their invite
  Upon his feet he rose.

"Sing us one more," the young men said,
   The singer hung his head,   30
Then glancing 'round with smiling lips,
   "You'll join with me," he said.

We'll sing that old familiar air,
   Sweet as the bugle call;
"All hail the power of Jesus name,   35
   Let Angels prostrate fall."

And wondrous was the old tune's spell,
   As on the singer sang;
Man after man fell into line,
   And loud their voices rang.   40

One cried out "my mother sings
   'Just as I am though tossed about;' "
And the crowd picked up the anthem —
   "With many a conflict, many a doubt."

The next said "I seem to hear,   45
   'It's rock of ages cleft for me,' "
And the boys joined in with feeling
   "Let me hide myself in thee."

Another said "I'm an outcast,
   But when I've nowhere to roam,   50
I think of mother and the city
   Which, long since she's made her home."

The next one said with tearful eyes
   "My mother's in eternity,
Her song was 'O rock of ages   55
   In thy cleft hide thou me.' "

Hush'd are her lips, the song's ended,
   The singer sleeps at last;
While I sit here in deep wonder,
   And think of days, long past.   60

The room still echoes with music,
  As singing soft and low,
Those grand sweet Christian carols,
  They rock her to and fro.

Safe hidden in the "Rock of Ages"   65
  She bade farewell to fear;
Sure that her Lord'd always lead her
  "She read her title clear."

Dear Saint in mansions long folded,
  Safe in God's fostering love,   70
She joins in the blissful chorus,
  Of those bright choirs above.

There she knows not pain, nor sorrow,
  Safe beyond Jordan's roll
She lives with her blessed Jesus   75
  The lover of her soul.

These boys are men, the stream still runs,
  Those songs, they still are heard;
And oh! the depth of every soul,
  By those old hymns is stirred.   80

And up from many a bearded lip,
  In whispers soft and low;
Rises the songs the mother taught
  The boy long years ago.

Harriet Beecher Stowe's Works

"Uncle Tom's Cabin."

That grand and noble woman dear,
    Called Harriet Beecher Stowe,
The book she wrote without a fear
    Drove slavery from our shore.
To know her works, to feel her worth,   5
    Go read that noble book
And see what dauntless words she wrote,
    What fearful risks she took.

It struck a blow to slavery's tree,
    That burned its very life;   10
It scorched the undergrowth around,
    And left it in a strife;
It parched the branches to a crisp,
    Withered the leaves in twain,
It drove the sap into the ground   15
    To never rise again.

. . . .

Men divine, wrote book upon book,
    Forcing restitution,
And tried to prove that slavery was
    A God sent institution.   20
To speak, to write, to think against
    This inhumanity,
Was nothing but a case of what
    Was called insanity.

It was at such a time as this   25
    That Harriet Beecher Stowe,
Called "Uncle Tom" upon the scene,
    And made him walk before
The gaze of all the countries 'round,
    She made him speak and cry,   30

In twenty diff'rent languages
   She made him pray and sigh.

She then asked all the world who heard
   His wild distressing prayer,
If 'twas not likely that a heart   35
   Humane is stationed there;
She brought forth George and showed his grand
   Affections for his wife,
His love for liberty, and how
   He fought the slavish strife.   40

She brought Haley, the Negro trader,
   Who had no human heart,
Who stole the virtue of his slaves,
   And then the lash impart;
Who took a newly wedded wife   45
   Before her husband's gaze,
Could the devil have seen all this,
   He would have stood amazed.

She then showed forth the Christian heart
   Of Mister Shelby's wife,   50
Who sympathized with all the slaves
   In their discouraged strife;
Who wept when she first heard the news
   From her dear husband bold,
When she asked where was Uncle Tom,   55
   He said "the brute is sold."

These things and hundreds, thousands more,
   This noble book had shown,
And there stood Harriet Beecher Stowe,
   Between pulpit and throne;   60
She stood nearer the Throne of God,
   Than all false priests before,
And turned the search light on to show
   The heartache and the woe.

She wrote brave words and spead them,   65
    Upon the human breeze,
That made pro-slav'ry clergymen
    Draw in their breath and sneeze;
Her shafts were sent hilt deep into
    The tender, human heart,   70
Just like the shepherd boy who smote
    The giant with his dart.

This book had made the world grow mad,
    With slavery and its crime,
Before the bloody battlefield,   75
    With marching tread did chime;
Before John Brown had died to save,
    Before great Lincoln's call,
Before brave Sherman reached the sea,
    Before Grant captured all.   80

She called from out its slumb'ring tomb,
    Affections of the soul,
She armed them with eternal light,
    And sent them forth so bold
Against the greed, the gain, the lust,   85
    That these two forces fought,
Like Wolfe and Montcalm on the plain,
    Till right had error wrought.

Notes

Coffin summons the novel's characters: *George* Harris and his wife Eliza (37–38); the Yankee slavetrader *Haley* (41); Tom's owner, Mrs. *Shelby* (50). 65. spread. 77. John Brown: see Williams's "At Harper's Ferry. . . ." 79. *Sherman:* General William Tecumseh Sherman (1820–91) led the Union armies' advance through Georgia in 1864 in the Civil War. 80. *Grant:* see Horton's "Gen. Grant. . . ." 87. *Wolfe and Montcalm:* Generals James Wolfe and Louis Joseph Montcalm fought for England and France, respectively, in the French and Indian War; both died in the Battle of Quebec in 1759.

Ajax' Conclusion

My friends, our race is ostracised,
Long standing tears are in our eyes,
And we as meek and humble doves,
Endure it all with smiles and love.
And those who try to crush us down   5
Return our smiles in hateful frowns,
So we must rise and strike a blow,
When e'er these demons block our door.

As long as we retreat from them,
They'll use us as their limber-jim,   10
But if we punishments resist,
The white man'll know that we exist,
And if we all united stand,
We can our rights as men demand;
But we must show determination,   15
Instead of meek disconsolation.

The red man showed that he would fight,
This country gave him certain rights,
They never lynch an Indian chief,
They know his friends come to relief,   20
The foreigner from 'cross the sea,
Has all the rights of liberty,
Because if humans take his scalp,
His countrymen will raise a scrap.

The rattlesnake, the white man dreads,   25
And on his body will not tread,
Because he knows the rattlesnake,
If touched, will to'ard the toucher make.
The harmless ant upon the ground,
Men trample on without a frown,   30
If we resist, we'll gain respect,
If we unite 'twill take effect.

There must be some blood shed by us,
When Southern brutes begin to fuss,
Some Brown and Turner've got to die, 35
To picture to the demon's eye
The fact that we are in this land
To stay, 'till God gives us command
To move away, and until then,
We must be recognized as men. 40

We made the South-land with our toil,
And we intend to share the spoil,
But sometimes it seems just as well
To have a residence in hell.
Poor men are cut and burnt like fuel, 45
The country does not call it cruel.
Someone must rouse this base-ball age,
To overcome this black outrage.

Who's more fit to defend this right,
Than we who've seen these wicked sights? 50
Stern freedom's voice bids us arise,
Our patient ways she does despise,
Contentment makes real life decay.
Brave discontent brings brighter day,
What we are now, the past has made, 55
The future's on our shoulders staid.

Notes

Ajax, a Greek hero in the Trojan War, is transformed by Coffin into an African-American activist who in a series of poems suffers discrimination and rallies his race to fight for justice. 35. *Brown and Turner've got to die:* John Brown (see Williams's "At Harper's Ferry. . . .") and Nat Turner, the slave leader of a bloody insurrection in Virginia in 1831 for which Turner was hanged.

JAMES EPHRIAM McGIRT

James Ephriam McGirt (1874–1930), a prolific author, publisher of his own magazine, and a prosperous businessman, never found the literary fame or woman to love that he sought. Born to Ellen (Townsend) and Madison "Mack" McGirt in Robeson County, North Carolina, McGirt worked on their farm, went to public school in Greensboro, and earned a B.A. from Bennett College there in 1895. He did manual labor until 1903; then he moved to Philadelphia to publish and edit *McGirt's Magazine*. The magazine printed McGirt's own poetry, stories, and articles urging race advancement along with writings by prominent African Americans and advertisements for McGirt's many business deals and books. When the magazine ceased publication in 1909, McGirt returned to live with his family in Greensboro, where he first established a profitable company that sold hair-grower and toiletries worldwide from 1909 to 1918, and then a realty business. Alcoholism marred his last years, and he died of nephritis.

With more than a hundred poems in his collections, McGirt never succeeded as a poet because his work is uniformly poor in all poetic skills. Despite some improvement over the years in language and technique, only a few verses have more than biographical or historical interest. McGirt wrote an equal number of martial-patriotic poems featuring the Spanish-American War; poems denouncing intra-racial color prejudice, slavery, and discrimination; sentimental verses that gush over love, nature, children, mothers, and boyhood; and didactic, pathos-filled confessions of personal failure and pleas for temperance, virtue, and world peace.

Avenging the Maine, A Drunken A. B. and Other Poems (Raleigh, N.C.: Edwards & Broughton, 1899); *Some Simple Songs and A Few More Ambitious Attempts* (Philadelphia: George F. Lasher, 1901); *For Your Sweet Sake* (Philadelphia: John C. Winston, 1906).

Memory of Lincoln and the Yankees

Among the dear old friends we people cherish
   Within the highest portals of our hearts,
The name that sounds as dear as dear old mother's
   Is Lincoln's name, from us 'twill ne'er depart.

When first I heard of Lincoln and the Yankee   5
   My heart then reached the zenith of its joy,
And in this heart of mine it quickly nestled,
   My love for them no force can quite destroy.

Lord, if these rolling waves of time and pleasure
   Should dash against their sacred nestling place,   10
Pray with Thy powerful hand stay it and guide us;
   May nothing from my heart their love erase.

Ye men that fought and still are living,
   And in whose veins the Yankee blood holds sway;
Within our hearts for thee there lives a kindness   15
   That will not be erased till judgment day.

Ye mortals now who lie in grave and trenches,
   Who fell to free this helpless negro race;
No mortal name like thine we hold in reverence,
   Within our hearts thou hast a sacred place.   20

It's not my wish to call your soul from heaven,
   But could I call your body from the ground;
On earth thou might'st live on in peace for ages,
   With sweetest oil I'd daily balm your wounds.

Oh, mothers, now so loving and so happy,   25
   Ye people whom the Northern race hast freed;
Pray grasp your loving infant from the cradle,
   And tell them of the Yankees' blessed deed.

(1899)

Nothing to Do

The fields are white;
    The laborers are few;
Yet say the idle:
    There's nothing to do.

Jails are crowded;   5
    In Sunday-schools few;
We still complain:
    There's nothing to do.

Drunkards are dying—
    Your sons, it is true;   10
Mothers' arms folded
    With nothing to do.

Heathens are dying;
    Their blood falls on you;
How can you people   15
    Find nothing to do?
                    (1899)

My Song

Why was I born if this ends all,
  All that I'll ever be;
To feel a spirit that's divine,
  No chance to let it free.

Unfortunate seems now my port,   5
  Drifting on poverty's sea;
The chains of need have bound me fast,
  Oh! would that I was free.

I'm struggling daily for the shore,
  The sea is vast and wide;   10
And when I stop to sing my lays,
  I'm threatened by the tide.

But if these rugged lays I've sung,
  Should cause some heart to move,
And bring to me freedom   15
  How could I then but love!

Accept these lays to you I bring,
  A token of my art;
Jangling though they seem to be
  Remember 'tis a start.   20

(1899)

The Century Prayer

Lord God of Hosts incline thine ear
To this, thy humble servant's prayer:
May war and strife and discord cease;
This century, Lord God, give us peace!
Henceforth, dear Lord, may we abhor   5
The thought of strife, the curse of war.
One blessing more, our store increase,
This is our prayer, Lord, give us peace!

May those who rule us rule with love,
As thou dost rule the courts above;   10
May man to man as brothers feel,
Lay down their arms and quit the field;
Change from our brows the angry looks,
Turn swords and spears to pruning-hooks.
One blessing more, our store increase,   15
This is our prayer, Lord, give us peace!

May flags of war fore'er be furled,
The milk white flag wave o'er the world;
Let not a slave be heard to cry,
Lion and lamb together lie;   20
May nations meet in one accord
Around one peaceful festive board.
One blessing more, our store increase,
This is our prayer, Lord, give us peace!
                                   (1901)

Tell Me, Oh Fate

Tell me, oh fate, is it decreed
  That I leave but a blot
To stain the pages of the past?
  Tell me, is this my lot?

Pray let a print of these sore feet   5
  Rest on the sand of time;
Pray let the print of these sore hands
  Upon the pages shine.

Years have I labored, toiled and fought,
  But yet no prize I see;   10
Tell me, oh fate, if this is all
  That I shall ever be?

(1901)

When de Sun Shines Hot

No, dere ain't no use r workin' in de blazin' summertime,
Whin de fruit hab filled de orchard, an' de burries bend de vine;
Der's enuf ter keep us libin' in de little gyarden spot,
An' der aint no use'n workin' w'en de sun shines hot.

Fur I'ze read it in de Bible 'bout de lilies how dey grow,   5
It was put in der er purpus dat de workin' men mout know,
Dat dis diggin' an er grabben, wusn't men't in our lot,
An' der ain't no use'n workin' we'n de sun shines hot.

Does yer heer de streams er callin' az it cralls erlong de rill;
Does yer se de vines er wavin', biddin' me ter kum an' fill?   10
Whar's m' hook and line—say, Hannah, give me all de bait yer got,
Fur der ain't no use'n workin' w'en de sun shines hot.

Des 'bout dark I kum hum, strollin' wid a binch er lubly trout;
Hannah she c'mmence er grinnin' little Rastus 'gin to shout;
Soon de hoecake is er bakin', fish er fryin', table sot.   15
No, der ain't no use'n workin' w'en de sun shines hot.

(1906)

Born Like the Pines

Born like the pines to sing,
  The harp and song in m' breast,
Though far and near,
There's none to hear,
I'll sing as th' winds request.   5

To tell the trend of m' lay,
  Is not for th' harp or me;
I'm only to know,
From the winds that blow,
What th' theme of m' song shall be.   10

Born like the pines to sing,
  The harp and th' song in m' breast,
As th' winds sweep by,
I'll laugh or cry,
In th' winds I cannot rest.   15

(1906)

SAMUEL ALFRED BEADLE

Samuel Alfred Beadle (1857–1932) was born in Atlanta, Georgia. He studied and practiced law in Mississippi. Beadle's topics include love (of many women), squandered youth, obedience to God, and race protest. Occasional variations in metric and stanzaic patterns break the monotony of his verse, but most of it suffers from prosaic and awkward language and rhymes.

Sketches from Life in Dixie (Chicago: Scroll Publishing and Literary Syndicate, 1899); *Lyrics of the Underworld* (Jackson, Miss.: W. A. Scott, 1912).

Lines

Suggested by the Assaults made on the Negro Soldiers as they passed through the south on their way to and from our war with Spain.

How I love my country you have heard,
    And I would you were noble and free
In spirit and deed, as in word,
    And your boasted humanity.
I love you, my country, I do,—   5
    Here's a heart, a soul that is thine,
Pregnant with devotion for you,
    And blind to your faults as to mine.

The standard of morals is high;
    When fixed by my brother for me,   10
It goes towering up to the sky
    With a dazzling purity.
For a bench he sits on a skull,
    And is a judge austere and stern,
With whom my demurrers are null,   15
    And my pleadings, though just, are spurned.

I've carried your flag to the front
    Through pestilence, battles and storms;
Of the carnage of war took the blunt,
    Obeyed your command, "Carry arms!"   20
And gone with you down to the death,
    With the thorns of caste on my head;
Defended your home and your hearth,
    And wept o'er the bier of your dead.

As the smoke of the fight goes by,   25
    And the bugle calls to repose,
By my countryman's hands I die,
    As well as by the hands of its foes;
Yet I love you, my country, I do,
    Here's a heart, a soul that is thine,   30

Pregnant with devotion for you,
And blind to your faults as to mine.

(1899)

Note

War with Spain: Spanish-American War (1898) by which the United States acquired Puerto Rico, Guam, and the Philippines.

After Church

Yes, May and I are friends,
　　Lovers, many have said;
For down the lane and o'er the lea
　　To church we often tread,
In that careless sort of way,　　　　　　5
　　That leads to love, they say;
And after church we often search
　　For garlands by the way.

Yes, May and I are friends,
　　And something more, they say;　　　10
Because along the curved strand,
　　Where we sat the other day,
I simply wrote her name,
　　And wrote it o'er again;
When after church we stopped to search　　15
　　For shells along the main.

More than friends are we,
　　My bonny May and I;
At least that's what our neighbors say
　　Whene'er they pass us by,　　　　　20
They smile and wink their eye,
　　And set their necks awry:
When after church we stop to search
　　For heart's ease, May and I.

　　　　　　　　　(1899)

Words

Words are but leaves to the tree of mind;
    Where breezy fancy plays;
Or echoes from the souls which find
    Expression's subtle ways.

A beaming lamp to idea's feet   5
    Where sentinel thought abides;
Or a guide to the soul's retreat,
    Where master man presides.

A jewel trembling on the tongue,
    The index of the heart;   10
The black mask from the spirit wrung,
    Revealing every part.

A ship upon the sea of life,
    With all her sails aswell;
Her cargo being the bread of life,   15
    Or the cindered dross of hell.

(1899)

Lines to Caste

The things I love I may not touch,
　But kiss the hand that shackles bring;
The thraldom of my soul is such
　I can but nurse my thongs and sing,
　　And hope and pray that destiny　　　　　　5
　　Will somehow yet unfetter me.

I simply trust fate as I ought,
　While hate defames, malice reviles,
And so distorts the public thought
　That even innocence defiles　　　　　　　　10
　　All who are not adjudged by caste,
　　Superior and nobly classed.

I may not ponder here nor muse,
　Nor let the plain truth designate
The things it would. The hangman's noose　　15
　Unmans, deters, doth reinstate
　　The inquisition and its hell
　　Of terror, tyrannous and fell.

Oh! that thou'd grant me grace, despair,
　My dread, my sore distress, my pain,　　　　20
Or I could breathe some form of prayer,
　Or might some suasive word obtain,
　　Through which to move to clemency
　　The iron hand that shackles me.

Fanciful thought; I must not hope,　　　　　　25
　Nor question prejudice and hate;
For they who read my horoscope
　Say that the stars which rule my fate
　　Designed me for vile tyranny,
　　And plunder while they fetter me.　　　　　30

They bid me grovel, squirm and whine,
  Nor strive against vile calumny;
And vain the thought that would decline
  Submission to such tyranny;
    For like a wild beast from its lair,   35
    The state doth hound me to despair.

My fancy, sure, revives at times,
  Soars, but to beat its weary wings
Against a bar, that basely limes
  Me in my hope; vilest of things,   40
    So dire, so fell, but strong my prison,
    Hope to escape it is derision.

And yet there often comes to me,
  I know not how, from whence nor where;
But comes the thought perpetually,   45
  That justice is not deft to prayer.
    Though it seems barren, yet for me,
    With good is pregnant destiny.

Then wherefore should my soul repine,
  Why be disconsolate and sad;   50
All things are well in Fate's design,
  Nor great, nor small, nor good, nor bad
    Has aught to boast of o'er the clay,
    Tyranny plunders, day by day.

Fret not, dear soul, whene'r the proud,   55
  The haughty proud, would press you hard.
Have they so far subdued the shroud,
  That clay can now assume the God?
    Whate'er its form, or hue, or clan,
    Clay's not the measure of the man.   60

The cup where dazzles bright the wine
  Was in some distant day and clime

Crysalis of a soul like thine;
   There spirit, daring, once did climb,
      There dwelt and thought itself a god—   65
      'Twas but a tenant of the sod.

Who is so great among mankind,
   His infancy knew not the womb;
And, coming thence, still is not blind,
   To wombed life, as he the tomb   70
      Enfolds within its dank embrace,
      Whate'er his prowess, clan or race.

And who's so small that, should he fall,
   Jehovah takes no note of him?
Though he be spurned by kings, and all   75
   Who frown men down with visage grim,
      Methinks he'll be as grand in clay
      As he who tortures him today.

I know not why I live or die,
   Nor why of me the Lord should reck,   80
When like the bruis'd reed prone I lie,
   The tyrant's heel upon my neck;
      I simply know that Caste is blind,
      And that its hope is vicious mind.

Because God loves He doth chastise,   85
   And makes another race the rod;
Then let the chasten race be wise
   And know the lash is not the God;
      'Tis not the rod's; chastisement is
      Eternally and justly His.   90

We have forgot our own household,
   To take our tribute to the strong—
The willing vassal, young or old,
   Deserve chastisement late and long;
      And ours is but the well-earned hell   95
      Of wanton, faithless infidel.

                              (1912)

PRISCILLA JANE THOMPSON

Priscilla Jane Thompson (1871–1942) was one of three poets born to Clara Jane and John Henry Thompson in Rossmoyne, Ohio. Priscilla, her sister Clara Ann, and brother Aaron Belford privately published seven volumes of verse among them between 1899 and 1926. Priscilla spent her life in Rossmoyne, living with Clara Ann and another brother, Garland Yancey Thompson, to whom Priscilla dedicated her second volume.

Christian faith and morality, love, and her race are Thompson's topics in both volumes. She peoples tributes to God and to lovers with the stuff of romantic novels: knights and royalty, chivalric sentiments, and gothic disasters. Thompson's two dozen verses on racial issues, half of them in dialect, look backward to life in slavery, escape to Canada, and Emancipation. In most cases, God is piously summoned to heal all ills. An occasional religious verse (and "The Muse's Favor") depart from the ordinary, but debilitating the literary value of all of Thompson's verse are her antiquated, ungrammatical, and incongruous diction, excessive punctuation, broken meters, and off-rhymes.

Ethiope Lays (Rossmoyne, Ohio: Author, 1900); *Gleanings of Quiet Hours* (Rossmoyne, Ohio: Author, 1907).

The Muse's Favor

Oh Muse! I crave a favor,
  Grant but this one unto me;
Thou hast always been indulgent—
  So I boldly come to thee.

For oft I list thy singing—   5
  And the accents, sweet and clear,
Like the rhythmic flow of waters,
  Fall on my ecstatic ear.

But of Caucasia's daughters,
  So oft I've heard thy lay,   10
That the music, too familiar—
  Falls in sheer monotony.

And now, oh Muse exalted!
  Exchange this old song staid,
For an equally deserving—   15
  The oft slighted, Afric maids.

The Muse, with smiles consenting,
  Runs her hand the strings along,
And the harp, as bound by duty—
Rings out with the tardy song.   20

The Song

Oh, foully slighted Ethiope maid!
With patience, bearing rude upbraid,
With sweet, refined, retiring, grace,
And sunshine ling'ring in thy face,
With eyes bedewed and pityingly   25
  I sing of thee, I sing of thee.

Thy dark and misty curly hair,
In small, neat, braids entwineth fair,
Like clusters of rich, shining, jet,
All wrapt in mist, when sun is set;　　　　30
Fair maid, I gaze admiringly,
　　And sing of thee, and sing of thee.

Thy smooth and silky, dusky skin,
Thine eyes of sloe, thy dimple chin,
That pure and simple heart of thine,　　　35
　　Tis these that make thee half divine;
Oh maid! I gaze admiringly,
And sing of thee, and sing of thee.

Oh modest maid, with beauty rare,
Whoe'er hath praised thy lithe form, fair?　40
Thy tender mein, thy fairy tread—
Thy winsome face and queenly head?
Naught of thy due in verse I see,
　　All pityingly I sing of thee.

Who've dared to laud thee 'fore the world,　45
And face the stigma of a churl?
Or brook the fiery, deep, disdain—
Their portion, who defend thy name?
Oh maiden, wronged so cowardly.
　　I boldly, loudly, sing of thee.　　　　50

Who've stood the test of chastity,
Through slav'ry's blasting tyranny,
And kept the while, their virtuous grace,
　　To instill in a trampled race?
　　Fair maid, thy equal few may see;　　55
　　Thrice honored I, to sing of thee.

Let cowards fear thy name to praise,
Let scoffers seek thee but to raze;
Despite their foul, ignoble, jeers,

A worthy model thou appear,   60
Enrobed in love and purity;
    Oh who dare blush, to sing of thee?

And now, oh maid, forgive I pray,
The tardiness of my poor lay;
The weight of wrongs unto thee done—   65
Did paralize my falt'ring tongue;
'Twas my mute, innate, sympathy—
    That staid this song, I sing to thee.

(1900)

The Vineyard of My Beloved

Now will I sing to my well-beloved a song of my
  beloved touching his vineyard.
My well-beloved hath a vineyard in a very fruitful hill.
                                        Isaiah 5:1

My Beloved hath a vineyard,
  In a very fruitful hill,
Where the choicest sunbeams glimmer,
  And the clouds their moisture spill;
And he fenced it round about,   5
  To keep the wild fox out;
And set a mighty host the field to till.

My Beloved hath a vineyard,
  In a very fruitful hill,
Where the earth is damp and fertile,   10
  And the harmful bee is still;
And he planted choicest vine,
  To yield the sparkling wine,
And set a mighty host the field to till.

But, despite the workers efforts,   15
  And the sunshine, and the rain,
Many of the choice vines withered,
  Making all His efforts vain;
So He took the blighted vines,
  And threw them to the wind—   20
Suff'ring not one barren grape-vine to remain.

We are grape-vines in that vineyard,
  And our opportunities,
Are the sunshine and the workers—
  Luring to eternity;   25
And, with conscience fenced about,
  To keep all bad deeds out,
Our hearts are ever pressed toward purity.

But despite our wary conscience,
   And our opportunities—   30
Many a one of us, are failures,
   Yielding rank impurities;
And at last, like backward sprouts,
Our just God casts us out—
For we slighted all our chances, carelessly.   35
                       (1900)

The Favorite Slave's Story

Well, son de story of my life,
　Is long, and full of shade;
And yet, the bright spots, here and tha,
　A heap of comforts made.

When fust my eyes beheld de light,　　　　　5
　'Twas on a Chris'mus day;
Twelve miles fum Richmond "on a fa'm,"
　As you young upsta'ts say.

We said "plantation" in de South,
　We black, and white folks too;　　　　　10
We wa'n't a changin' ev'ry day,
　Like all you young folks do.

My mother cooked de white-folks grub,
　Dat's all she had to do,
Ole Miss, she spilte her half to death,　　　　15
　And spilte her young ones, too.

Fah, well I mind me, in dem days,
　How I and Sue and Pete,
Would roll around Miss Nancy's cheer,
　And play about her feet.　　　　　20

Miss Nancy,—I kin hear her yet—
　'You Petah, Sue, an' Si!
I'll make yo' maustah whoop you sho!"
　(Wid laughtah in her eye.)

Ole mause, he'd whoop us soon as not;　　　25
　But, when Miss Nancy saw,
She'd run out, wid dat look, an' say,
　'I wouldn't whoop him, Pa.'

One day,—I nevah kin fahgit,
   Ole Miss wus sick in bed;   30
Ole Mause, he ripped, an' cussed, an' to',
   An' made himself a dread.

Somehow, I can't tell how it wus,
   He slapped my sistah Sue,
And mammy, coase she took it up,   35
   Den dah wus heap to do.

Pete lit right in wid tooth and claw,
   And so did little sis,
Fah me, I had anothah plan,
   I flew upstairs fah Miss.   40

I met Miss Nancy on de stairs,
   Wrapped in a great big shawl,
An' comin' down de steps so fast,
   Jest seemed as ef she'd fall.

I tried to tell her 'whut wus up,'   45
   She pushed me on befo',
Fah mammy's cries wus in her yeahs,
   An' she heard nothin' mo'.

She caught ole Mause, an' pulled him off;
   Her eyes dey fa'ly blazed;   50
Ole Mause commenced a silly grin,
   An' looked like he wus dazed.

I'd nevah seed Miss Nancy mad,
   Good Lo'd! She fussed an' to'e;
She raked ole Maustah o'er de coals,   55
   Until he begged an' swo'.

. . . .

An' aftah dat, I tell you, son,
   Ole Mause, he let us be,

An' doe he slashed de othah slaves,
   Pete, Sue, an' me went free.   60

An' so de time went spinnin' on,
   Wid not a keer nor plan;
I didn't know whut trouble wus,
   Till I wus nigh a man.

Ole Fairfax owned my fathah, son,   65
   Dey lived across de creek,
De white folks al'ays let him come,
   Three nights in ev'ry week.

Of coase he had his Sundays, too,
   Great days dey use to be,   70
Fah all de blessed day he'd have,
   We young ones, bout his knee.

Or else, he'd take us all to church,
   All breshed up neat an' new,
Wid Mammy hanging to his arm,   75
   An' leading little Sue.

An' Mammy's eyes 'ud be so bright,
   When she had Pappy near;
She'd laugh an' giggle like a gal,
   But tryin' times drawed near.   80

Ole Mause an' Fairfax wus fast friends;
   A pa' uv roscals dey;
In gamblin', cheatin', an' de like,
   Dey bofe had heap to say.

So bofe got mixed up in a scrape,   85
   Wid Richmond's bank, an' den,
Dey bofe sold ev'ry slave dey had,
   To keep out uv de pen.

I tell you son de good white-folks,
   Wus good in time uv ease;   90
But soon as hawd times cummed tha' way,
   Dey'd change, "quick as you please."

Soon as Miss Nancy seed de trap,
   Ole Mause had done walked in,
She changed right dah, an who but she!   95
   A-helpin' him to sin.

Dey talked an' planned togethah, long;
   An', as de days flew by,
Miss Nancy changed an' got so cross,
   Dat Mammy use to cry.   100

One mawnin', jest to pick a fuss,
   She said she missed a pie;
When Mammy said dey all wus tha,
   She said, she told a lie.

'Dat pie wus in her cabin, hid;   105
   She wus a vixen, bold;
An' ef she didn't bring it back,
   She'd have her whooped an' sold.'

Well, son, you see dat wus her scheme,
   To sell her, wid de rest;   110
An' aftah dat, she made it plain,
   To all uv us, I 'fess.

An' so, at last, de day rolled 'round,
   When all, exceptin' I,
Wus put upon de block an' sold,   115
   To any one who'd buy.

Oh, son! You don't know whut it is,
   To see yo' loved ones sold,
An' hear de groans, an' see de tears,
   Uv young, as well as ole.   120

An' see dem white men bus'lin' 'roun',
  A-feelin' uv yo' a'm,
An' havin' you to run an' skip,
  An' caper till you's wa'm,

An' all de while, wid questions, keen,   125
  An' wid a watchful eye,
Not keerin' how yo' h'a't might ache,
  Jest so you's strong an' spry.

Po' Mammy! How kin I fahgit,
  Her pa'tin' from us all?   130
Dat pa'tin', son, will 'bide wid me,
  Until de Lo'd will call!

. . . .

Ah well! De sun will sometimes shine,
  E'en in a po' slave's life;
De Lo'd healed up my broken h'a't,   135
  By sendin' me a wife.

Miss Nancy wus as good to her,
  An' spilte her jest as bad,
As she did mammy long befo',
  Sometimes it made me sad.   140

Ole Mause had prospered, bought mo' slaves,
  Ole Miss wus sweet an' kind,
My little ones an' Charlotte dear,
  Had pushed my grief behind.

I al'ays wus Miss Nancy's pet,   145
  She made it very plain;
An' I must say, in all my grief,
  She tried to ease my pain.

An' now, dat I wus gay once mo',
  An' happy as could be,   150

She petted Charlotte an' my chaps,
    An' seemed as pleased as me.

So time sped on widout a keer,
    Save whut had long since past,
Till Ole Mause's health begin to fail,   155
    An' son, he went down fast.

. . . .

De wah, dat had been grumblin' roun',
    Broke full about dis time,
De slaves begun a-walkin' off,
    To suit their own free mind.   160

Ole Miss wus cryin' day an' night,
    An' beggin' me to stay,
While Charlotte urged me, on de sly,
    To go North, fah away.

I looked into her pleadin' eyes,   165
    So helpless, trustin' me,
An' den, upon my little chaps,
    An' manhood said, "Be free!"

Ole Missus cumed down to de gate;
    To bid fahwell she tried,   170
But she jest held fast bofe our hands,
    An' cried, an' cried, an' cried.

An' so we cumed up to dis state,
    An' worked on, bes' we could,
A-trustin' al'ays in de Lo'd,   175
    An' tryin' to be good.

. . . .

(1907)

Bibliography

The Bibliographical Essay in *Invisible Poets* (1974) provided annotated descriptions of bibliographies, periodicals, books, articles, and manuscript guides available for research in nineteenth-century African-American literature, with emphasis on poetry. Sources of biography for individual poets also appeared in the text's footnotes and the Selected Sources of each chapter as well as in the appendixes. Because I examined those resources published before 1974 and incorporated their data into *Invisible Poets,* they are unlikely to yield new information to researchers in early black poetry. Moreover, recent publications have in many cases superseded earlier materials; therefore, I include in this Bibliography only the most valuable pre-1974 resources.

The Bibliographical Essay II in the 1989 edition of *Invisible Poets* annotated publications of 1974 through 1988. During these fifteen years little work of consequence pertinent to the early poets appeared in biography or literary history and criticism; research then and now focuses on twentieth-century African-American writers, black cultural history, and literary theory. These years, however, did bring publication of important bibliographies, finding aids and indexes to early black periodicals and to manuscript collections, and reprints of several poets' primary works. Such later resources, as well as publications since 1988, are included here in the hope that they will prove useful for further study of early black poets and poetry. Within each section of the Bibliography, sources are listed chronologically.

Bibliographies and Finding Aids

Books and Parts of Books

Guides to Bibliographies

Gubert, Betty Kaplan. *Early Black Bibliographies, 1863–1918.* New York, 1982.

Newman, Richard. *Black Access: A Bibliography of Afro-American Bibliographies.* Westport, 1984.

Stevenson, Rosemary M., comp. *Index to Afro-American Reference Sources.* Westport, 1988.

Bibliographies

Schomburg, Arthur A. *Bibliographical Checklist of American Negro Poetry.* New York, 1916.

Locke, Alain, ed. *The New Negro* [bibliographies by Arthur Schomburg]. New York, 1925.

Work, Monroe. *Bibliography of the Negro in Africa and America.* New York, 1928.

Porter, Dorothy B. "Early American Negro Writing." *Bibliographical Society of America Papers* 39 (1945): 192–268.

———. *North American Negro Poets . . . 1760–1944.* Hattiesburg, 1945.

Lash, John. "The American Negro and American Literature." *Bulletin of Bibliography* 19 (1946): 12–15; (1947): 33–36 [includes articles].

The National Union Catalog Pre-1956 Imprints. London, 1968–81.

Dumond, Dwight. *Bibliography of Anti-Slavery in America.* Ann Arbor, 1961.

Kaiser, Ernest. "Recent Books." *Freedomways* (1961–Fall 1985).

Dictionary Catalog of the Schomburg Collection of Negro Literature and History [New York Public Library]. 9 vols. Boston, 1962; Supplements: 1967; 1972; 1974. Annual supplements: *Bibliographic Guide to Black Studies.* Boston, 1976—.

Jahn, Janheinz. *A Bibliography of Neo-African Literature from Africa, America, and the Caribbean.* New York, 1965.

Porter, Dorothy B. *Working Bibliography on the Negro in the United States.* Ann Arbor, 1969.

Dictionary Catalog of the Arthur B. Spingarn Collection of Negro Authors [Howard University Library]. 2 vols. Boston, 1970.

Dictionary Catalog of the Jesse E. Moorland Collection of Negro Life and History [Howard University Library]. 9 vols. Boston, 1970; First supplement. 3 vols. *Dictionary Catalog* [Moorland-Spingarn Research Center, Howard University]. Boston, 1976.

Abajian, James de T. *Blacks and Their Contributions to the American West: A Bibliography and Union List of Library Holdings through 1970.* Boston, 1974.

Matthews, Geraldine O., and AAMP Staff. *Black American Writers, 1773–1949: A Bibliography and Union List.* Boston, 1975.

Bell, Roseann P. et al., eds. *Sturdy Black Bridges: Visions of Black Women in Literature.* Garden City, 1979. "Selected African-American Women Writers," pp. 379–409.

French, William P., Michel J. Fabre, and Amritjit Singh. *Afro-American Poetry and Drama 1760–1975: A Guide to Information Sources.* Detroit, 1979.

Hull, Gloria T., et al., eds. *All the Women Are White, All the Blacks Are Men, but Some of Us Are Brave: Black Women's Studies.* Old Westbury, 1982.

Clark, Edward. *Black Writers in New England: A Bibliography, with Biographical Notes, of Books By and About Afro-American Writers Associated with New England in the "Collection of Afro-American Literature."* Boston, 1985.

Davis, Nathaniel, comp. and ed. *Afro-American Reference: An Annotated Bibliography of Selected Resources.* Westport, 1985.

Foster, Mamie Marie Booth. *Southern Black Creative Writers, 1829–1953: Bibliographies.* New York, 1988.

Indexes to Poetry

Chapman, Dorothy Hillman. *Index to Black Poetry.* Boston, 1974.

Kallenbach, Jessamine S. *Index to Black American Literary Anthologies.* Boston, 1979.

Chapman, Dorothy Hillman. *Index to Poetry by Black American Women.* Westport, 1986.

Periodical Literature

Guide to Bibliographies

The Bibliographic Index: A Cumulative Bibliography of Bibliographies. New York, 1937—.

Finding Aids to Periodicals

Rowell's American Newspaper Directory. New York, 1869–80, 1885, 1890, 1900.

N. W. Ayer & Son's Directory of Newspapers and Periodicals. Philadelphia, 1880—.

Brown, Warren. *Checklist of Negro Newspapers in the United States.* Jefferson City, Mo., 1946.

Pride, Armistead S. "A Register and History of Negro Newspapers in the United States." Diss. Northwestern U., 1950; Ann Arbor; UMI, 1981.

————. *Negro Newspapers on Microfilm*. Washington, D.C., 1953.

————. *Guide to Microforms in Print*. Washington, D.C., 1971.

Hoornstra, Jean, and Trudy Heath. *American Periodicals 1741-1900: An Index to the Microfilm Collections*. Ann Arbor, 1979.

Bullock, Penelope L. *The Afro-American Periodical Press, 1838-1909*. Baton Rouge, 1981.

Campbell, Georgetta Merritt. *Extant Collections of Black Newspapers: A Research Guide to the Black Press, 1880-1915, with an Index to the Boston Guardian, 1902-1904*. Troy, 1981.

Daniel, Walter C. *Black Journals of the United States*. Westport, 1982 [magazines].

Suggs, Henry Lewis, ed. *The Black Press in the South, 1865-1979*. Westport, 1983.

United States Newspaper Program National Union List. 3d ed. Dublin, Ohio, 1989 [microfiche records of papers, 1842—].

Indexes to Periodicals

Analytical Guide and Indexes to "Alexander's Magazine," 1905-1909; "The Colored American Magazine," 1900-1909; "The Crisis . . ." 1910-1960; "The Voice of the Negro," 1904-1907. Westport, 1974-75.

Jacobs, Donald, ed. *Antebellum Black Newspapers: Indices to "New York Freedom's Journal" (1827-1829), "The Rights of All" (1829), "The Weekly Advocate" (1837), and "The Colored American" (1837-1841)*. Westport, 1976.

Blassingame, John W. et al., eds. *Antislavery Newspapers and Periodicals. An Annotated Index of Letters, 1817-1871*. 5 vols. Boston, 1980-84.

Carter, George E., and C. Peter Ripley, eds. *Black Abolitionist Papers 1830-1865: A Guide to the Microfilm Edition*. New York, 1981.

Bibliographies in Periodicals

African-American Literature: These ongoing American literature bibliographies have included black literature since 1974-76: *American Literature* (quarterly); *The American Humanities Index* (quarterly); *American Literary Scholarship* (annual); *Humanities Index* (quarterly); *Modern Language Association International Bibliography of Books and Articles* (annual).

The following African-American literature journals published bibliographies in only specific issues (dates given) and/or publish ongoing bibliographies, as noted: *Obsidian: Black Literature in Review* (1975-82; bibliographies:

Winter, 1975, 1976, 1977); *College Language Association Journal* (bibliographies: Sept. 1976, 1977; "Publications by CLA Members," 1984—annually, December); *Callaloo: A Journal of Afro-American and African Arts and Letters* (1984—annually, Fall); *Black American Literature Forum* (1988—quarterly); occasional bibliographies appear in: *Obsidian II* (1986—); *Phylon; Sage; Studies in Black American Literature.*

African-American Studies: Hallie Q. Brown Memorial Library and the Schomburg Collection, comps. *The Index to Periodical Articles By and About Negroes* (1950–72); *About Blacks* (1974–83); *Index to Black Periodicals* (Boston, 1984—annual).

Theses Bibliographies: Peebles, Joan B., ed. *Black Studies: A Dissertation Bibliography.* Vol 1, 1967–77; Vol. 2, *Black Studies II: 1977–80.* Ann Arbor, 1978, 1980; *Black Studies: A Catalog of Selected Doctoral Dissertation Research* [1979–84]. Ann Arbor, 1985.

Biography, Autobiography, and Criticism

Bibliographies, Indexes, and Guides

Bell, Barbara. *Black Biographical Sources.* New Haven, 1970.

Falk, Byron A., Jr., and Valerie R. Falk. *Personal Name Index to the New York Times Index, 1851–1974.* 3 vols. Verdi, Nev., 1976–82; Supplement, 1984.

Abajian, James de T. *Blacks in Selected Newspapers, Censuses, and Other Sources; An Index to Names and Subjects.* 3 vols. Boston, 1977; Supplement, 2 vols. 1985.

Spradling, Mary Mace, ed. *In Black and White: A Guide to Magazine Articles, Newspaper Articles, and Books Concerning More than 15,000 Black Individuals and Groups.* 3d ed. 2 vols. Detroit, 1980; Supplement, *Concerning More than 6,700 . . . Groups.* 1985.

Campbell, Dorothy W. *Index to Black American Writers in Collective Biographies.* Littleton, Colo., 1983.

Brignano, Russell C. *Black Americans in Autobiography: An Annotated Bibliography of Autobiographies and Autobiographical Books Written Since the Civil War.* Durham, 1984.

Andrews, William. "Afro-American Autobiography, 1760–1865," "Afro-American Biography, 1760–1865." *To Tell a Free Story: The First Century of Afro-American Autobiography, 1760–1865.* Urbana, 1986.

Burkett, Randall K. et al., eds. *Black Biographical Dictionaries, 1790–1950* [300 volumes on Microfiche, 3 vol. hard-bound *Cumulative Index*]. Alexandria, 1990–91.
(See also: Manuscripts and Records: Finding Aids.)

Reference Works and Dictionaries

Mather, Frank L., ed. *Who's Who of the Colored Race*. Chicago, 1915.
Logan, Rayford W., and Michael R. Winston, eds. *Dictionary of American Negro Biography*. New York, 1982.
Harris, Trudier, ed. *Dictionary of Literary Biography: Afro-American Writers Before the Harlem Renaisance*. Vol. 50. Detroit, 1986.
Young, Tommie Morton. *Afro-American Genealogy Sourcebook*. New York, 1987.
Craig, Tracey Linton, comp. and ed. *Directory of Historical Organizations in the United States and Canada*. Nashville, 1990.
Draper, James, ed. *Black Literature Criticism*. 3 vols. Detroit, [1992].

Biographical and Literary Studies

Brown, William Wells. *The Black Man: His Antecedents, His Genius, and His Achievements*. Boston, 1863.
Simmons, William J. *Men of Mark: Eminent, Progressive, and Rising*. Cleveland, 1887.
Mossell, Mrs. N. F. *The Work of Afro-American Women*. Philadelphia, 1894.
Kletzing, H. F., and W. H. Crogman. *Progress of a Race or the Remarkable Advancement of the Afro-American*. Naperville, Ill., 1901.
Brown, Hallie Q., comp. *Homespun Heroines and Other Women of Distinction*. Xenia, Ohio, 1926.
Loggins, Vernon. *The Negro Author: His Development in America to 1900*. New York, 1931 [with bibliography].
Brown, Sterling. *Negro Poetry and Drama*. Washington, D.C., 1937.
Redding, J. Saunders. *To Make a Poet Black*. Chapel Hill, 1938.
Wright, Richard. "The Literature of the Negro in the United States." *White Man, Listen!* New York, 1957.
Wagner, Jean. *Black Poets of the United States: From Paul Laurence Dunbar to Langston Hughes*. Urbana, 1973.

Sherman, Joan R. *Invisible Poets: Afro-Americans of the Nineteenth Century.* Urbana, 1974. 2d ed., 1989.

Redmond, Eugene B. *Drumvoices: The Mission of Afro-American Poetry, a Critical History.* Garden City, 1976.

Levine, Lawrence. *Black Culture and Black Consciousness: Afro-American Folk Thought from Slavery to Freedom.* New York, 1977.

Ensslen, Klaus. "The Status of Black Poetry from 1865–1914." In *American Poetry Between Tradition and Modernism, 1865–1914,* edited by Roland Hagenbuchle. Regensburg, Germany, 1984.

Bruce, Dickson, D. *Black American Writing from the Nadir: The Evolution of a Literary Tradition, 1877–1915.* Baton Rouge, 1989.

Jackson, Blyden. *The History of Afro-American Literature.* Vol. I: *The Long Beginning, 1746–1895.* Baton Rouge, 1989.

Articles in Periodicals

African-American and abolitionist periodicals are important sources of biography and criticism (and primary poetry and prose). Many periodicals are now available in facsimile reprints or on microfilm (see Periodicals, above). Some valuable periodicals are: Newspapers: *Freedom's Journal* (1827–30); *Liberator* (1831–65); *National Anti-Slavery Standard* (1840–70); *North Star* and *Frederick Douglass' Paper* (Dec. 1847–60). Magazines: *Douglass' Monthly* (1858–Aug. 1863); *Anglo-African Magazine* (Jan. 1859–March 1860); *African Methodist Episcopal Church Review* [AMECR] (1883–1927); *Voice of the Negro* (1904–7); *Alexander's Magazine* (1905–9).

Mossell, Mrs. N. F. "The Colored Woman in Verse." *AMECR* 2 (1885): 60–67.

Wilson, Joseph T. "Some Negro Poets." *AMECR* 4 (1888): 236–45.

Tillman, Katherine D. "Afro-American Poets and Their Verse." *AMECR* 14 (1898): 421–28.

White, Newman Ivy. "Racial Feelings in Negro Poetry." *South Atlantic Quarterly* 21 (Jan. 1922): 14–29.

Flint, Allen. "Black Response to Colonel Shaw." *Phylon* 45 (1984): 210–19.

Bruce, Dickson D., Jr. "The South in Afro-American Poetry, 1877–1915." *College Language Association Journal* [CLAJ] 31 (Sept. 1987): 12–30.

Anthologies

[Anthologies also contain biography, criticism, and bibliography.]

Haley, James T., comp. "Thoughts, Doings and Sayings of the Race." *Afro-American Encyclopedia.* Nashville, 1896.

Johnson, James Weldon, ed. *The Book of American Negro Poetry.* New York, 1922, 1931, 1958.

Kerlin, Robert, ed. *Negro Poets and Their Poems.* Washington, D.C., 1923.

White, Newman Ivy, and Walter C. Jackson, eds. *An Anthology of Verse by American Negroes.* Durham, 1924.

Brawley, Benjamin, ed. *Early Negro American Writers.* Chapel Hill, 1935.

Brown, Sterling, et al., eds. *Negro Caravan.* New York, 1941.

Stetson, Erlene, ed. *Black Sisters: Poetry by Black American Women, 1746-1980.* Bloomington, 1981.

Manuscripts and Records: Finding Aids

General (including African-American materials)

Downs, Robert B., comp. *American Library Resources: A Bibliographical Guide.* Chicago, 1951, 1962; *Supplement, 1971-1980,* 1981.

Library of Congress National Union Catalog of Manuscript Collections. Washington, D.C., 1959 —.

Robbins, J. Albert, comp. *American Literary Manuscripts: A Checklist of Holdings in Academic, Historical, and Public Libraries, Museums, and Authors' Homes in the United States.* 2d ed. Athens, 1977.

Ash, Lee, and William G. Miller, comps. *Subject Collections: A Guide to Special Book Collections and Subject Emphases as Reported by University, College, Public, and Special Libraries and Museums in the United States and Canada.* 6th ed. rev. and enl. New York, 1985.

National Archives Microfilm Resources. Washington, D.C., 1986.

Directory of Archives and Manuscript Repositories in the United States. 2d ed. Phoenix, 1988.

Index to Personal Names in the NUCMC, 1959-1984. 2 vols. Alexandria, 1988.

African-American

Lewinson, Paul, comp. *A Guide to Documents in the National Archives: For Negro Studies*. Washington, D.C., 1947.

Schatz, Walter, ed. *Directory of Afro-American Resources*. New York, 1970. *Black Studies: A Select Catalog of National Archives Microfilm Publications*. Washington, D.C., 1984.

Newman, Debra L., comp. *Black History: A Guide to Civilian Records in the National Archives*. Washington, D.C., 1984.

The Poets: Reprints and Sources

Reprints

Gates, Henry Louis, Jr., ed. *The Schomburg Library of Nineteenth-Century Black Women Writers*. 30 vols. New York, 1988. [Facsimile reprints of works by forty-five black women, with biocritical introductions; includes complete poems of Bibb, Fordham, Harper, Heard, Menken, Plato, Ray, and Thompson.]

Black Literature, 1827–1940. Alexandria, 1989—[Ongoing Microfiche publication of thousands of pieces of fiction, poetry, and book reviews in nine hundred black periodicals and newspapers.] Annual author and title index.

Reprints of some primary texts by the poets Bell, Cotter, Fordham, Fortune, Harper, McClellan, McGirt, Menken, Thompson, and Whitman are published by Ayer Company (Salem, N.H.); Books for Libraries Press (Freeport, N.Y.); AMS Press (New York); Beacon Press (Boston); and Irvington Publishers (New York).

Sources

For each poet, a few major pre–1974 sources are listed; other materials such as letters, school records, and death certificates, obtained by correspondence, are noted in *Invisible Poets*. Selected post–1974 sources are included. The poets appear in the same order as in this anthology, and sources are listed chronologically. Repeated references are abbreviated as follows; full citations, if not given here, are in the preceding Bibliography.

Brawley	Benjamin Brawley, *Early Negro American Writers*
DANB	*Dictionary of American Negro Biography*
DHU	Howard University Library, Moorland and Spingarn Collections
DLB	*Dictionary of Literary Biography*, vol. 50
Loggins	Vernon Loggins, *The Negro Author*
NNSch	Schomburg Collection of the New York Public Library
Simmons	William Simmons, *Men of Mark*
Schomburg	*The Schomburg Library of Nineteenth-Century Black Women Writers*
Shockley	Shockley, Ann Allen, *Afro-American Women Writers, 1746–1933: An Anthology and Critical Guide* (Boston, 1988)
TCLC	*Twentieth-Century Literary Criticism: Excerpts from Criticism of the Works of . . . Writers Who Died Between 1900 and 1960* (Detroit, 1984–88)
Wagner	Jean Wagner, *Black Poets of the United States*
WWCR	*Who's Who of the Colored Race* (1915)

GEORGE MOSES HORTON

Horton, George M. "Life." *The Poetical Works* (1845); Cobb, Collier. "An American Man of Letters." *The University [of North Carolina] Magazine* OS 40, NS 27 (Oct. 1909): 3–10; Walser, Richard. *The Black Poet: being the remarkable story (partly told my* [sic] *himself of George Moses Horton a North Carolina slave.* New York, 1966; Richmond, Merle A. *Bid the Vassal Soar: Interpretive Essays on the Life and Poetry of Phillis Wheatley and George Moses Horton.* Washington, D.C., 1974; Jackson, Blyden. "George Moses Horton, North Carolinian." *North Carolina Historical Review* 53 (April 1976): 140–47; Cobb, John L. "George Moses Horton's *Hope of Liberty:* Thematic Unity in Early American Black Poetry." *CLAJ* 24 (June 1981): 441–50; O'Neale, Sondra. "Roots of Our Literary Culture: George Moses Horton and Biblical Protest." *Obsidian* 7 (1981): 18–28; Manuscripts: Southern Historical Collection, University of North Carolina.

NOAH C. W. CANNON

Cannon, Noah C. W. *The Rock of Wisdom* (1833); Wayman, Alexander W. *My Recollections of African M. E. Ministers.* Philadelphia, 1881. Pp. 7–10.

CHARLES LEWIS REASON

Simmons; Payne, Daniel A. *Recollections of Seventy Years.* Nashville, Tenn., 1888. Pp. 46–48, 118, 327; Mayo, Anthony R. *Charles Lewis Reason, Pioneer New York Educator.* . . . N.D., n.p. 12 pages [NNSch].

ANN PLATO

Loggins; Williams, Kenny J.: *Schomburg.*

JOSHUA MCCARTER SIMPSON

Simpson, Joshua McCarter. "Note to the Public," "How I Got My Education." *The Emancipation Car* (1874).

JAMES MONROE WHITFIELD

Loggins; Brawley; Articles in *The North Star, Frederick Douglass' Paper, Liberator, Anti-Slavery Bugle, Pennsylvania Freeman, San Francisco Elevator, Pacific Appeal,* 1849–69; DLB.

DANIEL ALEXANDER PAYNE

Payne, Daniel A. *Recollections of Seventy Years.* Nashville, Tenn., 1888; Filler, Louis: *DANB;* Manuscripts: Payne Collection, Wilberforce University.

ALFRED GIBBS CAMPBELL

Paterson Intelligencer, Sept. 8, 1852; *National Anti-Slavery Standard,* May 16, 1856; *The Alarm Bell* [Princeton University Library].

FRANCES ELLEN WATKINS HARPER

Still, William. *Still's Underground Rail Road Records.* Rev. ed., 1872; Philadelphia, 1886; Chicago, 1970; Daniel, Theodora W. "The Poems of Frances E. W. Harper, ..." Master's thesis, Howard University, 1937; Hill, Patricia Liggins. " 'Let Me Make the Songs for the People': A Study of Frances Watkins Harper's Poetry." *Black American Literature*

Forum 15 (Summer 1981): 60–65; Walden, Daniel: *DANB; TCLC,* Vol. 14; Graham, Maryemma: *DLB* and *Schomburg;* Bacon, Margaret Hope. " 'One Great Bundle of Humanity': Frances Ellen Watkins Harper (1825–1922)." *The Pennsylvania Magazine of History & Biography* 113 (1989): 21–43; Foster, Frances Smith, ed. *A Brighter Coming Day: A Frances Ellen Watkins Harper Reader.* New York, 1990; Foster, Frances Smith. "Frances Ellen Watkins Harper." *African American Writers.* Ed. Valerie Smith, et al., New York, 1991.

JOSEPH CEPHAS HOLLY

Holly, Joseph C. *Freedom's Offering* (1853); Abajian, James de T. *Blacks in Selected Newspapers.* . . . Boston, 1977; 1985.

GEORGE BOYER VASHON

Delany, Martin R. "Letter to Frederick Douglass . . ." and Nell, William C. "George B. Vashon" [extract] *North Star,* January 18, 1848; "George B. Vashon." *North Star,* January 21, 1848; *Proceedings of the National Convention of the Colored Men of America.* . . . Washington, D.C., 1869; *Oberlin Review* [obituary], November 20, 1878; Manuscripts: Howard University Papers, DHU.

ELYMAS PAYSON ROGERS

Wilson, Joseph M. *The Presbyterian Historical Almanac . . . for 1862.* Vol. 4. Philadelphia, 1862; Manuscript letters (1860–61): American Missionary Association Archives, Amistad Research Center, Tulane University, New Orleans, La.

ADAH ISAACS MENKEN

Lesser, Allen. *Enchanting Rebel: The Secret of Adah Isaacs Menken.* New York, 1947; Gerson, Noel B. *Queen of the Plaza; a Biography of Adah Isaacs Menken* by Paul Lewis [pseud.]. New York, 1964; Mankowitz, Wolf. *Mazeppa: The Lives, Loves and Legends of Adah Isaacs Menken.* New York, 1982 [with bibliography]; Sherman, Joan R.: *Schomburg.*

JAMES MADISON BELL

Arnett, Benjamin W. "Biographical Sketch." In Bell's *Poetical Works* (1901); *DLB*.

CHARLOTTE FORTEN GRIMKÉ

Cooper, Anna Julia. *Life and Writings of the Grimké Family*. 2 vols. in 1. N.p., 1951; Forten, Charlotte. *The Journal of Charlotte L. Forten*. Ed. Ray A. Billington. New York, 1953; Logan, Rayford W.: *DANB; TCLC*, Vol. 16; Stevenson, Brenda: *Schomburg;* Manuscripts: Francis J. Grimké Papers, Negro Collection, DHU.

ALFRED ISLAY WALDEN

Winfield, J. L. H. and C. C. H. Introductions. In Walden's *Miscellaneous Poems* (1873); Taylor, William R. "Sketch of His Life." In Walden's *Sacred Poems* (1877); Manuscripts: Gardner A. Sage Library, New Brunswick Theological Seminary.

ALBERY ALLSON WHITMAN

Whitman, A. A. Prefaces. In *Leelah Misled* (1873), *Not a Man, and Yet a Man* (1877), *The Rape of Florida* (1884), *Twasinta's Seminoles* (1885); Simmons; Loggins; Brawley, Benjamin. *The Negro Genius*. New York, 1937; Marshall, Carl L. "Two Protest Poems by Alberry A. Whitman." *CLAJ* 19 (Sept. 1975): 50–56; Rowe, Anne E. *The Idea of Florida in the American Literary Imagination*. Baton Rouge, La., 1986; *DLB;* Letters: Houghton Library, Harvard University.

HENRIETTA CORDELIA RAY

Ray, F. T. and H. C. *Sketch of the Life of Rev. Charles B. Ray*. New York, 1887; Brown, Hallie Q., comp. *Homespun Heroines . . .* (1926); *DLB;* Sherman, Joan R.: *Schomburg*.

JOHN WILLIS MENARD

The Congressional Globe. 40th Cong., 3d sess. (1869: Jan. 5, Feb. 17, 27, March 3). Pp. 182, 1318, 1683–96, 1875–76; Barbadoes, F. G.

Preface. In Menard's *Lays in Summer Lands* (1879); Gibbs, Thomas V. "John Willis Menard, the First Colored Congressman Elect." *African Methodist Episcopal Church Review* 3 (April 1887): 426–32.

ROBERT C. O. BENJAMIN

Simmons; Taylor, Arnold H.: *DANB*.

TIMOTHY THOMAS FORTUNE

Slocum, A. Terry. "Timothy Thomas Fortune: A Negro in American Society." B.A. thesis, Princeton University, 1967; Thornbrough, Emma. *T. Thomas Fortune: Militant Journalist*. Chicago, 1972; Beasley, Maurine H. "T. Thomas Fortune." *Dictionary of Literary Biography: American Newspaper Journalists, 1873–1900*. Vol. 23. Ed. Perry J. Ashley. Detroit, 1983; Manuscripts: Bruce Collection and Fortune (Vertical File): NNSch.

JAMES EDWIN CAMPBELL

Woodson, Carter G. "James Edwin Campbell, a Forgotten Man of Letters." *Negro History Bulletin* 2 (Nov. 1938): 11; Wagner; Levstick, Frank R.: *DANB; DLB*.

JOSEPH S. COTTER, SR.

Kerlin, Robert. "A Poet from Bardstown." *South Atlantic Quarterly* 20 (July 1921): 213–21; Shockley, Ann Allen. "Joseph S. Cotter, Sr.: Biographical Sketch of a Black Louisville Bard." *CLAJ* 18 (March 1975): 327–40; Cain, Betty. "Wearing the Mask: Joseph S. Cotter, Sr.'s *Caleb the Degenerate*." *Melus* 5 (1978): 37–53; *DLB; TCLC*, Vol. 28; Manuscripts: Louisville Free Public Library, Western Branch, Louisville, Ky.

GEORGE CLINTON ROWE

Haley, James T., comp. *Afro-American Encyclopaedia*. Nashville, Tenn., 1896; *The Congregational Year-Book, 1904*. Vol. 26. Portland, Maine, 1904; Letters (1895–1901): Charles James McDonald Furman Papers, South Caroliniana Library, University of South Carolina, Columbia.

JOSEPHINE D. HEARD

"Historical Sketch of the Authoress." In Heard's *Morning Glories* (1890; 1901); Heard, William Henry. *From Slavery to the Bishopric in the A.M.E. Church: An Autobiography.* Philadelphia, 1924.

DANIEL WEBSTER DAVIS

Richmond Times-Dispatch, Oct. 28, 1913, p. 2; Oct. 29, 1913, p. 9; Harrison, Lottie Davis. "Daniel Webster Davis" (typescript). Condensed in *Negro History Bulletin* 18 (Dec. 1954): 55–57; Manuscripts: Virginia Historical Society, Richmond.

PAUL LAURENCE DUNBAR

Wiggins, Lida Keck, *The Life and Works of Paul Laurence Dunbar.* Naperville, Ill., 1907; Brawley, Benjamin G., *Paul Laurence Dunbar, Poet of His People.* Chapel Hill, N.C., 1936; Cunningham, Virginia. *Paul Laurence Dunbar and His Song.* New York, 1947; Wagner; Martin, Jay, ed. *A Singer in the Dawn: Reinterpretations of Paul Laurence Dunbar.* New York, 1975; Revell, Peter. *Paul Laurence Dunbar.* Boston, 1980; *TCLC,* Vol. 12; Rauch, Esther Nettles. "Paul Laurence Dunbar." *African American Writers.* Ed. Valerie Smith, et al. New York, 1991; Manuscripts: Ohio State Historical Society, Columbus; NNSch.

GEORGE MARION McCLELLAN

Catalogues of Fisk University. 11 vols. 1885–96; *DLB;* Manuscripts: Case Memorial Library, Hartford Seminary Foundation, Hartford, Conn.

ELOISE BIBB

WWCR; Beasley, Delilah L. *The Negro Trail Blazers of California.* Los Angeles, 1919; Shockley.

MARY WESTON FORDHAM

Braithwaite, W. S. Review of *Magnolia Leaves. Colored American* 3 (Nov. 1901): 73–74.

FRANK BARBOUR COFFIN

Kletzing, H. F., and W. H. Crogman. *Progress of a Race*. Naperville, Ill., 1901; *WWCR*.

JAMES EPHRIAM MCGIRT

Parker, John W. "James Ephriam McGirt: Poet of 'Hope Deferred'." *North Carolina Historical Review* 31 (July 1954): 321–35; Daniel, Walter C. *Black Journals of the United States*. Westport, Conn., 1982.

SAMUEL ALFRED BEADLE

Foster, Mamie Marie Booth. *Southern Black Creative Writers, 1829–1953: Bibliographies*. New York, 1988.

PRISCILLA JANE THOMPSON

Shockley.

Subject Index

Under each subject, poems are listed in order of their appearance in this volume. Some poems appear under more than one subject heading, and cross references are given to locate others. An asterisk denotes a poem in dialect.

Title and Poet Index